The Trout Pool Paradox: The American Lives of Three Rivers
Iraq's Crime of Genocide
Black Hands of Beijing: Lives of Defiance in China's
  Democracy Movement (with Robin Munro)
The Good Neighbor: How the United States Wrote the History
  of Central America and the Caribbean

Casting a Spell

RANDOM HOUSE   NEW YORK

Casting a Spell

The Bamboo Fly Rod and the American Pursuit of Perfection

George Black

Published in the United States by Random House, an imprint of
The Random House Publishing Group, a division of
Random House, Inc., New York.

RANDOM HOUSE and colophon are registered trademarks of Random House, Inc.

Portions of chapter 12 were first published
in *OnEarth* magazine, Winter 2006.

Illustration on page xxv by Irene Huang.
Photograph on page 133 courtesy of Per Brandin.

LIBRARY OF CONGRESS CATALOGING-IN-PUBLICATION DATA

Black, George.
Casting a spell : the bamboo fly rod and the American pursuit
of perfection / George Black.
p.   cm.
ISBN 1-4000-6396-5
1. Fishing rods—United States—Design and construction—History.
2. Fishing rods—United States—Design and construction—Biography.
3. Bamboo. I. Title.
SH452.B53 2006
688.7'912—dc22   2006045766

Printed in the United States of America on acid-free paper

www.atrandom.com

9 8 7 6 5 4 3 2 1

FIRST EDITION

Book design by Carole Lowenstein

*This book is dedicated to
Streamer, for obvious reasons,
Hoagy, for bridging the gap,
Per, for pushing the envelope,
Glenn, for Zen wisdom,
Jim, for pursuing crazy dreams,
Dana, for carrying on,
and
Sam, in memoriam*

Preface and Acknowledgments

When I was a kid, chewing my pencil over homework or organizing my stamp collection, I would often hear people say, "Oh, he's such a perfectionist." It was never clear to me whether this was intended as a mark of praise or exasperation. But there always seemed to be an undertow to the remark. *There's something a bit strange about that child.*

Perfectionism is described, more often than not, as a malady, something that gets bracketed together with substance abuse and Asperger's syndrome and obsessive-compulsive disorder. All manner of support groups and counseling centers and self-help books are out there waiting to help you vanquish your inner perfectionist. But I've never been inclined to see perfectionism that way—or at least not *exclusively* that way. Granted, there are people who are hostage to the illusion of perfection and then paralyzed by their failure to attain it. But then there's the other kind—the type B perfectionist, if you like. This kind knows that perfection doesn't exist, but uses the idea as a source of discipline, a spur to the incremental pursuit of excellence. The type B perfectionist accepts that mistakes and defects are inevitable but exalts the importance of learning from them, knowing that this process is, in some sense, what makes us fully human. When this kind of perfectionism brings brain, hands, and passion into proper alignment, the rewards can be very great—whether the tangible outcome is composing a string quartet, mastering a martial art, or creating an obscure object of desire like a bamboo fly rod.

There's no bright line, of course, between type A and type B perfectionism. It's the struggle between the two, in fact, that makes these people interesting—that, and the subcultures they create and inhabit. I've always admired writers who take you deep into these subcultures of perfection. That's what's so appealing about Thad Carhart's book, *The Piano Shop on the Left Bank,* for instance, which immerses you simultaneously in the history of the instrument, the hidden world in which it comes to life, and the aspirations of the musician and the maker. Another example would be John McPhee's *The Survival of the Bark Canoe,* which is both a portrait of a single craftsman and a physical journey through the world of water for which his craft was designed, so compellingly told that you want to take a magnifying glass to the appendix of technical drawings. McPhee's New Hampshire canoe maker, Henri Vaillancourt, definitely teeters on the edge of type A perfectionism, while Carhart's Parisian piano restorer, Luc, and Carhart himself, the pianist, have their feet planted more solidly on the ground.

Most of the bamboo fly rod makers I know have a touch of the Luc and a touch of the Henri. There are endless stories out there about craftsmen who complete a rod, show it to a delighted client, and then snap it over their knee because of some invisible blemish.

The world that rod makers populate is a classic subculture, a recondite corner of the larger culture of fishing. There are persistent, hardwired reasons why so many of us choose to fish, I think—in part it's the evolutionary residue of man as hunter and top predator, and in part it's the primordial, biological need to be in intimate contact with running water. Pretty soon, though, these deeply encoded reasons get tangled up with all sorts of social and cultural considerations: fly-fishing as an emblem of class and affluence; the self-regard that comes from mastery of a supposedly arcane skill; and the love of fine tools, which can turn so easily into a form of commodity fetishism. As an artifact, the bamboo fly rod has always had to navigate these currents, even though the rod maker usually wishes they'd just go away.

One of the marks of a society that has made the leap from sub-sistence to surplus is that essential functions take on these new, nonessential attributes. Thus fly-fishing becomes a recreational act, rather than simply a search for protein. This shift has probably been under way at least since A.D. 200, when the Macedonians, ac-cording to the Roman historian Aelian, first fashioned a hook and wrapped it with red wool and wax-colored feathers from beneath the wattle of a farmyard fowl. From the Middle Ages on, authors begin to write more systematically of the sport and its growing repertoire of tools and techniques—a fly fisherman makes an appearance, for example, in a thirteenth-century romance by Wolfram von Eschenbach; then there's the famous *Treatyse of Fysshynge wyth an Angle,* by the (probably apocryphal) fifteenth-century abbess Dame Juliana Berners; and finally, of course, Izaak Walton and Charles Cotton's *The Compleat Angler,* written at the time of the English Civil War.

It was at about this time that rural gentlemen in England began to develop the modern concept of organized leisure. For a couple of centuries after Walton, fly-fishing remained essentially an English habit, and the Masters of Empire carried it around the globe with them, making sure that their local streams, from the hill stations of northern India to the "white highlands" outside Nairobi, were always well stocked with trout. Legend has it that it was English military officers in Philadelphia who brought the sport to the New World in the early part of the eighteenth century. At least we know that's where the first recorded angling club and the first tackle shop were established, the latter stocking articles imported from England. Until the 1700s, supposedly, the local Pu-ritans had been either too preoccupied with survival or too intoler-ant of vanities to take up anything as shiftless as fly-fishing for pleasure.

But over the next hundred years, Americans distanced them-selves from the cultural tastes they had inherited from the mother country. By the time the American Civil War was over, the United States had evolved its own distinctive approaches to craftsmanship, to manufacturing, to wealth and material possessions, and to the outdoors. English craftsmen had made the first bamboo fly rods around 1800, but by the 1860s American artisans had appropriated the idea and made it their own. This cultural break involved various little wars of independence and petty snobberies. American gentlemen continued to favor imported fly reels—the English were good with metal, it was said, with some reason—but developed their own conceptions of what made a superior fly rod.

The seminal figure in this story was Hiram Lewis Leonard, a Maine craftsman who, in the 1870s, mastered the art of assembling six finely tapered strips of bamboo into an instrument of both strength and delicacy. More important, he and his apprentices rode the nineteenth-century wave of mechanical ingenuity to marry this exacting manual skill with the modern techniques of mass production.

Marriage it may have been, but it was also an enduring source of tension. Leonard and his preternaturally gifted disciples created both an industry standard and a paradigm of luxury. Their rods were very, very expensive—had to be, given the hours of skilled labor involved. But the rod makers never made much money themselves. And they never escaped the sucking force of the mass market, or the corporations that serviced its needs.

As a raw material for fishing rods, bamboo was the only game in town from the turn of the century until the 1950s. Then, thanks to the invention of fiberglass and cheap synthetics, coupled with the trade embargo that choked off the supply of the raw material from Communist China, the split bamboo fly rod was declared obsolete. A few resolute craftsmen—perhaps stepping across the line into type A perfectionism under these circumstances—clung to the old ways. But by the 1970s there were probably no more than a couple dozen survivors.

Then, astonishingly, the craft experienced a renaissance. Today there are more skilled rod makers than at any time in history. There are many reasons for this, including another wave of technological change and a backlash against the suffocating artificiality of corporate production. No bamboo fly rod ever carried a bar code. The most important factor in the renaissance, though, has been the sheer stubbornness of a new generation of perfectionists.

Along the way the sport itself has evolved and changed, and so has people's relationship to the places where it is practiced. As Americans and their automobiles spread out across the country, most of the country's formerly wild lands came within reach of ordinary people. Yet even as America in some respects democratized, its tastes and recreational activities stratified. Wild places have developed their own equivalent of the gated community. People who make a cult of one kind of fishing would not be seen dead engaging in another. Trout are the undisputed aristocrats of the sport; bass fishing is something people in the red states do, whizzing around in gaudy metal-flake boats festooned with the logos of corporate sponsors, NASCAR on the water.

Yet those distinctions may be more self-serving than real. In the last couple of decades fly-fishing, like so many other pursuits, has become needlessly complicated, encumbered with all the tinsel and swagger of modern marketing and social competition. Because a fine bamboo fly rod can cost thousands of dollars, it certainly isn't immune to those trends. An activity that has been prized for centuries as a source of grace and reflection and connectedness with the natural world has also become corporatized, commercialized, and overpopulated by alpha males. Shortly after completing this book, I was in a one-room, one-plane airport in a remote town in Chilean Patagonia when a group of American fly fishermen, fresh from a week of catching trophies in a high-priced wilderness lodge, came strutting into the place, submerging the locals in a tidal wave of boastful noise. Sad to report, the ugly

xiv | PREFACE AND ACKNOWLEDGMENTS

American not only is alive and well, but all too frequently seems to go fly-fishing.

The men I've written about here are another kind of American. Their lives represent a kind of rebellion, if a very quiet one, and that's something they share with those who invented the craft of bamboo fly rod making in the first place, almost as if the intervening century and a half of history had never taken place. That isn't to romanticize the past. The rod makers of the late nineteenth century weren't living in some ethereal state of nature; on the contrary, they struggled fiercely to retain their independence from the soulless corporate culture of their time. Often they lost; sometimes they fought the adversary to an honorable draw; but always they kept alive a set of values that have never been so important to preserve as they are today. Those values are the thread that runs through this story.

Hiram Leonard, as I say, is the seminal figure, and the story couldn't be told without him. Eustis Edwards I chose for deeply personal reasons, but also because he was the most underappreciated of Leonard's acolytes and a link, through his two sons, to the generations that followed. The incomparable Sam Carlson carried the torch a generation further. As for the contemporary rod makers, each of those I've chosen is a master of his craft, and each gave me fresh insights into the meaning of perfectionism.

My sincere gratitude, then, to all the craftsmen who let me intrude into their lives and their workshops. And thanks, too, to the many others who helped along the way with a helpful suggestion, a missing fact, a couple of beers, a bed for the night: Suzy Abrams, Hal Bacon, Rick Bannerot, Barbara Bright, Steve Brooke, Steve Campbell, Len Codella, Jeff Crouch, Joe Eldridge, Bruce Farling, Joe Garman, Phil Getchell, Jerry Girard, Sante Giuliani, Cynthia Graber, Bruce Handley, Dave Howell, Irene Huang, Julia Hunter, Sandy Ives, Martin Keane, Tom Kerr, Jeff Knapp, Jerry Kustich, Carmine Lisella, Brian McGrath, Dick Manning, Stephen Morgan, Tom Morgan, John Mundt, Amy Orlomoski, David Orr, John Randolph, Leslie Rose, Michael Sinclair, Jeffrey Smith, Phil Snyder, Dick Spurr, Tracey Stone-Manning, Archie Verow, and Carl-Erik Westberg.

My agent, Henry Dunow, believed extravagantly in this book from the beginning. So did Ileene Smith. Thank you both. At Random House, I'm grateful to Will Murphy and Matt Kellogg for guiding the manuscript painlessly to completion.

As always, my deepest thanks are to Anne, David, and Julia—who are the rock on which these little stick houses of mine are built.

New York City, March 2006

Contents

Some Important Dates

c. 200   Fishermen in Macedonia fashion the first artificial flies as a means of catching trout.

1496   Publication in England of *Treatyse of Fysshynge wyth an Angle*, attributed to Dame Juliana Berners.

1653   First edition of Izaak Walton and Charles Cotton's *The Compleat Angler.*

1732   Foundation of the Schuylkill Fishing Company of Pennsylvania, the first angling club in the American colonies.

1770s   Philadelphia tavern keeper Edward Pole opens the first American fishing tackle shop, selling rods and reels imported from England.

1831   Hiram Leonard is born in Sebec, Maine.

1845–1865   Pennsylvania gunsmith and violin maker Samuel Phillippe, his son Solon, and craftsmen Charles Murphy and Ebenezer Green from Newark, New Jersey, develop the first American split bamboo fly rods.

1857   Henry David Thoreau meets Leonard on Thoreau's third journey to the Maine woods; Eustis William Edwards is born in Portland, Maine.

1860s–1870s   Beginning of the "trout rush" to Maine's Rangeley Lakes.

1871   Leonard makes his first split bamboo fly rod.

1876   Leonard's gold-and-jewel-encrusted bamboo fly rod is exhibited at the Philadelphia Centennial Exposition.

1878   Loman Hawes and Hiram Leonard invent the beveling machine that allows for mass production of split bamboo strips; William Mills of New York City becomes sole agent for Leonard's rods.

1882   Leonard moves his rod shop to Central Valley, New York, bringing Eustis Edwards, Fred Thomas, Hiram Hawes, and Loman Hawes with him from Maine; casting tournaments begin in Central Park.

1885   Bangor metalsmith Ed Payne joins the Leonard group.

1890   Edwards, Thomas, and Loman Hawes break with Leonard and begin making the Kosmic rod.

1890   Montgomery Ward's catalog begins offering mass-produced six-strip bamboo fly rods for $1.25.

1892   Abercrombie & Fitch opens its Manhattan outfitter's store.

1893   The Kosmic rod is showcased at the World's Columbian Exposition in Chicago.

1895   Edwards moves to Los Angeles, abandoning rod making for the first time.

1897   Loman Hawes dies.

1898   Thomas and Edwards return to Maine and enter into a brief partnership building rods in Brewer.

1899   Thorstein Veblen publishes *The Theory of the Leisure Class*, coining the phrase "conspicuous consumption."

c. 1900   The Montague Rod and Reel Company of Massachusetts begins using "Tonkin Cane" as a trade name for the Chinese bamboo used in rod making.

1901   Edwards starts his photographic business in Brewer.

1907   Leonard dies at his home in Central Valley, New York.

1909   Hiram Hawes sets up his own rod shop in Canterbury, Connecticut.

1911   L. L. Bean invents his rubber-soled, leather-topped boots.

1914   Ed Payne dies; the following year his son Jim takes over the business.

1916   Edwards abandons photography and returns to rod making full-time.

1918   Edwards sells his rod shop to the Winchester Repeating Arms Company of New Haven, Connecticut, for $10,000 and agrees to a five-year contract as head of Winchester's rod-making operation.

1920   Publication of *The Idyl* [*sic*] *of the Split-Bamboo*, by Dr. George Parker Holden of Yonkers, New York; soon after, influenced by the book, Everett Garrison of Yonkers begins making rods.

1924   Eustis Edwards produces his Perfection rod.

1925   Edwards and his son Gene open their rod shop in Mount Carmel, Connecticut; Smithsonian botanist Floyd Alonzo McClure visits the Sui River Valley in southern China.

1927   Bill Edwards leaves Bangor to join E. W. Edwards & Sons; twelve-year-old Sam Carlson begins sweeping floors in the Edwards shop.

1929   The Winther-Stoner Manufacturing Company is founded in San Francisco.

1931   Eustis Edwards dies at his home in Hamden, Connecticut, shortly after optioning the family business to the Horton Manufacturing Company in the nearby town of Bristol; Hiram Hawes dies in Canterbury, Connecticut; McClure gives "Tonkin cane" its scientific name, *Arundinaria amabilis.*

1932   The Edwards rod shop in Mount Carmel is destroyed by fire; Gene and Bill begin work at Horton-Bristol.

1933   Californians Lew Stoner and E. C. Powell register patents for "hollow-built" bamboo rods.

c. 1936   Gene Edwards begins making fly rods for L. L.
              Bean, which by now has grown to become a million-
              dollar business.

1938   Fred Thomas dies.

1939   Bill Edwards quits Horton, designs the four-strip
              Quadrate rod, and opens his own shop with his son
              Scott.

1942   Horton-Bristol Manufacturing Company closes down
              its rod-making division and turns over its entire
              plant to war production.

1946   After the war ends, Gene Edwards opens his own
              rod shop in Mount Carmel, Connecticut, where he
              is joined by Sam Carlson.

1949   Mao Zedong's revolution triumphs in China.

1950   Bamboo rod making is devastated by the U.S. trade
              embargo against China and the introduction of fly
              rods made of fiberglass.

mid-1950s   The big mass-production companies—Montague,
              Horrocks-Ibbotson, South Bend, and Union Hard-
              ware—abandon bamboo rod making.

1955   Gene Edwards closes down his rod shop.

1956   Bill Edwards also closes down his business; much of
              the equipment is acquired by his senior rod maker,
              Ray Gambordella, who in turn sells it to Sam Carl-
              son at the end of the year.

1957   Carlson starts his own rod-making business.

1958   Carlson and Gambordella buy the F. E. Thomas
              Rod Company, but the partnership lasts less than a
              year.

1964   Fire destroys the Leonard plant in Central Valley,
              New York; although it resumes operations in 1965,
              all the old rod tapers have been lost in the fire.

1965   Entrepreneur Leigh Perkins buys the struggling

1992   Robert Redford directs the movie version of Norman Maclean's *A River Runs Through It.*

1996   Charles Schwab buys the E. C. Powell Rod Company and the Bitterroot Stock Farm in Montana.

1998   Steve Campbell of Brewer, Maine, buys the F. E. Thomas Rod Company from Sam Carlson.

2002   Sam Carlson dies in Greenville, New Hampshire; Dana Gray takes over the Carlson Rod Company.

2004   Despite employees' protests, Winston announces the outsourcing of some of its graphite rod production to China; the Plum Creek Timber Company announces development plans for almost half a million acres around Maine's Moosehead Lake.

2005   Jim Frank, Dave Decker, and Hal Bacon relaunch the Kosmic Rod Company; Glenn Brackett resigns from Winston.

2006   Glenn Brackett, Jerry Kustich, and Jeff Walker open a new shop, which they call Sweetgrass Rods, in Twin Bridges, Montana.

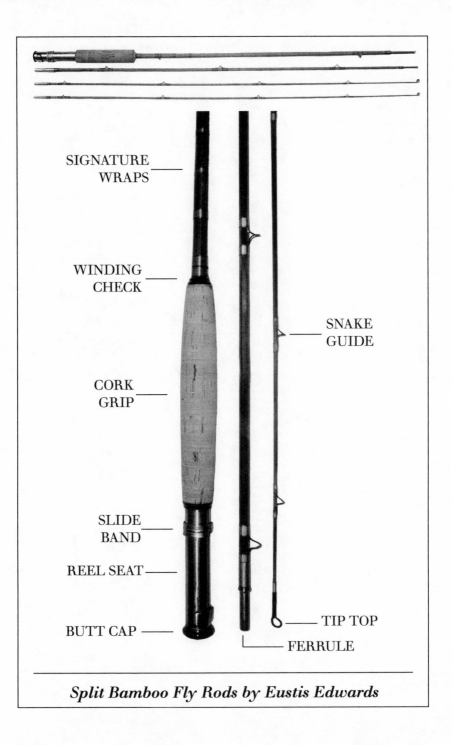

SIGNATURE WRAPS

WINDING CHECK

SNAKE GUIDE

CORK GRIP

SLIDE BAND

REEL SEAT

BUTT CAP

TIP TOP

FERRULE

Split Bamboo Fly Rods by Eustis Edwards

PART ONE

Old
Masters

Hiram Leonard at his bench, 1876.

I was born and reared in Hartford, in the State of Connecticut—anyway, just over the river, in the country.... So I am a Yankee of the Yankees, and practical.... Why, I could make anything a body wanted—anything in the world, it didn't make any difference what; and if there wasn't any quick, new-fangled way to make a thing, I could invent one.

—Mark Twain,
A Connecticut Yankee in
King Arthur's Court *(1889)*

We got curiously intimate with the peculiar needs of the neighborhood.... The dimensions we chose, the curves we followed, were imposed on us by the nature of the soil in this or that farm, the gradient of this or that hill, the temper of this or that customer.... What we had to do was to live up to the local wisdom of our kind; to follow the customs, and work to the measurements, which had been tested and corrected long before our time in every village shop all across the country.

—George Sturt,
The Wheelwright's Shop *(1923)*

CHAPTER 1

Wilderness with All the Comforts

My wife's hometown, Stillwater, Oklahoma—population forty thousand, home of the Oklahoma State University Cowboys and the National Wrestling Hall of Fame—is not the kind of place, at first blush, where you would expect a fly fisherman to have a life-changing experience. The old downtown is much like the core of a lot of American towns whose original logic has been bypassed by time and Wal-Mart. There are a few bars that cater to the student clientele from OSU, a couple of banks, an upscale home-furnishing franchise, a Christian bookstore or two, an ersatz Starbucks, some boarded-up storefronts, and a multidealer antiques mall, the kind you see these days in almost every town of comparable size.

The mall is much as you'd expect. Knickknacks and collectibles of all sorts. The stuff Grandma left in her attic. Used books. Farm tools, costume jewelry, fifty-cent ties, incomplete sets of glassware. A room full of ticking wall clocks. Barbie dolls and *Star Wars* action figures, as the cutoff line for the term "antique" creeps steadily forward. And then a dealer's stand I'd never noticed before: vintage fishing tackle.

At this point I'd been fly-fishing for three or four years, I suppose—long enough to graduate to my first hundred-dollar graphite fly rod and make the transition (in my own mind, at least) from rank beginner to semicompetent amateur—by which I mean that once in a while I even caught a few trout. So I stopped to take a look.

In one corner of the booth was a narrow wooden box about three feet long, its hinged lid secured with two brass clasps. I popped them open. Inside, boxwood partitions divided the container into several compartments, on much the same principle as a case of wine. Seven sections of hexagonal bamboo were nestled into the notched dividers. The handle was reversible. There was a stout butt section, two midsections, and three tips of varying thicknesses. This meant you could configure the rod a couple of different ways, as either an eight-foot fly rod or a five-and-a-half-foot bait caster—a kind of rod that is used for throwing heavier lures. This struck me as a neat arrangement.

Each segment of the rod was coated in a deep cherry red lacquer. The ferrules—the male and female parts that connected the sections—gleamed as chrome-bright as the trim on an old Cadillac. The snake-shaped line guides were attached to the bamboo with silk thread windings in elaborate patterns of lime green and lemon yellow. The guides themselves were of some gold-colored alloy. An inch or two above the cork grip, a lozenge-shaped acetate decal depicted a snowcapped mountain, perhaps a volcano, against a blue sky, with the initials "NFT." You could be forgiven for calling the whole thing gaudy, but to me it was magically redolent of the 1940s, a decade for which I've always felt a special affinity, perhaps because I was born at its tail end.

Suffice it to say that I fell in love with this fly rod, even though it would end up jilting me. The price tag said $87.50. I paid cash.

I fished the rod a couple of times that spring. Once I took it out on a smooth-flowing chalk stream in the south of England, where it landed a handsome sixteen-inch rainbow trout. After that I used it to catch some wild brook trout in Connecticut.

Feeling quite pleased with myself, I took the rod into a local fly shop to get the reading of an expert. He took the pieces from the box, sighted along each section in turn, put them together, squinted at them some more, made small humphing noises to himself, then gave me a long, appraising look. "Well, it's very pretty, isn't it?" he said. "The lacquer's nice, very decorative."

"But?" I said, knowing from his tone that the real verdict was still to come.

"Well, of course, as a fly rod it's worthless, it's a piece of junk." He pointed to the volcano decal. "NFT—Nippon Fishing Tackle. That's Mount Fuji in the picture, I guess. They churned these things out by the thousands in Japan after World War Two, for G.I.'s to take home as souvenirs, mainly. It's not even the right kind of bamboo...."

The man in the fly shop went on talking some more. I missed most of it—no doubt because embarrassment had kicked in. But I do remember the gleam in his eye, the lyricism in his voice, and the gist of what he said. The right kind of bamboo, he told me, was something called Tonkin cane. The raw material was Chinese, but the art of transforming it into a fly rod was a peculiarly American accomplishment; and in the hands of a master craftsman . . . well, if I ever had the good fortune to experience the real thing—as opposed to the piece of junk I had just dumped on his counter—I would surely agree that it was a kind of perfection.

I resolved then and there that I would go in search of this peculiarly American vision of perfection, never suspecting that it would take me all the way back to Henry David Thoreau.

In July 1857, Thoreau set out on his third journey from Walden Pond to the Maine woods. He'd traveled there for the first time in 1846, to Bangor by railroad and steamship and thence up the West Branch of the Penobscot River to Mount Katahdin, the second highest peak in New England. His second trip, in 1853, had taken him via Moosehead to Chesuncook Lake. But it seems to have been a little anticlimactic after the ascent of Katahdin, which had inspired his celebrated meditation on raw nature as

something savage and awful, though beautiful.... Here was no man's garden, but the unhandselled globe. It was not lawn, nor pasture, nor mead, nor woodland, nor lea, nor arable, nor

*waste-land. It was the fresh and natural surface of the planet
Earth, as it was made for ever and ever.*

Thoreau and his companions dined on Maine brook trout,
freshly caught. "In the night," he wrote, "I dreamed of trout fishing; when at length I awoke, it seemed a fabled myth this painted
fish swam there, so near by couch, and rose to our hooks the last
evening, and I doubted if I had not dreamed it all."

There was something restless and improvised about Thoreau's
third trip to Maine, and he was debating his itinerary right up to
the last minute. At first he considered exploring the Saint John
River from its source to its mouth, but then he changed his mind,
opting instead for Moosehead, the lakes of the Saint John, and the
Penobscot again. Just nine days before he left Concord, he was still
casting around for a traveling companion. He wrote to his cousin
George Thatcher, of Bangor, asking for suggestions. Perhaps his
nephew Charles would agree to join him, since he had "some
fresh, as well as salt, water experience?" But in the end, Thoreau
settled on his Concord neighbor Edward Hoar, late of California.

The interesting thing about Thoreau's account of this third
journey is that Hoar—his companion for 60 miles by stagecoach,
another 265 by canoe, and twelve rough nights under canvas—is
virtually invisible, never once mentioned by name. From Thoreau's
subsequent correspondence, you can infer that his neighbor was a
bit of a pain. Two weeks after his return to Concord, Thoreau
wrote to a friend that Hoar had "suffered considerably from being
obliged to carry unusual loads over wet and rough 'carries.' " Hoar
came back from Bangor with a set of moose antlers, a gift from
George Thatcher, which he used as a hat stand, and that's the last
we hear of him.

In contrast, another character, with whom Thoreau had only
the briefest of encounters, positively leaps from the page. It was
July 23, and Thoreau, Hoar, and their Penobscot Indian guide, Joe

Polis, had just boarded the stage that would take them from Bangor to the remote outpost of Greenville, which lies at the foot of Moosehead Lake.

Given the number of guns on display in the coach, Thoreau wrote, "you would have thought that we were prepared to run the gauntlet of a band of robbers." But it turned out that the occupants were the members of a hunting party who were embarking on a six-week trip to the Restigouche River and Chaleur Bay, in the remotest reaches of the Canadian province of New Brunswick.

Their leader was a handsome man about thirty years old, of good height, but not apparently robust, of gentlemanly address and faultless toilet; such a one as you might expect to meet on Broadway. In fact, in the popular sense of the word, he was the most "gentlemanly" appearing man in the stage, or that we saw on the road. He had a fair white complexion, as if he had always lived in the shade, and an intellectual face, and with his quiet manners might have passed for a divinity student who had seen something of the world.

Thoreau subsequently discovered that appearances were deceptive. Far from being a divinity student, his coach mate was in fact a celebrated gunsmith, and "probably the chief white hunter of Maine." But he never learned the man's name, which was Hiram Lewis Leonard.

Leonard belongs to that great American series of heroic archetypes—the lineage that includes Johnny Appleseed and Horatio Alger, but above all Daniel Boone and Natty Bumppo. One historian described him as "a millwright, gunsmith, daguerrotypist, flutist, trapper, moose hunter, taxidermist, and one of the very early manufacturers of split bamboo fishing rods"—which we'll come to in a moment. You could add a string of other accomplishments to that list: Leonard was also an expert canoeist, a fur trader, a pioneering fish culturist who was one of the first people to breed

salmon in a hatchery, and a gifted self-taught civil engineer who
was put in charge of the machinery department of the Pennsylvania Coal Company when he was still in his teens. On top of all that
there was his physical bravery. As Thoreau's coach to Greenville
crossed the Piscataquis River, his companions told him the story of
how, during the previous spring, Leonard had plunged into the
frigid, swollen waters of a nearby brook to rescue a Mr. Stoddard,
the owner of the Bangor-to-Moosehead stage, from drowning.

The Leonards were one of those old New England families
who could trace their ancestry back to the *Mayflower*, specifically
to three brothers who traveled together from England and settled
in Massachusetts. After a dismal spell as a sheep farmer, Hiram's
father, Lewis Leonard, became a master oar maker, leading a peripatetic life that took him from one stand of native ash trees to another—Sebec, Maine (where Hiram was born in 1831); Ellenville,
New York; and Honesdale, Pennsylvania—moving on each time
the supply of raw material for his oars was exhausted. Hiram's
younger brother Alvin joined his father in the family business, and
together they became the most celebrated makers of racing oars in
the country, their fame spreading even to England. A family diary
records that Lewis and Alvin "made nearly all of the oars used
by the professional rowers of the country and most of the noted
amateurs."

Many of the Bumppo-flavored legends about Leonard come
from his obituaries and postmortem reminiscences, and I suppose
such accounts should always be taken with a grain of salt. They're
evocative, nonetheless.

> *In the woods he always carried his flute with him and played
> it well. Many is the night I heard him wake the wilderness
> with "Nellie Gray," "The Irish Washerwoman," "Old Ken-
> tucky Home," and other tunes now seldom heard.*

> *Mr. Leonard's powers of endurance were beyond belief,
> judging from appearances. He never seemed tired and would*

tramp all day through the forest, returning at night seemingly fresh.

The men are scarce who could carry as heavy a load as long a distance as he could. In 1856 he carried a quarter of moose weighing 135 pounds from Little Spencer Pond to Lobster Lake, a distance of seven miles.

Thoreau himself had struggled to combat ill health with bouts of intense physical activity. As he wrote to his cousin George Thatcher, his decision to undertake a third journey to the Maine woods was the result of "finding myself somewhat stronger than for 2 or 3 years past." It's hard, then, not to imagine that it was Leonard's combination of physical prowess and apparent frailty ("a fair white complexion, as if he had always lived in the shade") that made such a powerful impression on the naturalist.

The fact was that Leonard's health had always been delicate. His first problems were respiratory, and there's some speculation that this may have been the result of exposure to coal dust during his stint with the Pennsylvania Coal Company. Then, not long after his encounter with Thoreau and his marriage to Lizzie Head, a classically educated minor poet who knew French, Latin, and Hebrew, Leonard contracted measles—not a laughing matter in an adult. His doctor advised Leonard and Lizzie to move away from Bangor and live full-time in the woods.

That's of some significance, I think, because traffic into the wilderness for health reasons—otherwise known as "taking the airs"—was beginning to be a fad. The doctor's prescription was an early hint that the Maine woods, in this period leading up to the Civil War, were not quite as "unhandselled" as Thoreau (not to mention his later fans) liked to imagine. There are plenty of other clues to this in Thoreau's own account of his travels. Paddling across the lakes of Piscataquis County, he was struck by the radical fluctuations in water level that had left miles of dead and exposed stumps along the lakeshore. To reach the raging currents of Web-

ster Stream—the "thunder-spout" where he and the Indian guide
Joe Polis spent a cold and anxious night separated from Edward
Hoar—Thoreau had first to navigate a mile-long artificial canal
that had been dug at the outlet of Telos Lake. Both the Telos canal
and the dead stumps were, in fact, visible symptoms of the impact
of the logging industry, which had tampered extensively with
Maine's waterways in order to sluice its product efficiently from
forest to market.

Maine, you might say, was fast becoming an idea as well as a
place. The timber industry was responsible for most of the scars,
but it opened roads that others quickly followed. The Victorian
upper-middle classes converged on the Maine woods from the
three great urban centers of the East Coast—Boston, New York,
and Philadelphia. These people had both means and motive. They
had plenty of disposable income; they were eager to escape from
the summer heat and pollution of the cities (much of it caused, no
doubt, by the industries they owned and operated); and they were
enthusiastic converts to the cult of the outdoors, in part because
they had absorbed Thoreau's message that urban life had made
them soft and corrupt and alienated them from the natural world.

For this WASP gentry, Maine summers were partly a matter of
aesthetics, partly an opportunity for adventure, and partly a reflection of status. The leading men of the time were in thrall to social
Darwinism, seeing nature both as a source of wealth and as a challenge to be overcome if civilization was to move forward. But in
Maine they also found, in the words of the environmental historian Max Oelschlager, that "wild nature still offer[ed] opportunity
for contemplative encounters, occasions for human beings to reflect on life and cosmos, on meaning and significance that tran-
scends the culturally relative categories of modern existence." And
as they grew attuned to the ancient rhythms of these wild places,
they became avid recruits for the first stirrings of conservationism.

In the process, they invented something that would come to be called outdoor recreation. These people didn't just walk, they *hiked*, and the purpose of the exercise was something different from and more profound than simply getting from point A to point B. In the world they created, hunting and fishing were no longer just means of obtaining protein; they were a *hobby*, a *sport*. And men like Hiram Leonard were there to provide them with the tools they required, which would be nothing but the best, with money no object.

The "sports" also needed an infrastructure, of course. They needed to be housed and fed. Contemplative encounters with nature were all well and good, but leaky tents had limited appeal. The rudiments of this infrastructure had been there since the mid-1840s, when the timber companies began constructing a string of sluice dams above and below Lake Wellekennebacook (today's Lower Richardson Lake)—Upper Dam, Middle Dam, and Lower Dam—to facilitate their log drives. These were lonely places: as a condition of employment, the dam keeper had to be a married man, so that a second person would be on hand in case of accident or injury.

The radical man-made change in the lake level flooded out a picturesque character named Joshua Rich, who was living in deep solitude on a point of land off Metallak Island, hunting, fishing, and trapping game, some of which he shipped out as research specimens to Louis Agassiz at his Museum of Comparative Zoology in Cambridge, Massachusetts. After the flood, Rich decamped to Middle Dam, where he found some dilapidated huts that had been thrown together to house the workers who built the sluice. Rich considered the dam, considered the huts, considered the gigantic native brook trout that teemed in the lake—Thoreau's "painted fish"—and a lightbulb went on. He built some cabins and called the place Angler's Retreat.

The classic early account of Joshua Rich's camp was written in 1864 by a physician named Elisha Lewis. He reached Middle Dam on the steamer *Union,* which hissed and clanked its way across Lake Umbagog at five miles per hour, steam pouring from its leaky boiler, wreathed in the smoke of burning hemlock logs. In Dr. Lewis's description, the *Union* was a craft

> *more curious and ingenious in its conception than anything which had yet been constructed on our seaboard... a nondescript abortion or cross between a mud-scow and a locomotive; it might very properly, in accordance with naval nomenclature, have been christened a hermaphrodite locomotive.*

Although Joshua Rich livened up the evenings with "his recital of wild adventures with deer, wolves, bears, caribou, panthers, moose and elk," Dr. Lewis made it clear that the Angler's Retreat was not yet the Waldorf-Astoria:

> *Soon after our arrival we were informed that the Camp was poorly supplied with food—nothing to be had in the way of edibles save slices of strong-tasted [sic] pork fried with tough bread. I must confess I was quite startled by this announcement, in consideration of the beautiful visions of wild-game, corn-cakes, hot buckwheats, ham and eggs, and other like delicacies which Mr. Rich's flaming circular had conjured up in my mind's eye.*

The help also left a lot to be desired. The doctor complained about the "sulky guides" and the "impertinence from the campboy and boorish incivility on the part of the half-tipsy *maître de cuisine*" (though, to be fair, camp cooks in the Maine woods probably weren't accustomed to being thought of as *maîtres de cuisine*). At the end of his stay, Dr. Lewis offered the proprietor of the Angler's Retreat some parting advice.

> *Mr. Rich, if he really wishes to make his camp a resort for sportsmen and tourists, should engage the services of a cou-*

ple of middle-aged, steady women, one as a cook, the other as housemaid and waiter, and not be dependent on low, foul-mouthed ship scullions and saucy, dirty boys for such duties. He should teach his gentlemanly guides to be civil, patient, good-natured and obliging, and above all, should have them under proper control, and under no circumstances permit them or his kitchen scullions to bully and control him. . . . When such arrangements are made, I will be glad to visit "The Angler's Retreat" once more.

Ouch.

Over time the accommodations did improve, especially after Rich sold out to new owners. By 1879, a flier was promising that "all the sleeping rooms are nicely finished, lathed and plastered." It was no longer just the gentleman "sports" who came to the booming camps. Maine was now becoming an enticing vacation spot for the entire family, and the demand for comfort increased accordingly. In 1887, after the Angler's Retreat was taken over by the Androscoggin Lakes Transportation Company, a brochure painted this picture of what the visitor could expect for $2 a night:

The house contains sleeping accommodations for forty people, the rooms being furnished with handsome bedsteads, woven wire springs, and 40-lb hair mattresses. The ladies' sitting room, dining-room, office etc. are conveniently located on the first floor, and long, roomy piazzas, overlooking the lake, offer a pleasant retreat for the idlers.

Of course, hordes of tourists don't materialize in a place by spontaneous generation. First they have to be identified, solicited, cultivated, flattered. The place itself, the destination, has to be packaged and sold. In the last two decades of the nineteenth century and the early years of the twentieth, the state of Maine was the object of an aggressive marketing and branding campaign, largely driven by the expansion of the railroads. The Bangor, Aroostook, and Maine Central reached Moosehead Lake in 1884; ten years later a narrow-gauge line cut the travel time from Boston to the Rangeley Lakes to ten hours. The discerning, well-heeled visitor would be whisked away to a tranquil, balsam-scented paradise—"wilderness with all the comforts." The Gilded Age would come to the Maine woods, which would be transformed into the "Play Ground of the Nation."

The person who coined this slogan was a singular character named Cornelia Thurza Crosby. Born in 1854 in the tiny western Maine town of Phillips, Crosby had succumbed to tuberculosis as a young woman. Like Hiram Leonard, she followed her doctor's advice to trust in "the healing power of nature." Out in the woods, she quickly made her reputation as a sharpshooter, the first woman ever to bag a caribou and an intimate friend of Annie Oakley. But trout fishing was her consuming passion. While recuperating from her illness, Crosby caught her first brook trout with an alder pole, and she never looked back. By 1891 she was famous as the woman who had broken all records by catching fifty-two trout in forty-four minutes. She acquired the nickname "Fly Rod," and it stuck.

Fly Rod Crosby cut a memorable figure in her knee-length leather boots, navy blue serge suit, red felt hat, and midlength skirt, which was furnished with an assortment of concealed hooks and eyes to keep it from trailing in the mud. "It is the easiest thing in life to describe me," she wrote. "I am a plain woman of uncertain age, standing six feet in my stockings. I scribble a bit for various sporting journals, and I would rather fish any day than go to heaven." (The last comment, while perfectly understandable, got her in trouble later in life when she converted to Catholicism.)

Each spring Fly Rod took her Maine exhibit to the Annual Sportsmen's Exposition at Madison Square Garden in New York. It was quite a package. She brought live specimens of trout and salmon in specially designed, air-cooled railcars supplied by the

U.S. government. She brought the finest examples of Maine taxidermy. She brought spruce gum samples and prize potatoes and, on one occasion, a 107-pound squash. The centerpiece of the exhibit was always a peeled-log cabin—Camp Oquossoc one year, Camp Rangeley or Camp Penobscot the next—its walls decorated with all manner of rods, nets, and snowshoes, dead antlered animals and giant mounted trout. Owls and eagles perched on the roof. Stuffed cougars bared their teeth, looking real enough to take a bite out of your leg. Fly Rod acted out scenes of camp life, while Mrs. Etta Dill demonstrated her skills at the fly-tying bench, Penobscot Indians in full regalia wove baskets, and fishing guides with bristling mustachios stood around holding canoe paddles and looking exotic and vaguely menacing.

Although the railroad was Crosby's main backer and the principal beneficiary of her efforts, she rarely if ever mentioned it directly. The "Play Ground of the Nation" campaign was a triumph of indirection in advertising. Fly Rod didn't spend time describing the punctuality of the Maine Central or the luxury of its Pullman cars; instead, she concentrated on the enticements of the destination, knowing full well that her audience had only one way to get there.

And they came by the thousands. By the end of the century there were dozens of sporting camps–cum–resort hotels in the Maine woods, most of them concentrated in the Rangeley Lakes area. Hard fried pork was a distant memory. This was an era of candlelit dinners and white linen, and the menu at the Angler's Retreat offered all the fare that Elisha Lewis had hoped for, plus fresh oranges and bananas, lyonnaise potatoes, sirloin steak, lamb chops, tenderloin, and honeycomb tripe.

And the fishing . . . the fishing was all that Joshua Rich had promised. Six-pound, seven-pound, even eight-pound brook trout abounded in the Rangeley Lakes and in the Rapid River, which snarled its way down through five miles of whitewater from Middle Dam to Lake Umbagog. Visitors penciled details of their catch on the cabin walls. One party from Smithville, New Jersey, reported they had landed five hundred pounds of trout. ("Smithville Hogs," someone else scrawled underneath.) Others pinned up outline drawings of their biggest catches on panels of birch bark. And at night, when they retired, the "sports" hung their rods on pegs on the rough board walls of the Angler's Retreat. There were "rods of high and low degree," one visitor reported. But the finest of them were made by Hiram Leonard.

CHAPTER 2

A Useful Thing, Beautifully Made

After my humiliating encounter with the man in the fly shop, I began to move cautiously up the ladder of quality, nosing around for rods that—whatever their other merits—were at least made of what he had called "the right kind of bamboo." I started to notice small ads tucked away in the back pages of the fly-fishing magazines, and in time these led me into one of the infinite subcultures of American life—a small but thriving world of collectors, dealers, and working craftsmen who continued to practice the traditional art of bamboo rod making in apparent defiance of all economic logic.

I found there was an intense schedule of vintage tackle shows and auctions all over the northeast, in Pennsylvania, New Jersey, Connecticut, and Massachusetts. I began to travel on weekends to high school auditoriums, convention centers, and Holiday Inn ballrooms, where I fingered the rods on display and struck up nervous conversations with men (for there was not a woman among them) whose eyes gleamed with a kind of benign fanaticism as they held forth on arcane subjects like ferrule welts, node spacing, and swelled butts. I came to recognize a regular cast of characters, and most of what they said was at first incomprehensible to me.

I subscribed to dealers' catalogs and blanched at the prices. Rods that bore the name of Leonard usually ran well into the four figures; rods by other craftsmen I'd never heard of could bring five. Ten, twelve, even fifteen thousand dollars for a fishing rod! Confused and intimidated, I bought a few rods that were in a friendlier price range. For the most part these were "production rods"—factory made, in other words, rather than handmade by an individual craftsman. Dating mainly from the 1930s and 1940s, these rods had been turned out in the hundreds of thousands by the likes of the Montague Rod and Reel Company of Montague City, Massachusetts; the Horrocks-Ibbotson Company of Utica, New York ("World's Largest Manufacturer of Fishing Tackle"); the South Bend Bait Company of South Bend, Indiana; and the Union Hardware Company of Torrington, Connecticut.

These rods were made of split bamboo—they were even "the right kind" of bamboo—but it turned out that still wasn't enough. My informants told me that my new acquisitions, too, were junk, barely a step up from cherry red lacquer and decals of Mount Fuji. I was badly deflated.

One rod, however, which had been made by the Horton Manufacturing Company of Bristol, Connecticut, elicited a flicker of interest. It was a tool of modest attributes, one dealer told me. However, it did have a relationship, albeit of the most tenuous kind, with the great Maine tradition. At the time it was made, in the 1930s, the rod-making operation at the Bristol Horton factory had been supervised by two half brothers named Edwards. And their father, a man named Eustis William Edwards, had been one of Hiram Leonard's earliest and most gifted apprentices. That was three degrees of separation, but it was enough. I was, so to speak, hooked.

At about this time, my daughter came into the room where I had my modest trove laid out on a table for inspection. She rolled her eyes in a way that only an eight-year-old can master, and said, "Yeah, Dad, but, like, what's all the fuss about? I mean, they're just a bunch of wooden poles with metal bits stuck on the ends."

Well, Julia, yes. And then again, no.

The best concise description of a split bamboo fly rod I ever heard—one that is both a description and an aspiration—is that it is "a useful thing, beautifully made." The man who said this was named Hiram Hawes, and he was both a nephew and a son-in-law of Hiram Leonard's. When Leonard started up his rod-making business in Bangor, Maine, in 1871, young Hiram Hawes, like Eustis Edwards, became one of his first apprentices.

The Haweses and the Leonards had always been close, ever since the Leonards moved to Honesdale, Pennsylvania, in 1840. Both families made guns, both prized fine craftsmanship, and both had a passion for music. Hiram Leonard himself played the flute (and not just any flute, but a good one, a Boehm) and the bass viol. His brother Alvin—after his father died and the family oar business came to an end—became a music teacher in Scranton. His sister, whose name has never been established, married a local gun maker and music teacher named Dwight Hawes. Hiram Leonard's daughter Cora, a talented concert pianist, married Dwight's son Hiram. And Hiram and his four musical brothers were locally famous around Honesdale as "the Hawes Boys."

When I learned all these biographical details, it seemed to me that they helped place the fly rod on the spectrum of crafts, and fly-fishing on the spectrum of activities. If you were to marry a shotgun and a violin, the offspring, in terms of form and function, might look a lot like a bamboo fly rod.

I should say right away that I've never been one of those who believe that fly-fishing elevates the practitioner to some higher order of humanity—I mean, Dick Cheney is a fly fisherman, for heaven's sake, and is even reputed to favor bamboo rods. Nonetheless, those who fly-fish flatter themselves, with some reason, that theirs is the most artistic and literary of outdoor pursuits. More has been written about fly-fishing than any other sport—some of it quite good (although much of it very bad). Artists have painted other sports—think of the Douanier Rousseau and his football players or Frederic Remington and the Winchester shotgun—but I can't think of another artist who has captured the spirit of a sport as thoroughly as Winslow Homer did in his watercolors of fly-fishing for brook trout in the Adirondacks.

There are also powerful similarities, which others have written about, between fly-fishing and music, both in their endless potential complexity and in the meditative state each can induce, the sense of powerful underlying harmonies that are both mathematical and poetic. It may seem pretentious to compare a tool for catching trout with an instrument for making music. You can't play a Bach solo partita on the fly rod, or the cadenza from the Mendelssohn concerto; there's no such thing as a Jascha Heifetz of the fly rod, or a Stéphane Grappelli. But a split bamboo fly rod, used well, is also a small embodiment of human grace.

Part of this grace is mechanical. Bamboo is an organic material with its own natural frequency, and the basic satisfaction of using a split bamboo fly rod is to attain harmony between this and the frequency of your own musculature, your own casting rhythm. The rod feels, in this sense, like a natural extension of your physical being. The illusion that is created is of suddenly having an arm thirty, forty, fifty feet long. You can, metaphorically speaking, take hold of a fly—a tiny, deceptive confection of fur and feather— between thumb and forefinger and place it on the water, in more or less the exact spot you want. *As lightly as thistledown*—that's the usual cliché.

If you ask an engineer, or a technically minded craftsman, what is going on here, he's likely to start tossing around terms like "moment of inertia," "wave linear action," and "modulus of elasticity." Some will say you can measure the action of a particular rod—the way it does its basic job of accelerating the speed of the fly line in the air—by means of static deflection tests and stress curves, or by plotting rate-of-change graphs. My eyes tend to glaze over quickly at this kind of talk.

If you want to be poetic about it, on the other hand, you could do worse than Norman Maclean's definition in *A River Runs*

Through It. A bamboo rod, he writes, is "the four-and-a-half-ounce thing in silk wrappings that trembles with the underskin motions of the flesh." (You should bear in mind, reading this, that the opening line of his famous novella reads, "In our family, there was no clear line between religion and fly fishing.")

Eventually I talked to one New England rod maker who laid out the technical essentials in terms that I found easier to grasp. He told me that the best way to think of a bamboo fly rod was as an unorthodox combination of lever and spring, designed to propel a long, thin weight (the fly line) that culminates in a weightless object (the fly).

"It's a lever," he explained, "but a lever that works quite the opposite of most of the levers we use as tools. It isn't designed to *intensify* the efficiency of your arm movement when you cast; its job is actually to *dissipate* that energy over a long distance. To distribute the stress evenly along the length of the rod, it has to be thicker where the stress is greatest—at the butt—and thinner where the stress is least, at the tip."

So what about the spring? I asked.

He explained, "The spring is designed to absorb the shock of the change in direction of the cast, and on top of that it allows the lever to bend. Ideally that will make the fly line travel in a flattened arc. And the spring is also used to store the energy of the cast"—the energy then being unloaded when you bring your wrist to a dead stop at the completion of the casting stroke.

The balance between lever and spring, the rate at which the diameter of the rod is reduced from butt to tip—these variables are what make up its *taper,* and the taper can be modified and tweaked in infinite ways to suit both the caster and the circumstances. For the craftsman, this is where the real fun starts.

If all goes well, you will employ these mechanics to catch a trout, one of the loveliest of creatures, at the point of intersection of two worlds, the visible and the invisible. The place where this occurs is also likely to be beautiful, since trout favor such settings. This is a fine experience; you will strive for words to express it; and once you have experienced it, you will want to repeat it, again and again.

Even in the static moments before the cast is made, there is the question of aesthetics. There is the pleasure of handling organic materials. There is the subtle contrast of fine silk thread against bamboo; the rings of dense, flor-grade Portuguese cork that form the grip; the dull sheen of nickel silver in the ferrules; the polished wood of the reel seat—walnut, cherry, butternut, African mahogany; the patina that varnish takes on with age. Rods can even be said to have a nose, like wine. Some experts claim they can distinguish individual makers by the smell of the aged varnish on a rod; in the case of one legendary craftsman, this has been compared to the odor of burnt orange rinds. And then there is the ghost in the machine: the sense of association with a particular maker and what is known of his character and values; the visible signs of his perfectionism; the imagined hints of where the rod has traveled, what it has been made to do in the hands of earlier owners.

There are also strong affinities between the bamboo fly rod and the stringed instrument, particularly the violin, as human artifacts. For either to succeed, the maker must extract function from a limited inventory of natural raw materials with very specific physical properties. The making of both calls for a high degree of manual skill, and once the basics have been mastered there are no limits to where that skill can be pushed. There's a wonderful moment in Martin Scorsese's film *The Aviator* where Howard Hughes, played by Leonardo DiCaprio, passes his hand over the rivets on the fuselage of a newly built airplane. He wants them flat—absolutely flat—so that the craft can be perfect, air resistance cut to an absolute minimum. His designers exchange looks. But fly rod makers and violin makers are like that: they want the rivets to be perfectly flat. The goal of perfection pervades every step of the process, even though most craftsmen know that by definition it can never be attained.

As I pressed deeper into the world of the bamboo fly rod, every maker I talked to or read about articulated a vision of perfection, even though the terms they used varied enormously. You'd think that such a specific skill would call for a certain consistent personality. But other than their perfectionism, these men had nothing visible in common. I came to know one rod maker who was a motormouthed recovering alcoholic; another who was a practicing Buddhist; another who was an urbane intellectual; another who was a cold and cerebral engineer, short on basic human skills. Some entered a world of Zen calm when they sat down at their workbenches; others were driven to poverty, divorce, or the brink of madness by the demands they placed upon themselves.

In 1869 Hiram Leonard felt well enough to leave the Maine woods for good with his poet wife, Lizzie, and set up in business as a gunsmith in two upstairs rooms on Main Street in Bangor. Leonard left almost nothing in the way of written records—few craftsmen did; these were workingmen and they weren't sitting around keeping diaries like Virginia Woolf. But he did dictate one brief memorandum, a year or two before his death, in 1907. Written in Lizzie's hand, it recalls that Leonard made his first fly rod within a year or two of returning to Bangor, using joints of ash—his father's old oar-making material—and lancewood.

Ash (the best of it bone white and sometimes scavenged from old billiard cues) and lancewood (bright yellow in color and renowned for its strength and elasticity) were two of the more popular woods being used to build fly rods—their properties allowing them to function as both lever and spring—at the time of the Civil War. Some of the others, like cedar, hickory, shadblow, ironwood, and bois d'arc (or Osage orange), were from American native trees. Cuba (still in the hands of the Spanish) offered mahoe, *dagame,* and *júcaro prieto.* But the best woods were the harvest of Britain's imperial trade. The Asian colonies—India, Burma, Borneo—yielded up obscure timbers like *kranji* and *pingow, pyengadu* and *chow.* The tropical forests of British Guiana, in addition to lancewood, produced greenheart, which was dense and heavy and came in light and dark versions; *bethabara,* which could be planed very fine but was "difficult and disagreeable to work"; paddlewood, salmon pink and light in weight; and *bourra-courra,* the handsomest of them all, whose fine-grained crimson wood was variegated with irregular black spots, giving it its French name of *bois de lettres* and its English name of snakewood.

Each of these woods had its merits and its shortcomings, its supporters and its detractors. Many were beautiful as well as strong, and the best were used for violin bows as well as fly rods. But all of them, with the single exception of lancewood, shared a common defect: none was resilient enough to be trusted for the finest part of the rod, the tip. For that purpose, and increasingly for the rod as a whole, informed opinion was heading in a new direction, toward another part of the British Empire. The top-quality fly rod would no longer be made from a tree, but from a grass—bamboo.

Hiram Leonard wasn't the first to work in this new medium. His 1905 memorandum recorded that a salesman from the Boston sporting goods house of Bradford & Anthony had seen his first effort in ash and lancewood and exclaimed, "The man who made that rod understood the business and ought to be able to make split bamboo rods." Leonard's memorandum went on, "I had never seen one, he showed me two; I examined them; he asked me if I could make them. Answered, 'Yes, and better than those.' " And, incredibly, he did so. I say incredibly because the structure of the new material, the properties of density, strength, and flexibility that made it so desirable, also made it a nightmare to work with hand tools. And Hiram Leonard, further adding to his Natty Bumppo–like legend, made his first bamboo rod with no tools other than a small vise, a hatchet, a rasp, and an Ojibway crooked knife.

There are more than a thousand species of bamboo, in some fifty genera, ranging from feathery decorative miniatures a few inches tall to rugged monsters reaching 120 feet. Bamboo is the fastest-growing thing on the planet: a Japanese scientist once measured a stalk, or culm, of a species called *Phyllostachys bambusoides* that grew almost four feet in twenty-four hours.

In India, bamboo is called "poor man's timber"; in China, it is one of the "three winter friends," along with the pine and the plum. Nineteenth-century craftsmen settled on one particular species, which was classified at the time as *Bambusea arundinacea*, though it was later redesignated as *Bambusa bambos*. But the identification of species is notoriously difficult in the case of bamboo, since it flowers so rarely—only once every 120 years in one case. Scientists eventually decided that *Bambusea arundinacea* was a misnomer; the species that rod makers were using was actually *Gigantochloa macrostachya*, a native of northeastern India whose culms grow to fifty feet or more. Not that any of this mattered much to the craftsmen, who simply called it Calcutta cane.

The origins of the split bamboo fly rod vanish into the mists of apocrypha, but Calcutta cane seems to have entered the British market when it was used as ballast in the holds of East India Company ships returning home empty. It had some modest value in the marketplace for its use in cabinetwork and basketry; and then, around 1800, someone making fishing rods decided that it might have value for that, too. Not the whole culm, which could be anything from an inch and a half to four inches in diameter, but narrow strips—"rent and glued-up," as the British said—which could then be planed to the desired shape.

By the time it reached London, or Philadelphia, Calcutta cane was covered in dark, irregular burn marks from a hot iron. Why these were present, no one quite knew, although theories abounded: they were strictly for ornament; they were to kill the larvae of boring insects; they were to straighten the crooked culms; they were the result of burning off vines and tendrils; they were tied up with some pagan Oriental religious ceremony. Four of these five theories had some foundation in reality.

Like all brilliant ideas, the split bamboo fly rod in its modern form—made from six strips planed at a sixty-degree angle to form a hexagonal cross section—seems to have had no single inventor, although the consensus these days is that either Samuel Phillippe of Easton, Pennsylvania—another gunsmith and a prize-winning violin maker—or his son Solon was the first to make an entire rod in this way, in 1859. (Phillippe and other craftsmen had also experimented with rods made from three and four strips of Calcutta cane.)

The locus of all this early activity was a triangle roughly bounded by New York City, Philadelphia, and the Catskill Mountains. Tradition says that it was eighteenth-century British officers stationed in Philadelphia who introduced fly-fishing to the United States, and the streams of eastern Pennsylvania and the Catskills are generally described as the cradle of the sport in this country. Easton, where Samuel Phillippe lived, is about seventy-five miles south of Honesdale, where the Leonard and Hawes families made their home. Another two of the early pioneers, Charles F. Murphy and Ebenezer A. Green, lived sixty miles from Easton in Newark, New Jersey. Green made rods only for himself and his friends, while Murphy, who is thought to have made about four hundred rods altogether, seems to have been the first to make them for the market.

Murphy and Green underline my earlier point about the wide range of personalities who have dedicated themselves to the idea of perfectionism in split bamboo. Green was "a retired mechanic of large means" who spent most of his time hunting, fishing, and tending his estate. Murphy was a pugnacious little volunteer fire-man who liked his drink, a man "who would rather fight than eat" and was "a little given to brag of his exploits and to think that no man can equal them."

From the historian's point of view, Murphy's bragging was a good thing, since he tended to buttonhole strangers and tell them in great detail what he was up to. In 1865, a writer named Fred Mather ran into Murphy as he was holding court in Conroy's tackle shop on Fulton Street in lower Manhattan.

I listened with wonder to the talk of angles, tapers, gluing and other details, until I thought that the building-up of a split bamboo rod required more careful attention than the grinding of a lens for a great telescope, and I looked with ad-miration on a man who could make one with a good, even ac-tion.... As to a single hand-made rod I can't understand how one can be made perfect unless with elaborate tests of each strip in each joint, which seems nearly impossible.

Braggadocio aside, the little firefighter knew what he was talk-ing about, and he had immediately understood the qualities of Calcutta cane as a rod-building material. In structural terms, bam-boo is totally different from wood. Wood consists of more or less uniform and homogeneous patterns of hollow cells, denser in the annular rings and more open-grained toward the center of the trunk than just beneath the bark. Bamboo, on the other hand, is a three-layered tube, punctuated at intervals by swollen leaf nodes, with soft pith on the inside, hard enamel on the outside, and, sand-wiched in between, the fibrovascular bundles, separated by ther-moplastic resin, that rod makers worship as the "power fibers."

After looking at one of Phillippe's creations, Murphy told Mather:

I showed the rod to Mr. E. A. Green, of Newark, and he got some Calcutta bamboo and made a rod of three pieces for his

*own use, of carefully selected material, and it was an extra
good rod for its day. Then we talked the matter over. Says I,
"there is a lot of waste material in that rod, and the joints in
the cane are no good." And so it came about that I split the
cane, only into four parts at first, shaved down the pulpy inside and glued the pieces together, and had a rod that was
springy enough to cast a fly and had the backbone to fight a
salmon.... I soon found that four strips left far too much pulp
on the inside... and I made rods of six and eight strips.*

As Fred Mather understood, this was work that required an inordinate amount of skill. That translated into man-hours (anything from forty to a hundred, depending on whom you asked),
not to mention the years of unpaid sweat equity before the requi-
site skills were mastered and you could actually charge money for
your product.

" 'Murphy,' says I"—Mather speaking—" 'what price did
these rods bring in that early day?' "

"Well," Murphy answered,

*the trout rods sold for $40, and for an 18-ft. salmon rod I got
as high as $125; but it was all hand-work, careful measure-
ments and tests from start to finish, with much material that
was rejected. And please remember that every rod was made
to order... though prices were high, we earned every dollar
we got; but there were a few men in those days who wanted the
best that could be had, and would pay for it. If that had not
been the case, the split bamboo rod would never have been invented.*

Those are astonishing sums. In current dollars, one of Murphy's salmon rods would cost at least $2,000. But that's actually a
gross underestimation of the real cost, since purchasing power has
increased so much over the last century and a half. It might be

more illuminating to say that it would have taken close to six months of an average worker's earnings to buy Murphy's salmon rod. When I read this passage, the central paradox of the craft became clear: the buyer was almost inevitably a person of wealth, someone capable of influencing tastes and behaviors in the Maine woods and beyond, while the maker . . . well, look no farther than Murphy himself. Despite the fantastic prices he was able to charge, and although he was known as "a very conscientious, careful workman," he was "spending more time on his work than is profitable, and consequently is poor."

The irony of this situation was not lost on Hiram Leonard.

CHAPTER 3

The Worm in the Bud

There's no shortage of ways to make a fool of yourself while fly-fishing—in addition, that is, to taking red-and-green lacquered rods into snooty Manhattan fly shops for appraisal. Perhaps the commonest trick is to snare your back cast high in a nearby tree and then attempt to untangle the resultant macramé while the anglers who are sharing the pool with you studiously look the other way and pretend to be deeply absorbed in their own affairs.

While this happened to me all the time, my real specialty was to attract the satirical attention of passersby when I tested out new rods in the park outside my apartment building in Manhattan. The park is a small strip of open ground, shaded by tall trees, with an equestrian statue of Joan of Arc at one end. In the eighties, when my wife and I first lived here, the park was basically off limits to civilians. Prostitutes yelled incoherently in the bushes, and the ground was perilous with needles and crack vials; sometimes there were gunshots in the night. In the nineties, the park was briefly seeded with grass, and my son David and I would spend hours out there going through the rudiments of baseball. More recently the place has turned into a dog run, and the ground is almost as treacherous as it used to be in the days of the crack dealers. But the center of the dog run is a strip of bare earth about a hundred feet long, and it's an ideal place for some unobstructed casting.

Friendly neighbors will often lean out of windows and yell encouragement when I'm hard at work on the dog run. On the fourteenth of July each year—Bastille Day—parties of uniformed French sailors on shore leave come to the park to pay homage to Joan. Once I saw a group of them shooting covert glances in my direction and muttering to one another. I imagined them saying:

"Merde alors, qu'est-ce qu'il fait? Il est fou, celui-là!"
"Mais, écoute, il pêche à la mouche, n'est-ce pas?"

The dog walkers are the worst. Unerringly, they will call out, "Catching anything?" chortling as if Oscar Wilde himself would applaud their wit. Most of the time I just smile politely, though if I'm feeling cranky, I may glower at them and mutter something like "Chinook salmon."

On one particular occasion, however, I was oblivious to all the insults. The reason was that I was testing out a rod built by Eustis Edwards. By now I was a full convert to split bamboo. I'd given away the last of my graphite rods: no more plastic for me! Fishing with graphite, I'd decided, was like playing baseball on Astroturf. Graphite rods might be able to hurl a fly line an inordinate distance in a straight line, and then snap back to attention like a marine on parade the instant the casting stroke was completed. But to me their efficiency seemed cold and hard, maybe even a little malevolent. I had no interest in fishing with something that originated in the military-aerospace industry and was advertised by the Orvis Company as being made from the same material as Trident nuclear submarines. Trout fishing and high-tech weaponry seemed to me to belong to separate spheres of existence.

The Edwards rod took my breath away. It was like a feather in my hand; it seemed to cast itself. In places the bamboo was flamed as black as a spent match head. I had never seen or felt anything like it.

It was the 1930s Bristol rod, with its tenuous links to the great Hiram Leonard, that had first stirred my interest in the Edwards family. A short time after I bought it, I shelled out a ridiculous amount of money—more than most of my rods had cost at that point—on a book called *Classic Rods and Rodmakers*. Long out of print and greatly sought after on the antiquarian market, it was written in the mid-1970s by a collector and dealer named Martin Keane, and it's still regarded as the gold standard of books on the subject.

While I read the whole book avidly, I kept coming back to the photograph on page 99, of Eustis William Edwards. I don't know what it is that makes a face mesmerizing, but this one mesmerized me. The photograph, taken in 1902, shows a man in his mid-forties (though he appears younger), dressed in a tweed Norfolk jacket and a high, rounded celluloid collar. The hair, which is thick and worn slightly long for the period, is parted a little off center. The mouth is soft and almost feminine. The eyes are gentle but at the same time intense. They followed me round the room, as people sometimes say about the eyes in paintings.

Edwards had been dead for more than forty years when Keane wrote his book, but the author found sources in the New Haven area, where Edwards spent the last thirteen years of his life, who still remembered him clearly. They recalled him as "a highly unusual man—quiet, unassuming, sincere, and honest beyond question," with a "tranquil, yet straightforward manner." Those are all qualities you could infer from simply looking at the photograph.

Eustis Edwards was born in Bangor, Maine, on July 27, 1857— just four days after Thoreau had encountered Hiram Leonard in the stagecoach to Greenville. It's an odd name, Eustis, but it carries the hint of a fishing connection from the start, since Eustis is a small town on the Dead River in western Maine, just a few miles from the Rangeley Lakes.

Keane had uncovered few details of Edwards's early life beyond enigmatic fragments in the Bangor town register. In 1875, he was still a student, living in a quiet neighborhood near the Bangor Theological Seminary; in 1879, proprietor of a fruit and confectionery store; by 1881, a bookkeeper. When I poked around a little more in the Bangor records, I found that his employer at this time was a man named Pierre McConville. I found a photograph of

McConville in a Bangor commercial publication of the time, a plump little man standing in front of an office window that proclaimed him as "Ship Broker—Notary Public—Haytien Consulate—Port Warden." His ad promised, "Special attention given to orders for all kinds of White Pine, Spruce Lumber, Deals etc. Also Penobscot River and Fresh Pond Ice, packed for any voyage, by the cargo or larger quantity." There's nothing there, in other words, that says craftsman, let alone bamboo fly rod maker. Yet by the following year, 1882, Eustis Edwards was installed as one of the first and most brilliant of Hiram Leonard's apprentices—recruited while Leonard was still in Bangor.

In the years after the Civil War, with peacetime prosperity and millions of new immigrants pouring in, the United States was alive with invention. In the 1870s, Alexander Graham Bell invented the telephone; Thomas Edison came up with the electric filament lamp and the phonograph; Henry Heinz gave the world bottled ketchup. American consumers could barely keep up with the flood of new industrial products, which were marketed to them in ways the world had never seen.

At the same time, the outdoors beckoned. In 1868, John Muir reached Yosemite; four years later, Yellowstone Park was established; on the East Coast, the White Mountain Club and the Appalachian Mountain Club followed in short order. The new recreational market was saturated with travel memoirs, guidebooks, photographic albums, and how-to manuals, and 1873 saw the inaugural issue of the most important of the nineteenth-century sporting-and-conservation magazines, *Forest and Stream*. No region received more intense coverage than Maine's Rangeley Lakes.

From his vantage point in Bangor, it must have been easy for Hiram Leonard to see the gross imbalance between supply and demand. The small city acted, so to speak, as a kind of choke point in this process of defining, selling, and consuming the American wilderness experience. The gentleman "sport" traveling to Maine from Boston, Philadelphia, or New York was almost forced to pass through Bangor: that was where the steamer dropped him. Bangor was where he got his maps and railroad schedules and hired his guides before striking out on the trek into the Maine woods. Increasingly the Leonard rod was the object he craved, the ultimate indicator of his taste.

The potential market was enormous, but how many rods could Leonard build? Only so many hours could be invested in the painstaking business of building a split bamboo rod by hand. But given the specialized skills involved, was there any alternative? *Forest and Stream*, for one, didn't think so: "The bamboo rod maker can employ no assistants as competent as himself to execute the nice details of his delicate work. He is the artificer of his own handicraft."

Hiram Leonard, with the help of his extended family, set out to prove the skeptics wrong. He knew from hands-on experience that one of the special qualities of Calcutta bamboo was that its organic structure allowed it to be planed to precise tolerances. In theory, this meant that there was no limit to the ways in which it could be worked and tapered. But what if the work could be done by a machine?

Leonard expanded his small shop by hiring a stolid young man named Fred Thomas, who was barely twenty but already the foreman of a Bangor lumberyard. Then four of the Hawes boys— Hiram, Loman, Merritt, and Frank—decamped to Bangor from Honesdale, Pennsylvania, to join their uncle in his promising new business. Loman came first, it seems, "a great tall fellow with stooped shoulders and prominent cheekbones"; Hiram followed a year later, giving up his job as a trombone player with a traveling circus.

It was Loman who turned out to be the mechanical genius, and in 1878, he and his uncle Hiram designed their machine. It was a crude affair to look at, constructed mostly of wood, and with few metal parts other than the cutting blades. But it could cut bamboo to tolerances of a few thousandths of an inch, and do so reliably time and time again. *Scribner's Monthly,* a magazine favored by New York sophisticates, sent a reporter up to Maine to write about Leonard's marvelous machine. Under an engraving of a bearded Leonard bent over a spartan-looking workbench, the magazine described how the beveler fed strips of bamboo into a pair of rotary blades set at a precise angle of sixty degrees, while a separate mechanism raised each strip progressively as it drew closer to the blades, thus achieving the desired taper.

The thing was revolutionary. While Charles Murphy labored to turn out four dozen rods a year by hand, the Leonard shop could now manufacture close to a thousand. And their quality was consistently spectacular. An incredulous physician, it was reported, was "unable by the closest scrutiny to find any evidence of the rod being made from split bamboo." So, using a surgical saw, he

> made a thin section which he put under his microscope, using a 60 power objective. There was no trace of any joining; the structure was without a seam. This would have convinced most men that the name of "split bamboo" was a fraud, but the doctor determined to give the rod another test. He boiled the section and saw it fall into six pieces. The workmanship was so perfect as to defy the microscope.

This was a waste of a good rod, but it established beyond doubt that Leonard was doing something that was without precedent.

He drew on his early training as a mechanical engineer to work out a set of mathematical formulas for a variety of tapers— different permutations of lever and spring—which have served as a conceptual starting point for virtually every other rod maker who has practiced the craft for the last 130 years. And the beveler gave Leonard his competitive advantage, his proprietary secret.

The machine was kept in a locked room, off-limits to all but its two inventors. For the rest of Leonard's evolving team of craftsmen, prying into its secrets was a firing offense.

Something distinctively, deliberately, even defiantly American was taking form here. Men like Leonard and Hawes, and Samuel Phillippe before them, were products of the artisan culture of guns and stringed instruments, with its bonded apprentices and father-to-son laying on of hands. In post–Civil War America there was a growing reverence for their can-do self-reliance, a cult of the inventor and the entrepreneur, a conscious rejection of the English roots of the rod-making craft, and of Anglophilia more generally. While Leonard's rods crossed the Atlantic and broke down English prejudices about the quality of workmanship in the ex-colonies, it became fashionable for Americans to deride English fly rods as heavy, clunky, Rube Goldberg affairs. (If you couldn't use an English rod to catch trout, the angling historian A. J. Campbell has written, at least it might come in handy for clubbing to death any passing muskrats.)

Where the outdoor pastimes of an English gentleman spoke to a legacy of country estates and privately owned waters, the wealthy elites of post–Civil War America aspired to the conservation of public land and were intent on self-renewal through encounters with the wilderness. The emerging aesthetic of the fly rod was closely tied, moreover, to the specific landscapes of Maine, Pennsylvania, and the Catskills.

Bangor was a small town in a remote location, but it had a rich history of logging and shipbuilding, and Leonard was able to find a ready supply of talented woodworkers and metalworkers. By the mid-1870s he was employing eleven men, plus a bad-tempered lady named Mrs. Pitcher who wound the ornamental silk wraps on each rod that left the workshop. The labor force, then, was not his problem. The tough part was marketing.

With hindsight, you can see the contradictory pressures with which Leonard must have struggled. As long as he made rods by hand, one at a time, economic logic dictated a personal relationship between the craftsman and the client. He knew the client's needs and whims, knew the places where the rod would be taken, could offer advice drawn from his own experience—half a lifetime's worth—of the Maine woods. But the beveling machine, churning out raw blanks for a thousand rods a year, changed all that. It was now in Leonard's power to feed the beast of the market. But the same question loomed for him as for any craftsman in the same position: would the beast devour him?

Not much is known about Leonard's business dealings in the 1870s. For a couple of years he allowed the venerable New York tackle house of Abbey & Imbrie to act as his sole agent. After that there was an even briefer spell with a silent partner, a Boston investor named Hidder, or Kidder, or Ridder—even the man's name hasn't been established with certainty. But in the absence of documented history, layers of mythology tend to grow up to fill the empty spaces. At one of my Holiday Inn tackle shows, I sat down to dinner with a group of collectors and raised the question of how Leonard had moved his product to market. I was surprised by the intensity of the response. Lips were pursed; heads were shaken. Someone set down a beer bottle a little too hard. Leonard had been snookered by smarter and worldlier types, one man complained. He made bad business decisions, another growled: the company had been stolen away from under him. A third collector said he refused to buy any but the earliest Leonard rods as a statement of conscience.

A hundred and thirty years on, it all seemed a little out of proportion. Hidder, Kidder, Ridder . . . for all I knew, the man could equally well have been a cutthroat wheeler-dealer who beat his wife, or an uxorious milquetoast with a wooden leg. But the collectors' minds were made up. We were back in the world of Natty Bumppo again: Leonard was an American original, a principled backwoodsman betrayed by the blind forces of commerce and greed. That isn't to say the collectors were wrong—only that it made me more determined to learn everything I could about the man.

There would have been no lack of commercial outlets for Leonard's work in Boston and Philadelphia, a city that a nineteenth-century writer had described as a "paradise for artisans." But it was New York that exercised by far the strongest gravitational pull. This was where the Carnegies and Morgans and Rockefellers were concentrated, where money was emerging as *the* American value. If I'd needed evidence of how this ambience affected Leonard, I found it in a story that *Forest and Stream* ran in 1875. The magazine reported that the celebrated Maine craftsman was making an exhibition rod for Abbey & Imbrie, which would be put on display at the 1876 Centennial Exposition in Philadelphia. The rod was to have a solid-gold reel-seat set with amethysts and precious stones, gold ferrules and guides, and gold silk windings. The cost would be "about $2,000." Gilded Age, indeed. There's no record of whether anyone actually bought the rod, but there were plenty in New York in 1875 who had the means to do so.

If Leonard was guilty of anything, it seems to have been the sin of naïveté. His reason for parting ways with Abbey & Imbrie, my collector friends told me, was a desire to protect the Leonard name from being swallowed up by a corporate logo. But in hooking up with Mr. Hidder (or whatever his name was), Leonard may have jumped from the frying pan into the fire. For in allowing the Boston investor to buy a share of the business, he may not have realized that the man had also acquired equal rights to dispose of the name—and in 1878 that's exactly what he did, selling his interest in the company to a New York City businessman named William Mills.

Mills didn't just sell fishing rods. He sold camping supplies and picnic baskets and Wood's Improved Lollacapop, "the greatest known antidote for mosquitoes, black flies and gnats in the world."

A new recreational culture was starting to emerge here, in which fashion, style, and merchandising were all important parts of the mix. The man of means needed not only a rod, a reel, and a box of flies, but the right clothes, the right suitcases, the right rain gear and tent and mosquito net, and he wanted to find the whole package under one roof. For wealthy New Yorkers, the ultimate gentleman's outfitter, Abercrombie & Fitch, was just around the corner. Opening its doors in 1892 in lower Manhattan, it kitted out Teddy Roosevelt in tropical battle gear for the charge up San Juan Hill, and then in later years catered to the likes of Ernest Hemingway, Howard Hughes, Emilia Earhart, and the duke of Windsor.

In a quarter of a century we'd come a long way from Thoreau, who had asserted, in *Walden,* that "most of the luxuries, and many of the so-called comforts, of life are not only indispensable, but positive hindrances, to the elevation of mankind." By 1880 or so, the style of the times was what Thorstein Veblen would soon be calling "conspicuous consumption." James Twitchell, a contemporary commentator on advertising, has written about this very well. Paraphrasing Veblen, he says, "As wealth spreads, what drives consumers' behavior is increasingly neither subsistence nor comfort, but the attainment of 'the esteem and envy of other men.'" In the late 1800s, the cult of outdoor recreation was an important arena in which these consumer choices were made.

William Mills, who became Hiram Leonard's sole agent in 1878, had a pretty shrewd understanding of how the process worked. The intrinsic value of the Leonard rod was, of course, rooted in the quality of its manufacture. But to an important degree the value of the rod lay not in the object itself, or its immediate utility as a tool, but in how it was perceived. Mills published ads that said, "If a fisherman wishes **Perfection** in his rods . . . he **must use a Leonard rod.**" A little later, he coined a strikingly modern tagline: *"H. L. Leonard—The rod you will eventually buy."* The name Leonard acquired a mystique; it came to mean

artist as well as artisan; it was a byword for skill, integrity, and perfectionism, with a price tag to match. By purchasing a Leonard,
you showed appreciation of those values. The selling of the
Leonard rod was an early example, in other words, of what a modern marketing theorist would call successful branding.

For the urban "sports," the taxing journey to Maine by steamer,
railroad, and stagecoach was all part of the great adventure. For
William Mills, however, Bangor's remoteness was a major pain.
After a couple of years, he asked Leonard to come down and check
out a location closer to Manhattan, in a village called Central Valley. Mills explained that he had a sister there, as well as part ownership of an abandoned fishing rod factory that could easily be
refurbished.

I drove out to Central Valley one day to take a look at the place.
I'd driven past it dozens of times before without paying much attention. Once you're on the Palisades Parkway, just outside Manhattan, you follow the winding road over Bear Mountain, then
cross over the New York State Thruway, until all of a sudden the
ground drops away to the north and you find yourself looking
straight down onto the flat valley floor and the vast Woodbury
Common mall with its two-hundred-plus designer outlets—
Burberry, Calvin Klein, Coach, Dolce & Gabbana, Fendi, Giorgio
Armani, Ralph Lauren, and the like. Thinking about the Leonard
rod as an early example of luxury branding, I thought it a rich
irony that the site of his workshop should now be given over to this
extravagant display of what Twitchell calls "opuluxe."

The timing of the move to Central Valley wasn't great—
within months of Leonard's arrival the U.S. economy slipped into
a prolonged recession—but the location was spectacular. Central
Valley lies on the eastern edge of the Catskills, the sacred territory
of American fly-fishing, and is hemmed in by the parallel ridges

of Schunnemunk Mountain and the Cornwall Highlands. The U.S. Military Academy, at West Point, is a few miles away, over the hills to the east. By the time Leonard arrived, a new spur line on the Erie Railroad had cut the journey into Manhattan to an hour, with seven or eight trains a day during the week and four on Sundays.

To be strictly accurate, Central Valley was only one of three hamlets that were strung along Woodbury Creek like pearls on a string. The other two were Highland Mills and Woodbury Falls, and together they made up the township of Monroe, their joint population barely twelve hundred. The railroad changed the valley in substantial ways, though it still retained its bucolic charm. Prosperous city folks came for the weekend, many of them drawn by the excellent fishing and shooting, and summer boarding-houses did brisk business.

There were celebrities, too. The most famous resident of Central Valley was the exiled Cuban revolutionary Tomás Estrada Palma, who came here to recuperate from his ill treatment in a Spanish dungeon, opened a school—the Palma Institute—and laid plots for Cuban independence with fellow conspirators such as the great nationalist poet José Martí and the hot-tempered General Calixto García, who had a large bullet hole smack in the middle of his forehead as the result of a botched suicide attempt. In 1902, Estrada Palma would become Cuba's first elected president.

Then there was the railroad czar E. H. Harriman, whose great properties lay nearby in Arden. Harriman was a passionate hunter, and in time he struck up a friendship with Hiram Hawes, offering him the position of overseer of the Adirondack-style camp that he had built on his Arden House estate. For two seasons "Hi" Hawes ran the camp and taught visiting kids how to fish and canoe.

Central Valley had character, in other words, and the arrival of Hiram Leonard gave it more. Leonard was employing about sixteen people in his workshop now. Some of them he recruited locally; others, including Eustis Edwards, Fred Thomas (the shop foreman), and Edward Payne, came down from Bangor to join him, as did Hi and Loman Hawes. Their brother Merritt, who had gone back to Honesdale, Pennsylvania, for a spell, now rejoined the group. As time went on, most of them married local girls from Central Valley or Highland Mills. Eustis Edwards (modestly registering his profession as "laborer") took as his wife a young woman named Jennie Gordon, whose brother William worked in the Leonard rod shop.

If his obituaries can be believed, Leonard "used to say that no man who did not love music and who could not play at least one musical instrument could make a good fishing rod." Accordingly, he had no sooner unpacked his bags than he formed the Central Valley Mechanics Band, drawing most of its members from the rod shop. By February 1882, the band was ready to give its first performance at the Institute Hall, which was "pronounced by all a great success" and raised $35. Leonard had spent a lot of money outfitting the ensemble in plumed helmets and long overcoats with a gold stripe down the side. Loman Hawes was the bandleader, and played the cornet. His brother Hiram played the violin and "received much applause for his version of the *Mocking Bird*." Leonard himself played the flute, the clarinet, and the bass viol. And Eustis Edwards was said to be a talented multi-instrumentalist, switching between the flute, the cornet, the clarinet, and the violin.

Ed Payne, an expert metalworker who had been making fly reels in Bangor, was lured down to Central Valley three years later than the others. In addition to playing the clarinet like Edwards and Leonard, he seems to have been something of a cutup, a song-and-dance man who acquired the nickname "Joe" from his celebrated performances of the sentimental Stephen Foster song "Old Black Joe." Payne also liked to act in burlesque. In a local show called *The Duchess of Dublin* ("laughable throughout"), he played a character called Silas Sharpset, "a second Barnum."

Reading fragments like this from the local news sheets, you have the sense of Hiram Leonard—who was now in his early fifties—hovering in the background as a benign patriarch, a man of unusual discipline and a kind of controlled passion. He reviled alcohol and tobacco, and had not eaten meat since his days in the Maine woods. He had a keen interest in spiritualism. He was an active mason, a Red Man, a Knight of Pythias. He had a quasi-paternal relationship with the three surviving Hawes boys, who all lived in his home, Lionsden. When his daughter Cora eventually married Hi Hawes, she gave Leonard a nephew and son-in-law all in one.

When they weren't building rods and making music, Leonard and his acolytes were busy adding a new highlight to the Manhattan social calendar. In the balmy days of early fall, starting in 1882, gentlemen and their ladies strolled up Fifth Avenue to Olmsted's Harlem Meer, at the northeastern tip of Central Park, for a fly-casting exhibition and competition sponsored by *Forest and Stream*.

This was something quite different from fishing in the conventional sense—fishing, that is, for the purpose of catching fish. Tournament casting per se was not new; it had started in the United States around 1864, and much earlier in England. But its origins were distinctly down-market, and casting contests were often held in conjunction with the organized slaughter of the passenger pigeon. The champions of the sport were folksy characters like Reuben Wood—"genial, jolly, lovable Uncle Rube," in the words of Fred Mather—who smoked a long-stemmed pipe that he called a "flugemocker," referred to a big fish as an "old codwalloper," and declared something excellent "just exebogenus."

The affairs in Central Park, by contrast, were part pure contest of skill, part marketing exercise to show off the latest in rod design, and part fashion statement. The superintendent of the park provided seating for two hundred and danced attendance on Roosevelts and Rockefellers. William Mills provided Leonard's top-of-the-line fifty-dollar Catskill model as the top prize. Afterward, the participants and a select group of spectators repaired to the Metropolitan Hotel for dinner.

The rules called for the contestants to stand on a wooden platform thirty feet from shore and cast their flies out parallel to a rope line studded with small buoys and tin distance markers. Judges and referees paddled alongside in rowing boats, scoring the casts for distance, accuracy, and delicacy of presentation of the fly.

The event was invariably dominated by Hiram Leonard himself ("probably the handsomest fly caster in America") and his extended family. His nephew Dr. A. D. Leonard, who had opened a drugstore and soda fountain in Central Valley; Hiram and Merritt Hawes; and the doctor's brother Reuben Leonard were all champion casters. In the women's division, Leonard's daughter Cora generally held off the challenge of her archrival, Miss Helen Stoddard. Cora's casting outfit was "a black skirt and a silk waist of Gordon tartan"; Miss Stoddard wore "a black dress and a blue waist with black lace, white lace and other trimmings quite impossible for a man to describe." Since the spectators had difficulty telling them apart, *Forest and Stream* advised them to focus on the hair color: "Miss Stoddard is a decided and handsome blonde, whereas her opponent is a striking-looking brunette."

Hiram Hawes in particular turned in performances that defied all conventional wisdom about the natural limits of bamboo, casting unheard-of distances—eighty-five feet and more—with lighter and lighter rods, designed both to compensate for the inherent weight of the raw material and to suit the conditions of the small, rocky rivers of the Catskills. Critics inveighed against these new tools, deriding them as unmanly and un-American, condemning the "aesthetic craze for effeminate toy rods." But Hawes kept on winning contests and converts. After yet another victory in 1884, *Forest and Stream* wrote, "Comment on his style is superfluous, it is simply perfect, yet we wish someone would beat him to break the monotony of his winning year after year."

It all sounds like an idyll, but in truth it wasn't. The worm in the bud was apparent from the beginning, and it prefigured the struggles that every dedicated rod maker would experience over the next century: perfectionism versus economics. It was Hiram Leonard's name that gave the product its cachet, but now it was Mills who owned the name, and Leonard was kicked upstairs, more and more marginalized from the business decisions. Acting rather like an intrusive publisher with a brilliant but temperamental editorial staff, Mills insisted on meeting the demands of a growing market by producing rods that Leonard would have rejected as seconds back in Bangor. These were the rods that my collector at the Holiday Inn had refused to buy.

The pressure came not only from customers clamoring for the Leonard rod but from direct and indirect competition, and in the end even from competition from within. Although Leonard's marvelous machine remained locked away in its secret room, others figured out the basic principles and began to construct bevelers of their own. While Leonard still represented the acme of quality, the split bamboo rod was beginning to lose its mystique of exclusivity. Mass production and direct marketing were bringing bamboo within the reach of the common man, not just the Central Park elites. By about 1890, Montgomery Ward, which had sent out its first mail-order catalog to Midwestern farmers in 1872, was offering six-strip bamboo rods for $1.25. Like my red-lacquered Japanese rod, these may have been junk, hastily slapped together from mismatched sections of cane and with cheap plated-brass fittings. But they were affordable, and the customers were enticed into buying them with flamboyant advertising claims and often fraudulent names like Hindu Vine and African Steel Vine.

There was pressure, too, from the higher end of the market.

Captain Thomas Henry Chubb, who had come to New England to find "clean water and bracing air" after a bout of yellow fever in Galveston, Texas, began cranking out thousands of good as well as tens of thousands of not-so-good rods from his highly mechanized factory in Post Mills, Vermont. Leander Bartlett opened his Montague City Rod Company on the Connecticut River in Massachusetts. And in the resort village of Manchester, Vermont, where he built the Equinox House hotel, a man named Charles F. Orvis added split bamboo to the list of wooden rods he had been making for more than twenty years.

Mills responded to all this with a production schedule that sat poorly with a group of men who had been handpicked for their perfectionism. Even though the beveling machine had cut down on many of the more tedious aspects of the production process, this was still work that demanded intense concentration and meticulous attention to detail, and was unforgiving of the smallest errors. Mills was always in a hurry; the craftsmen's motto might have been "Don't rush me." And in the end, in 1890, their patience gave out, and Fred Thomas, Eustis Edwards, and Loman Hawes decided to strike out on their own. Leonard's supergroup had lasted just eight years.

CHAPTER 4

The Stormy Petrel

The more I learned about Eustis Edwards, the more my fascination grew. The rod I'd fallen in love with was a model called the Perfection, and the name seemed entirely appropriate. As far as I could tell from Martin Keane's book, it had been made in about 1924, which left me a lot of detective work to do if I was to piece together the details of Edwards's life in the thirty-four years after he parted ways with Hiram Leonard in 1890.

Given the virtues of my new rod, the most astonishing thing to me was that I could actually afford it. Not so with those of Payne, Hawes, and Thomas, the other superstars of the Leonard group. With the exception of one or two Thomases, their rods by and large were out of my financial reach. But it seemed that the value that the market placed on the work of Eustis Edwards had nothing to do with its intrinsic worth. It was tied up instead with the vicissitudes that the Edwards family faced in later years.

The other reason for the affordability of my Perfection was more prosaic: it was in lousy shape. For a start, it had only a single tip section (bamboo rods traditionally come with a spare, as a hedge against breakage). Then some rocket scientist had replaced its original silk wraps with nylon thread, which to rod makers is the equivalent of pairing a Château Margaux with a bag of Doritos. Worst of all, there was an ugly repair on the butt section, which looked as if it was concealing some pretty major damage.

I showed it to a couple of rod makers to get a second opinion. One of them flexed the broken part, and I winced as I watched the repair wrap stretch and strain like the skin on the palm of your hand when you bend your fingers back. After two or three rounds of this, there was a faint creaking sound, and then a snap. The rod maker said, "Oh dear."

Now I needed someone to repair the repair, or, as it turned out, to build me a whole new section. I asked around, and eventually someone steered me toward a man who went by the name of Streamer.

I was told that Streamer (whom his wife, but apparently no one else, called Bill Abrams) shared my obsession with Eustis Edwards. In fact, he was one of only a few contemporary rod makers—perhaps the only one—whose rods drew their inspiration directly from original Edwards designs. He also shared my passion for a Connecticut trout stream called the Shepaug, which I had written about in a previous book. His sobriquet came from a style of fly (as well as a fly shop he had once owned) that had been made famous by a flytier named Carrie Stevens, who perfected her craft at Upper Dam in Maine in the 1920s. Eustis Edwards, the Shepaug River, the Rangeley Lakes—here were three auguries. Streamer and I were clearly destined to become friends.

Streamer turned out to be a genial type with a certain natural diffidence and unfashionably liberal politics that closely matched my own. He generally had a corncob pipe clenched between his front teeth, which had a distinct gap. He commuted to the river in a funky Jeep Wrangler from which he had carefully removed the letters *Wr*.

Streamer lives in a large cedar clapboard colonial in the woods. It looks as if it dates from the eighteenth century, but in fact he built it himself. Next to it is a strip of lawn of roughly the same dimensions as Joan of Arc Park, where he tests out his rods.

The first thing you notice on entering Streamer's workshop is a pair of ornately framed nineteenth-century hand-colored lithographic portraits. These are not, as you might imagine, his ancestors. They are Hiram Leonard's father, Lewis, the oar maker, and his wife, Hannah. Streamer rescued the portraits from a Massachusetts auction.

A couple of weeks after our first meeting, he sent me an e-mail. He had dismantled the broken joint of my Perfection, separated it by some mysterious alchemy into its six component strips, and then poked around inside like a forensic pathologist conducting an autopsy. The butt was partly hollow, he told me, for the sake of lightness. He was excited by this discovery, since the "hollow-building" technique was something that was developed only much later by rod makers on the West Coast. This was typical Eustis Edwards, he said—characteristically adventurous and experimental. We agreed that in the absence of documentation, you had to look for clues like this to the character of the man. If I was to write about him, I was faced, in other words, with the challenge of piecing together a kind of *inferential* biography.

Over the months that followed, I got to know Streamer better. We went out a few times together on the Shepaug and the Housatonic. He took me to wild, secret corners of Connecticut. On one occasion he strapped a holster to his belt before we left the house. "You don't mind, do you, two die-hard liberals?" he asked, seeing my questioning look. "Bear." When we reached the ravine he had in mind, high in the folds of a rocky hillside, he pointed to a huge fallen tree and told me he'd seen cougar scat there on his last visit, deposited on the trunk as a territorial marker. In Connecticut!

Streamer's casting skills were a joy to watch, and almost invariably he caught two or three trout for every one of mine. I noticed in him an intense sense of place, of being in the right landscape. That's a rare characteristic in our mobile, postmodern world, but I found it was common among rod makers. Once they've put down roots, they tend to become trees.

As we were sitting together one spring evening at the edge of the Housatonic Railroad tracks, looking down on his favorite pool and watching a big trout rise to sip Hendrickson mayflies from the surface, I asked him to tell me something of his life, and how he had come to be a bamboo rod maker.

"My mother's family goes back to Pennsylvania," he said. "They were Amish, Mennonite. They came to the U.S. for religious reasons, and—" He broke off abruptly. "Oh God, look at that fish. . . ."

"Come on, concentrate," I said.

"OK. Then on my father's side it goes back to Vilnius, Lithuania. My grandfather took his mother's name, which was Abram, and added the *s*. There are these rumors in the family that he was the bastard son of a Lithuanian prince. So I tell my son Ian he's the heir apparent."

After that it was a classic nineteenth-century immigrant story. Grandfather was a machinist in the industrial town of Torrington, in Connecticut's Naugatuck Valley, center of the world brass industry; later there was a farm in Greenfield, Massachusetts, that was repossessed by the bank during the Depression; then a spell peddling fruit from a pushcart outside the Hartford railroad station. Streamer's father was chagrined by this decline in the family's fortunes, and would cross the street to avoid the fruit cart.

The fish below us was still rising; then another appeared a few feet below the first, its head and shoulders clearing the water as it picked off the mayflies.

"That one's even bigger than the first one," I said.

"Yeah, I know him," he answered. "That's Ralph the Wonder Trout."

He went on, "So anyway, Dad decided he wanted to paint and he wanted to fly. When the war broke out, he enlisted, learned to fly trainers, first a Steerman biplane, then the Vultee, and ended up down at Eglin Field shortly after Doolittle left for his bombing raids on Tokyo. That cleaned out all the B-25 instructors—all the best ones went off with Doolittle—so Dad was given a crash course on flying a B-25, practicing takeoffs and landings on the markings they'd put on the tarmac for Doolittle to simulate take-off from carriers."

In an odd moment when Herbert Abrams wasn't flying, one of his commanding officers began musing about a design problem. Japanese planes had that big red circle painted on their sides; the Royal Air Force had its red, white, and blue roundel. American planes had a white star in a blue circle. That didn't do much to distinguish them from the enemy, which meant you worried a bit about shooting down one of your own. So Abrams invented the U.S. Air Force logo—the encircled star with two tabs that has been painted on the side of every American warplane since 1942.

After the war Streamer's father came to New York, studied at the Pratt Institute, then joined the Art Students League, married a woman named Lois, who had jumped into his lap at a masquerade party, moved to northwestern Connecticut, and became a well-known portrait painter. In the White House, the presidential portraits of Carter and George Bush the elder are both by Herbert Abrams; so is a portrait of Arthur Miller in the National Gallery, as well as one of General William Westmorland that hangs in the Pentagon.

The father-son attachment had obviously been intense, for me enviably so. The two began to go fishing together when Streamer was four or five, catching small native brook trout from the streams that course through the Litchfield Hills. It was strictly meat fishing, free trout for supper when times were hard.

"But then I saw guys down on the Housatonic," Streamer said. "And I said, 'Daddy, what are they doing?' And he said, 'Well, they're fly-fishing. That's a whole different thing, it's not the kind of fishing we do.' He was implying that these guys would come up from the city with their Abercrombie & Fitch outfits, get into the river, and do it for show. The irony is that he was an artist, and fly-fishing is an aesthetic pursuit. But he saw it as very utilitarian: you caught fish to eat. But the artist in me started saying, I want to do that, because it's beautiful."

Streamer went to a small private school called Rumsey Hall, which sits on the Bantam River, near its confluence with the Shepaug. He'd spend recess on the river; a memorable teacher named William Wishart taught him to tie flies. There were rumors that Eustis Edwards had once fished the Shepaug.

Later he went to art school for a while, painted a little, ran out of money, spent time in software marketing, ran a fly shop, learned the rudiments of carpentry. He and his wife, Suzy, who is an actress, opened a furniture business in Kent, a snooty weekenders' town on the Housatonic.

"We made a fortune during the summer and fall," he said. "And then in winter we scraped for pennies to pay the oil bill."

They almost went bankrupt, almost lost the house he'd built. Suits from the IRS walked around his workshop and wrote down numbers.

It was a man named Van Winkle—a direct descendant of Washington Irving's publisher—who had first mentioned the name of Eustis Edwards.

"His opinion was that Payne got more glory than he deserved, and Edwards was just as good, if not better. And then I found a 6166"—a model that Edwards made in the early 1920s—"and I restored it and started fishing it, and . . . that was the rod. I just felt that it fit my *anatomy* somehow. There was something about it that connected, that little finesse. And that was my first experience with the magic of a cane rod taper." (Rod makers use the terms "cane" and "bamboo" interchangeably.)

Along the way, he formed a clear impression of the man. First of all there was the aesthetic stamp that Eustis Edwards put on his fly rods, giving them an utterly unique appearance. He was the first maker to sign his work, inscribing a spidery "E. W. Edwards" in white ink on the rod shaft. The reel seat in most cases is of simple nickel silver, ornamented by details of black hard rubber, with a delicately turned and knurled wedding band to secure the reel. Many rod makers will use a distinctive pattern of decorative "signature wraps" just above the cork grip, and again, the Edwards version is idiosyncratic and beautiful, three or four bands of silk thread, each narrower than the last.

"My dad used to talk a lot about 'massing' in painting," Streamer went on. "If you don't have the massing, the painting won't carry aesthetically. To me, Edwards put it all together; he had the aesthetic end and he had the functional end."

It was clear that Edwards reminded him of his father in other ways, too. Despite the novelistic quality of Herbert Abrams's life, "he was so private in so many ways, like Eustis Edwards, he wasn't a self-promoter."

Edwards's aesthetics were a clear statement: these rods are different. Yet that wasn't the same as an act of commercial branding.

"Eustis wasn't concerned with marketing," Streamer said. "He didn't have that in his mind. His interest was in making a fishing rod; it was that simple."

Yet I found I was still facing the same problem. How much of this view of the man was inferential, and how much could be borne out by the biographical record? Most important, when you were dealing with an anonymous workingman who lived a century ago, how was that record to be established? I still had no more than the rudiments to go on. Born in Portland, Maine, July 1857; worked for Hiram Leonard from 1882 to 1890; died in Hamden, Connecticut, on New Year's Eve of 1931.

I wondered whether the libraries and public records of Maine, or of Central Valley, New York, might reveal anything I didn't know. And three generations later, was there any surviving family?

I called Martin Keane, but he said all he knew was in his book, and that had been based on a single interview with Edwards's younger son Gene—himself a rod maker—more than thirty years earlier. I called a series of bewildered people named Edwards in the Bangor area. On top of my frustration, I began to feel a little foolish. But Keane had mentioned that Gene Edwards had retired to Florida, and after many more false leads I found myself talking to a woman there named Barbara Bright. She told me she was Gene Edwards's daughter, Eustis's granddaughter. She had nothing, she said, only a few photographs of her father. But there was a great-grandson in a small town called Pilot, Virginia, and a box of family papers in his attic.

I broke the journey to Pilot at my friend Joe's cabin on the slopes of Old Rag Mountain in the Shenandoah National Forest, and spent a morning fishing for native brook trout of a genetic strain that has remained intact since the retreat of the glaciers. As I headed deeper into rural Virginia, the hollows were choked with garbage, and thunderstorms rolled around in the mountains, which were obscured with fog. But then the sun came out, there was a rainbow over I-81, and I saw the sign to Pilot.

Stephen Morgan brought the box down from his attic. The first thing I pulled out was a batch of photographs. The first was a Civil War–era tintype of a boy of seven or eight, wearing what appeared to be the fanciful uniform of a Zouave in the Union Army. The second, which bore the logo of a photographer in Saint Louis, showed a handsome young man in his late teens, dressed in an expensive-looking coat with a velvet collar. And the third was a formal studio portrait of a middle-aged man in a rattan chair— dated 1902 and clearly from the same session as the photograph in Keane's book. Each of the three photographs had a set of penciled initials on the back: "E.W.E." The script was familiar to me from the distinctive signature on the shaft of his fly rods.

These images spoke of money, and the next document in the box explained why. It was an outsize sheet of paper, folded in four. I spread it out on Stephen Morgan's kitchen table. God bless the American passion for genealogy, I thought to myself.

According to the typescript that went with the chart, most of the family history had been put together by Eustis Edwards's father in the mid-1800s. It had then been brought up to date in the 1970s by Eustis's grandson Scott.

You could not have designed a more textbook New England lineage. On his father's side, Eustis Edwards was the great-great-great-great-great-great-great-grandson of John Winthrop, the founder of the Massachusetts Bay Colony; on his mother's side, a direct descendant of John Dwight of Dedham, Massachusetts. There were also more tenuous family ties to two presidents, John and John Quincy Adams.

Later generations of the family had been packed with judges and lawyers, doctors and dentists, engineers, merchants, and clergyman. There were colorful characters like Great-Uncle Sherlock, a shipbuilder who had settled in the West Indies, and Great-Uncle Sparhawk, "a gentleman, a scholar and a hero" of the War of 1812. There was Uncle Scott, a physician in Saint Louis (and thus, I thought, the likely source of the portrait of Eustis as a teenager). There was also an eighteenth-century Boston craftsman named John Edwards, one of the most celebrated silversmiths of his time. I found that one particularly interesting.

The closer the generations came to Eustis, the more distinguished they became. Great-grandfather: Thomas Edwards, judge advocate general in the Continental Army. His son: William Eustis, editor and part owner of the *Portland Advertiser* in Maine. *His* son: William Scott, a successful civil engineer in Bangor. And William Scott Edwards's only child: Eustis William, bamboo rod maker extraordinary.

Yet when he signed his certificate of marriage to Jennie Gordon in 1886, Eustis had given himself only the most modest of titles: "laborer." A year later, his first child was born—a boy who took his grandfather's name, William Eustis. The attending physician was Dr. A. D. Leonard, Hiram Leonard's nephew. Eustis Edwards had been in Leonard's shop for five years now; barely three more to go.

The crackup seemed to happen all at once. If there was an intellectual author of the split, it was probably Fred Thomas. But it was Eustis Edwards and Loman Hawes who provided the technical means of breaking away from the Leonard-Mills operation. Hawes, of course, was in the unique position of being able to build a machine that would compete with the beveler that he and Leonard had designed together. Eustis Edwards's part was smaller, though absolutely crucial, and like a lot of small American dramas it worked itself out in the corridors of the U.S. Patent Office.

When Edwards and his colleagues decided to break with Leonard, the country was celebrating the centennial of the first patent statute, in April 1790. Orville H. Platt of Connecticut, chairman of the Senate Patent Committee, marked the occasion with a speech in which he noted that until the Constitutional Convention had acted, "there were no 'mechanics' in the meaning of the word as now used. . . . Mechanical knowledge was monopolized by the blacksmith, the carpenter, the millwright, and the village tinker." A hundred years later, more than four hundred thousand patents had been granted, and the patent system was hailed as the key to the country's growth and prosperity.

There was nothing about split bamboo per se that you could patent; what gave the Leonard rod its competitive advantage (apart from its sheer quality, for which Thomas, Edwards, and Hawes were largely responsible) was the design of its ferrules, which were strong, waterproof, and impeccably machined. Old Hiram had a pair of patents on his ferrule design that would not expire until 1895—a problem that had to be circumvented by any competitor. Eustis and Loman came up with some minor technical tweaks, but they were enough to establish their intellectual property rights and thus the independence of the new firm of Thomas, Edwards, and Hawes from the commercial stranglehold of the Mills family.

The three star craftsmen of the Leonard shop set up their rival business at the falls on Woodbury Creek, just a couple of miles downstream from their old workplace. In a township of barely a thousand, with so many interrelated by friendship or marriage, this must have been an uncomfortable situation, to say the least. Nor was it necessarily a craftsman-artist-aesthete's dream. Even though Thomas, Edwards, and Hawes represented the cream of the talent, they were still anonymous to the public, and they were taking on the carefully branded household names of Leonard and Mills in a brutally competitive marketplace. What they ended up doing, in effect, was to trade one corporate sponsor for another. They found that sponsor in Chicago, in a newly established company called A. G. Spalding & Brother.

This new arrangement gave the three rod makers instant name recognition, since the "A. G." part of the company's name referred to Albert Goodwill (Al) Spalding, who had been the premier baseball pitcher of the 1870s and onetime captain of the Boston Red Stockings. ("His face is that of a Greek hero," a *New York Times* reporter wrote, "his manner that of a Church of England bishop.") In 1876, Spalding had won a phenomenal forty-seven games for the Chicago White Stockings, and he was eventually inducted into the Baseball Hall of Fame in 1939. Spalding retired from the game in 1877 to found his sporting goods company, and after that his name adorned the mitts worn by generations of American boys. In 1889, when he began conversations with Thomas, Edwards, and Hawes, Spalding had just returned from the first-ever international baseball tour, which took him to such improbable destinations as Hawaii, Australia, Ceylon (now Sri Lanka), Egypt,

Italy, and Paris. There's always been speculation that it was base-ball that accounted for the connection with Thomas, Edwards, and Hawes, since Loman Hawes was a talented semiprofessional ballplayer.

In January 1890, even before the Hawes and Edwards patents had been granted, Spalding launched an advertising blitz promising "the most perfect split bamboo rod ever made." He called it the Kosmic rod and cited the new ferrule design—"a new and in-genious device never before used in the construction of a rod"—as its major selling point. His first ad proclaimed that "the ferrules also are PRACTICALLY DOUBLE, and fitted OVER the bamboo is a WATERPROOF cushion of ZYLONITE, while over that are set the fer-rules thus adding MATERIAL STRENGTH AT THE JOINTS." This was ac-tually a bizarre and not terribly functional feature, but it was certainly distinctive.

Loman stuck with the others for only a year. Some combina-tion of bad health and a bad temper seems to have provoked this latest split, and Ed Payne left the Leonard shop to take his place with Thomas and Edwards. For two years the new workshop hummed along without incident; then, in 1893, the Chicago con-nection gave the Kosmic rod its most brilliant showcase.

The whole world seemed to flock to Chicago that summer to visit the great White City that stretched along the shore of Lake Michigan. The population of the United States at the time was 65 million; an astounding 27.5 million paid to see the World's Columbian Exposition. The Kosmic rod almost feels like a metaphor for the whole affair, which gave Chicago the opportu-nity to shake off its inferiority complex and best what the *Tribune* called "the hawks, buzzards, vultures, and other unclean beasts, creeping, crawling, and flying," of the nation's cultural and intel-lectual capital—New York.

The fair was beyond extravagant. Set in a faux natural land-scape by Frederick Law Olmsted were a Moorish palace, a Ferris wheel 264 feet high, and a pavilion big enough to house the Great Pyramid of Giza, the U.S. Capitol, Saint Paul's Cathedral, Winchester Cathedral, and Madison Square Garden. There was copy of the Statue of Liberty chiseled out of salt, a giant map of the United States made out of pickles, and a life-size knight on horseback sculpted entirely from prunes. Thomas Edison came to the fair, and Archduke Franz Ferdinand of Austria. So did Clarence Darrow and Ignace Paderewski and Buffalo Bill Cody. And so did Fly Rod Crosby's bosom friend, Phoebe Anne Moses of Tiffin, Ohio—aka Annie Oakley.

People sampled exotic new foods such as Juicy Fruit chewing gum, Cracker Jack popcorn, and a cereal called Shredded Wheat. And they experienced the vicarious thrill of visiting a Cairo street and Algerian and Turkish villages, and witnessing dances by alleged cannibals from Dahomey in French West Africa. *Forest and Stream* sent two of its correspondents to provide color reporting on the spectacle, and their dispatches give some hint of the, shall we say, uneven politics of nineteenth-century conservationism. The reporters took a dog with them, reasoning that "there's lots of things on the Midway that you want to try on a dog first"—one example being the putative Dahomey cannibals.

"These may be genuine Dahomans," one of the journalists sneered, "fresh from the realm of King Benzine, but to me they look a mighty lot just like plain Mississippi niggers. I kick on paying a quarter to see thirty-eight niggers. I've seen 700 for nothing."

The fisheries section of the fair was housed in a magnificent series of buildings—"an architectural poem"—on an artificial lagoon. Within the complex, the Romanesque-style Anglers' Pavilion bore a striking resemblance to the French Benedictine abbey of Cluny. Inside it, the visitor was encouraged to inspect "the primitive apparatus of the savage, and the most approved appliances and methods evolved by many cycles of scientific progress." The New York tackle house of Abbey & Imbrie, which had once briefly marketed Hiram Leonard's work, exhibited another of its gold-trimmed display rods with a cut topaz the size of a pigeon egg set into the butt. But Spalding's display of thirty luxuriously appointed Kosmic rods, which Fred Thomas traveled to Chicago to promote and which took the exposition's gold medal, was the highlight of the exhibit for local loyalists (even if the rods were the work of New York craftsmen). *Forest and Stream* gushed about the display, "This is *de luxe, fin-de-siècle, fin-du-monde,* anything you like."

Shortly after I read these descriptions I was invited to lunch at the Anglers' Club of New York. After we had eaten, one of the club officers asked me if I would like to see two very special Kosmic fly rods that were in their collection. As soon as I laid eyes on them, I was convinced that one of these rods had to have been the centerpiece of Spalding's display—an eight-piece gold-filigree-ornamented "trunk rod" (so-called because it was designed for ease of carrying), nestled in a blue-satin-lined leather case. Everything about this rod and its companion—from the distinctive ferrules to the color of the silk wraps to the slightly rounded corners on the hexagonal bamboo—positively screamed Eustis Edwards. On the outside of the leather case was a brass plate that identified the rod as the property of the Standard Oil Company magnate C. M. Pratt. An old card inside said that Mr. Pratt had once been heard to say, "If Queen Victoria can have a gold fly rod, so can I!"

Yet this fin-de-siècle opulence—whatever pleasure it may or may not have given Eustis Edwards—did not last. In barely six months the Spalding-Kosmic enterprise unraveled. The economic crash that had begun in May 1893 deepened into the most severe and prolonged depression the United States had ever experienced, and in April 1894 Spalding announced that he was selling the Kosmic line to a Brooklyn company called U.S. Net and Twine—Charles M. Pratt, president.

The other two Bangor men, Fred Thomas and Ed Payne, began

the daily commute from Woodbury Falls to Brooklyn, where they produced Kosmic rods for another four years; Eustis Edwards stayed with them for only a few months. Then, for totally unexplained reasons, he took off for the West.

Whatever animosity there might have been over the breakup of the Leonard group, his friends gave Eustis and his wife, Jennie, a classic Central Valley send-off. It's easy to imagine the Hawes brothers on violin and cornet, Ed Payne making everyone laugh with his song-and-dance routine, perhaps even Hiram Leonard himself playing "Nellie Gray" on his Boehm flute.

The couple and their six-year-old son Billy

> *were tendered a kind farewell ovation on the eve of their departure for Los Angeles, California, where they are henceforth to reside. Thirty friends turned up as a surprise amidst packing trunks. The party dissolved into a game of whist in one room. Not so in the next room . . . where everybody, under the spell of Terpsichore, was tripping through the Virginia Reel to the jiggy rhythm produced by the "Fisher's Hornpipe" and "Devil's Dream," as they alternately disported themselves on the piano keys.*

But the moment was ephemeral, just like the economic good times. Within a month of their departure, Eustis, now thirty-seven, lost his beloved Jennie, and there's no evidence that he ever settled in Los Angeles after her death. For the next four years, he is lost to the historical record. Again, I was left with little but fragments and inferences. But they suggested unhappiness. The man was newly widowed with a young child, the country was in the throes of an economic depression, and he'd inexplicably chosen to walk away from his craft at the very moment when his stock was at its highest. After the lush green landscapes and marked seasonal changes of New York and New England, Eustis recalled the West, according to Keane, only as "a wasteland of sand and desert." For twenty years after his return to the Northeast, he flitted from place to place, sometimes dabbling in rod making, sometimes fiddling at dances, and sometimes pursuing a second career, in photography. Because he never settled on any one thing for long, Hiram Leonard's daughter Cora called him "the stormy petrel."

After that, my research trail went cold, until a collector I knew in Maine called to say that he had acquired some papers relating to the Hawes family.

Hiram Hawes and his wife, Cora, had left Central Valley in 1909, bringing Hiram Leonard's poet widow, Lizzie, to live with them. They settled in Canterbury, Connecticut, where Hawes started his own rod-making business. He tried to market his product as the "Leonard-Hawes rod," which was no more than the technical truth. But William Mills & Co., jealous of its sole rights to the Leonard name, swiftly put an end to that. It isn't clear whether it actually came to a lawsuit, but there was at least a stern message to cease and desist.

I found that surviving remnants of the Leonard-Hawes family still lived in Canterbury. It's one of those small New England towns that looks, with the exception of the traffic lights, as if life had been frozen in place in the early nineteenth century. Hiram Hawes's grandson Jeffrey Smith was waiting to meet me at the door of his 1842 colonial house; next door was Prudence Crandall's School for Negro Girls, built in 1833.

As he walked me through the generations of the Leonard-Hawes family, I mentioned the portraits of Hiram Leonard's parents that hung at the entrance to Streamer's workshop. Smith laughed loudly and said, "Come with me."

We walked down the slope to a dilapidated barn and ascended a creaking wooden staircase. Smith waved his arm. "This was the old Hawes rod shop," he said. He pointed at a spot on the wall, above the workbench: "And that's where those portraits hung for years until my mother got rid of them. I can't believe they've turned up again." Then he went over to a corner of the room and dusted off a long, heavy wooden object: "And this is one of Lewis Leonard's oars, made of ash." The place was full of ghosts.

Back at the house, Smith went off to fetch two scrapbooks that had belonged to Lizzie Leonard. They were stuffed full of sentimental and patriotic poems and newspaper clippings, most from the 1890s. There were reminiscences of nineteenth-century Maine sporting camps; there was an 1898 portrait from the *New York Daily World* of Leonard's daughter Cora wearing her black competition blouse and waving a bamboo fly rod; there was an article entitled "The Only Caribou Killed by a Woman"—the woman in question being Fly Rod Crosby.

There were recipes for rhubarb, elderberry, and dandelion wine. There were instructions for preparing Uncle Simon's home cure for rabies (rue, garlic, lead, molasses, and beer—"never known to fail"). There were several articles on spiritualism and meditation. One of them advised the reader, "Empty your mind of its contents. Be receptive to the higher forces. Wait. Rest absolutely upon the bosom of infinite being."

I scanned the rest of the headlines: *"Pasteur, Benign Microbes: The War They Wage with Pernicious Bacilli in Our Midst." "Christ Was Known in Asia: A Russian Traveler Finds Evidence That the Christian Messiah Was Identical with the Buddhist Issa." "How Thought Is Photographed: An Explanation of the Latest Marvel of Science."*

I looked up from my reading to see Jeffrey Smith standing in the doorway. "Here," he said, "this is Lizzie's diary for 1905. No one outside the family has ever seen it. It's the only one we have—the rest were lost." He handed me a notebook with fragile, yellowed pages.

The diary was suffused with an old woman's melancholy, filled with her fears for the health of friends and family, the anxieties of a time before antibiotics and antibacterials. On every page, it seems, someone is sick or dying. Four of the five Hawes boys are dead now, as well as both the sisters. Of the seven siblings, only Hiram survives. Loman Hawes, dead of tuberculosis; his brother Merritt, dead of tuberculosis; Cora's young daughter, dead of tuberculosis.

Leonard is seventy-four now. He dictates a memorandum to Lizzie, describing his rod-making career; it has the feel of a deathbed document. Lizzie writes that her husband still trudges down to the workshop once or twice a day when his health permits. But the summer heat oppresses him; he often feels weak and suffers from unexplained pains; he takes sitz baths, which offer some relief; his nephew Dr. A. D. Leonard makes regular visits, conducts unspecified operations, debates whether to prescribe cocaine.

The family's economic fortunes also seem to have declined. On May 13 Lizzie reports distressing news: the Central Valley bank has failed. "I had $1,450," she writes. "Probably never get a cent. Everybody feeling badly about the bank and losing their money, quite a blow to Central Valley." The Leonards rent out Lionsden to a New York family called Blotter and move into the carriage house. They go to Lake Pleasant in the Adirondacks for six weeks, taking the cheaper train to save a few dollars. While they are there, Eustis Edwards—Billy, as they call him—puts in a brief, tantalizing appearance as their houseguest. Lizzie is relieved to return to Lionsden, and even happier to see the Blotters go. Mrs. Blotter's horse has kicked Cora; in general, the summer renters have treated the Leonards' daughter abysmally.

On January 30, 1907, barely a year after Lizzie's diary ends, Lionsden was in deep mourning; the patriarch was dead. Many years later, his daughter Cora told a visitor, "My father was not a businessman; he was a genius."

CHAPTER 5

The Tea Stick

When I got back from Pilot, Virginia, I brought Streamer a copy of the 1902 photograph of Eustis Edwards. He matted it, framed it, and hung it on the wall of his workshop, between his beveler and a rack of raw bamboo culms.

Bevelers have come a long way since the huge, heavy wooden contraption that Hiram Leonard and Loman Hawes built in the 1870s. Streamer's is a deceptively simple-looking machine, based on a design by the mid-twentieth-century Michigan craftsman Lyle Dickerson, who stands right up there with Eustis Edwards in Streamer's personal pantheon of genius. The beveler is only about thirty inches long, and basically consists of an adjustable steel traveling bed and a pair of cutting blades set, like Leonard's, at a sixty-degree angle. Once you master the technique, you can turn out a roughly milled, tapered strip of bamboo in about a minute. If all goes well, you should get a strip that is a perfect equilateral triangle in cross section, cut to a tolerance of about one-hundredth of inch.

"It's fast," Streamer explained, "and it gets the job done to the point where I can take the strip to the planing form to finish it off quickly."

He told me that a small coterie of rod makers preferred to do the whole operation by hand-planing, but that seemed to me to cross the line from perfectionism into the realm of something closer to fanaticism, not to mention carpal tunnel syndrome.

Depending on who's doing the counting, making a perfect bamboo fly rod involves anything from thirty to a hundred steps—even a thousand, if you count every time you stop and scrutinize what you've done and, if necessary, do it over. Hoagy Carmichael Jr. once told me, "The thing about making bamboo rods is that you spend the entire day trying not to make a single mistake. And a good rod, a really good rod, is one where you make maybe... *nine* mistakes." (For readers whose ears prick up on hearing the name Hoagy Carmichael, be patient; we'll come to Hoagy's story later.)

In *The Idyl [sic] of the Split-Bamboo,* a well-known book about rod making from the early 1920s, Dr. George Parker Holden wrote:

> *The making of a split bamboo rod is readily within the accomplishment of anyone who can handle a few of the simpler carpenter's tools, with patience. Admittedly, the process involves some manipulations of delicacy but none of discouraging difficulty, as all there is to it may be summed up in careful attention to details in their proper sequence and not one of which truly is difficult in itself—and what could be better exercise for youth? For the same constitutes the successful conduct of life.*

That blithe description seemed like a lot of hooey as I watched Streamer work and listened to him tick off the steps in the process and the fine calculations involved. To be honest, I felt a little like old Fred Mather listening to the cross-talk in Conroy's tackle shop at the end of the Civil War and concluding that "the building-up of a split bamboo rod required more careful attention than the grinding of a lens for a great telescope."

By the time Streamer gets to the beveling machine, he's already air-dried the original culm of bamboo, then split it into anything from eighteen to twenty-four raw strips, depending on the thickness and quality of the stalk. Some rod makers accomplish this task with a knife, others with a saw, others with a specially designed tool that's commonly known as a "pie splitter"—a name that will convey an idea of its shape.

The next steps in the process are to apply direct heat to the rough-cut strips of bamboo to straighten them into a workable form, and flattening out the leaf nodes in a vise so the final sections of the rod won't have any bumps or irregularities. The straightening in particular seemed to me to require the patience of a saint. To straighten a strip, you heat it over a flame, which softens the pectins in the bamboo; when they cool, they will set in a new position. Heat the strip too much and you can snap it like a piece of uncooked spaghetti.

"Isn't that hard to do?" I asked him. "I'll bet you must lose some through trial and error."

"Yeah, a few," he admitted. "It's like any art or craft, or painting—in the beginning you overwork it. You're trying to get it just perfectly straight. But you go too far and then you have to come back. It's like a child learning how to steer a car; they oversteer and then they correct."

After a couple of passes through the beveler, Streamer tempers the roughly tapered strips by heat-treating them in an oven he built himself, which hangs from the ceiling of his workshop and looks like an oversize lipstick tube.

"It's amazing how much ambient temperature and humidity affect the bamboo," he told me. "Hot air removes the humidity. If there's anything I would consider a special, secret way that I make rods, it'd be the way I use hot air. I have an eye for getting it right. There's a magic spot in there that you hit. Eustis found it; that was his discovery. And Dickerson did it, too."

Remembering that Streamer had once been a carpenter, I asked him how working with bamboo compared to working with wood.

"Oh, it's totally different," he replied. "The only thing that's similar is being aware of the direction of the grain. You always have to be conscious of that when you're working with bamboo. The whole thing about bamboo is the structure, the strength of it, which is what you're working to preserve. Especially on the outside, that's the part of it you never want to invade."

"And wood?"

"Wood, you can take a chunk out of it anywhere you like. At the same time, stresses in wood are very important, like the movement you get with water saturation. With bamboo there's very little of that. It kind of works like teak, or *ipe*—Brazilian walnut. That has a cell structure that doesn't take in water, it's almost crystalline."

And what about Holden's comparison to carpentry? Was it really that simple?

He thought about it for a moment. "Well, I think a decent cabinetmaker, given the time and the tools, wouldn't have too much difficulty making a rod. But making a *good* rod—that to me is more of a challenge than making a piece of Queen Anne furniture, as far as the intensity of the concentration you have to have, the focus. With wood, I always found that some of the most challenging projects were some of the simplest. People would sometimes come into the shop and say, 'I don't want anything expensive or fancy, just something simple like a Shaker table.' And you had to explain to them that what makes a Shaker table so beautiful is the geometrical precision. But math and precision—in a natural, organic material, those things don't go well together. So that simple perfection is much more complicated than any of the ornate Chippendale carving and cabriole legs that you can imagine."

There was that word again, the one I kept hearing—"perfection." But the pursuit of perfection isn't just in the working of the bamboo; it goes right back to the very start of the rod-making process, to the search for the ideal piece of cane. I asked Streamer what made a good culm, the kind you'd choose for making the perfect rod.

"Here," he said, reaching up to the drying rack and taking down a six-foot culm. "It's the density of the power fibers and the straightness of the grain. That's it."

"Can you tell that just by looking?" I asked. "I've heard people say that you can also tell by the sound, that if it's good it rings like a bell."

"Yeah, kind of." He tapped the culm several times with a knuckle. "I mean, they make musical instruments out of this stuff. You can hear it, it's harmonic." He struck it again in several places, producing three distinct musical notes.

"But how it looks is much more important," he continued. "Looking at the power fibers is a bit like judging the quality of a fur, or even the hair on a dog. You look at the power fibers, and if they look nice and neat and tidy, and denser toward the outside, that's a good piece of bamboo. But if the power fibers are big, and scattered all around inside the lignum, like a mangy dog, that's not the quality I want."

"And where does the best bamboo come from?" I asked.

"Well," he said, "there's Demarest, of course."

I found Harold Demarest living in chipper semiretirement at the age of ninety in a beautiful lakeside house in rural New Jersey. He told me that his family's intimate relationship with bamboo went back almost a hundred years. It had been an accident, really, he said, fetching me a leather-bound ledger in which his father and his uncle had documented the early years of their business. The careful columns of handwritten notes recorded a potpourri of the early-twentieth-century trade in exotica, with ports from Odessa, Russia, to Lourenço Marques, Mozambique, supplying the American market with camphor, citronella, quinine bark, green snail shells, mother-of-pearl, buffalo horn for buttons, goatskins, ferns, menthol, walnuts. For the China trade, Harold told me, his father, Charles H. Demarest, worked through a German broker in Shanghai at first, switching later to a locally owned firm in Hong Kong.

In the half century that followed the Opium Wars, the opening of the Chinese treaty ports, and the British seizure of Hong Kong,

British and American traders became well acquainted with the qualities of Chinese bamboo, especially those species that grew in the southern part of the country. These could be easily harvested and shipped down the Pearl River delta to the godowns of Hong Kong, where you could use the stuff for furniture, for ornamental plantings to shade the gardens of colonial officials, or as scaffolding stronger and lighter than steel to prop up new construction. (In fact, this green latticework of bamboo scaffolding is still one of the first things that strike you when you arrive in Hong Kong today.)

Somewhere along the line, the traders happened on a nameless Chinese species that transformed the art of making bamboo fly rods, fueled a revolution in design and taste, and tied the craft to a unique degree to the vagaries of international economics and politics, since the new bamboo grew only in a single remote valley in the Chinese province of Guangdong. I could think of no other craft that was so dependent on raw material from a single source of supply—except perhaps the making of fine violin bows, which requires *pau-brasil*, or pernambuco, a dense, resilient, and flexible wood that grows only in the the Atlantic coastal forests of Brazil (and indeed gave that country its name).

Until well into the twentieth century, the old Calcutta cane, with its distinctive scorch marks, had virtually monopolized the craft of bamboo rod making. That wasn't to say that the new species was unknown, and Demarest certainly wasn't the first to bring it to the United States. Loman Hawes supposedly came across the Chinese cane one day in a set of umbrella spokes, and was blown away by its strength and flexibility. One of the earliest bamboo rod makers, William Mitchell of New York City, recalled that when he made his first rod in 1869, it was "not of Calcutta bamboo but of Chinese, which is harder, more homogenous and more difficult to obtain than the former."

The new species wasn't given a scientific name until 1931, when Floyd Alonzo McClure, an American botanist at the Smithsonian Institution, called it *Arundinaria amabilis*—the lovely reed. In Wade-Giles Chinese, it was *tsing li;* in Cantonese, *cha kan chuk*—the tea stick. But in the trade it also acquired a lay name, albeit one that was totally inaccurate—Tonkin cane. I had seen the name in the old Demarest ledgers, where it appeared as early as 1907, though it seems to have been used almost a decade earlier than that by the Montague Rod and Reel Company, a mass-production outfit in Massachusetts. Whether someone actually thought it came from the Gulf of Tonkin, or whether the folks at Montague just thought the name would have exotic appeal in the marketplace, who knows? But it stuck.

McClure tracked the new bamboo to its source in 1925. He marveled at the "austerity and magnificence" of the culms that grew forty feet high in the acidic soils of the Sui River Valley. The tea-stick region—an oval no more than twenty-five miles long— is drenched by seventy inches of rain each year and battered by ty-phoon winds. But it's that brutal microclimate from which the species derives its elastic power.

These days a top-quality twelve-foot culm of bamboo, cut from the base of the stalk, where the nodes are farthest apart, may cost a rod maker anything up to $60. In the hands of a skilled crafts-man, that can yield enough strips for two complete rods. The thirty, or hundred, or thousand steps that someone like Streamer has to execute are what accounts for most of the final cost of a rod, but even by the time it reaches the American craftsman, the value that has been added to the raw culm by human labor—skilled, semiskilled, and unskilled—is considerable. By value, I mean not only the monetary kind, but the deeper value that a natural or-ganic material acquires when it is worked. Certainly very little of the money sticks to the hands of the Chinese peasants who do the hard work.

Harold Demarest walked me through the process. "When they cut it, they judge the maturity," he said. "In its first year the bam-boo has a sheath around every section, and then in the second year the sheaths fall off, and in the third year the whole culm develops a dark mold. The third and fourth years are when they cut, and you see it stacked up along the roadsides, all covered with dirt and mold. Up in the hills you'll hear them cutting the cane with a big, heavy knife with a flat, curved blade. You'll hear the *chop-boom.*"

After the culms are felled, boatmen lash them into rafts, like old-time loggers in the Maine woods, and pole them downriver to collection points where other workers scour them with sand to remove the accumulated growth of fungus and lichen. By sampan or truck, the culms—now a light sage green color—are taken to the processing plants, where they're heated and roughly straightened over an open fire. Less skilled workers then wrap the culms in matting, label them, and prepare them for export.

Notwithstanding its miraculous qualities, the customers wouldn't give the stuff the time of day when it first arrived in American rod shops. It wasn't just that they had grown accustomed to Calcutta cane; that material was also well suited to the style of fishing that had prevailed ever since Americans first discovered the artificial fly. The softer, more pliable structure of the Indian *Gigantochloa macrostachya* was ideal for the slow-flexing stroke that was needed to drift a pair of flies beneath the surface of the water to imitate a drowned or hatching insect. And that was how Americans were accustomed to fishing.

But then habits began to change, in ways that had a lot to do with the odd, ambivalent relationship between American and English elites and their respective views of what constituted gentlemanly outdoor sport. For the English gentleman, the dry fly was de rigueur; using the American-style wet fly was a terrible social gaffe, the equivalent of not knowing which way to pass the port. Theodore Gordon, who was probably the most influential of all American writers on the subject, said that he caught the English "dry-fly fever" in about 1890. Returning the compliment, the most sophisticated of English sportsmen became converts to the cult of Hiram Leonard. One of their leading eminences christened his personal Leonard "W.B.R."—world's best rod.

There was a problem, however. The English gentleman for the most part was casting his imitation mayfly on the placid surface of one of the spring-fed streams that flowed gently over the soft, chalky limestone of the home counties. American anglers in the Catskills, on the other hand, had to contend with turbulent, boulder-filled rivers that had been formed when the retreat of the glaciers scoured out their valleys. Under those conditions, a fly quickly became waterlogged, and the old Calcutta cane, with its deep, slow flex, wasn't able to compensate. Flick a stiffer Tonkin cane rod back and forth a few times, however, and your fly was miraculously dried off and ready for the next cast.

Theorists of the sport—as well as smart rod makers like Loman Hawes—quickly grasped the advantages of the new material. But consumer tastes often lag behind specialized knowledge, and it took another quarter of a century for popular attitudes to catch up. When they eventually did, it was in large measure thanks to Eustis Edwards.

This was surprising, to say the least, since Edwards had been out of the rod-making game for the better part of twenty years. After his blank biographical page in the wasteland of the West, Eustis resurfaced in Central Valley in 1898, the year of the Spanish-American War. The small town was abuzz with the doings of Tomás Estrada Palma, its most famous resident. Estrada Palma, Cuba's future president, was immersed in revolutionary intrigue while his friend Calixto García was taking command of the Cuban rebel forces and Undersecretary of the Navy Teddy Roosevelt was shopping at Abercrombie & Fitch for the duds he would need to lead his Rough Riders up San Juan Hill.

It isn't clear how long Eustis Edwards stayed in Central Valley the second time around, but it was long enough to open a short-lived photographic studio, and certainly long enough to fall in love with a schoolteacher named Bertha Ford. Bertha belonged to the most prominent family in Central Valley; her uncle Charles T. Ford was E. H. Harriman's "confidential man," charged with overseeing the development of the railroad magnate's Arden House estate, where Hiram Hawes ran the Adirondack sporting camp.

Eustis found that his colleagues from the old Leonard group were still in turmoil. Loman Hawes had succumbed to TB the previous winter. Ed Payne had tired of the daily commute to work for U.S. Net and Twine in Brooklyn; he had bought up the old Kosmic rod-making machinery, including Loman's beveler, and set up his own shop in Highland Mills. Fred Thomas had married, had a baby, and returned to Maine. When Payne decided to build a new beveler of his own design, Thomas had snapped up Loman's old machine and had it shipped up to Bangor. Or, more precisely, to Brewer, where he had business interests.

Bangor and Brewer are twin cities, one on either bank of the Penobscot, but they are quite different in character, and Brewer has always been the junior partner. In the 1890s, Bangor was the largest lumber port in the world, a thriving commercial center of twenty-five thousand people, its economy based on the pine, spruce, and hemlock that could be extracted from the Maine woods, the ice that could be cut from the Penobscot River and the inland lakes, and the railroads and steamship lines that made all this business and recreational activity possible. Brewer, just across the covered bridge, was a much smaller community, of five thousand, its identity shaped more by industry than by commerce. For employment, Brewer people looked to the town's shipyards, brickyards, icehouses, mast and spar makers' shops, carriage manufacturers, and small mills.

Fred Thomas set up his new rod-making enterprise on Center Street in Brewer and invited Eustis Edwards to come in with him. The two men have often been described as best friends, but I was beginning to have my doubts about that. In personality and in business sense, there seemed to be almost no points of convergence. Eustis was a diffident man from a prosperous background; he had a restless streak; his craftsmanship was constantly experimental, with a powerful sense of aesthetics. Thomas had been born into poverty in a small village in the Maine backwoods and spent his early years as a river driver; he was a stolid and conservative character; he came out of twenty uninterrupted years of rod making with a clear sense of how to turn out fly rods that suited the tastes of Maine "sports"; and he had a long-term business plan.

The partnership didn't last long—certainly not more than a year and a half, and perhaps less. As a result, Thomas and Edwards rods are rare and highly prized—out of my price range, in other words. Eustis's stormy-petrel side soon took over and he struck out on his own again. In October 1900 he was briefly back in Central Valley, remaining there just long enough to marry Bertha Ford. But the couple came straight back to Brewer.

Eustis had another of his brilliant and colorful sets of relatives in the town, the Tefft family. His great-uncle the Reverend Benjamin Franklin Tefft had been a celebrated preacher, a member of the Maine legislature, and an outspoken opponent of slavery. Eustis's cousin Charles Eugene Tefft, who lived in a handsome old mansion just around the corner from the Edwards family, was a nationally known sculptor. One of his best-known works was a statue in downtown Bangor of three river drivers breaking up a logjam on the Penobscot River. Charles Tefft was also a fanatical sportsman and a devotee of Thoreau. His brother said of him that he liked nothing better than "fishing from a boat on Sebec Lake, or frying venison and onions in the wilds of Old Katahdin." During the early part of the fishing season, Tefft virtually took up residence in the famous salmon pool below the Bangor Waterworks Dam on the Penobscot. In 1905 he spent eleven straight days there before he eventually hooked a twenty-two-pound salmon. He had so much trouble landing the fish that he held the rod in one hand, grabbed a target rifle in the other, and shot it in the head.

The conventional wisdom among American sportsmen had been that you could catch only a trout on an artificial fly, not a salmon. The man who debunked that myth was Hiram Leonard, who returned to Bangor in 1880 with a fresh-caught salmon from Wassataquoik Stream, a tributary of the East Branch of the Penobscot. Five years later, the first salmon was taken on a fly from the Bangor Salmon Pool, and a year after that the Penobscot Salmon Club was founded—the first of its kind in the United States.

The Bangor Waterworks Dam is long gone, and so are most of the salmon, but the clubhouse is still there. One of the members invited me to visit and showed me some of the club records. Often braving ice and sleet, members used to gather here on April 1 each year, "each with a setter dog, a pound of beefsteak and a quart of whiskey, the steak being for the dogs." Wearing coats and ties and soft hats, the gentlemen anglers fished from cedar-planked, canvas-covered boats, while their guides held them steady in the roiling waters of the salmon pool, keeping out of the way of the ice floes that came careening downstream. I say gentlemen anglers, but the Penobscot club was actually a rare instance for its time of men from different classes mixing socially, with bankers, doctors, lawyers, and corporate executives taking their place in the salmon pool next to boatbuilders, factory workers, and millwrights. In later years, as Atlantic salmon grew scarce and many of the best waters passed into private hands, that social diversity ebbed.

I looked at the display of photographs on the clubhouse walls. Many of them depicted the most famous of the club's traditions— the habit of sending the first Penobscot salmon of the year to the president of the United States. William Howard Taft was the first to get one, in 1912. The practice continued until 1954, with only one interruption—in 1938, when a militant Bangor Republican paid a premium for the presidential salmon to prevent the dishonor of having it sent to Franklin Roosevelt. After Eisenhower, the tradition ended; the salmon had succumbed to the pollution of the river and overfishing of ocean stocks. But it was revived in the early 1980s. There's a picture of Ronald Reagan on the clubhouse wall, dressed in a white suit and wearing his customary genial but clueless expression, as an emissary from Bangor holds up a large and very dead salmon beneath a portrait of FDR.

Nearby there hangs a portrait of Fred Thomas, seated in an ornate mahogany chair with a dog at his feet and looking every inch the patriarch, as well he might, for the F. E. Thomas rod ruled the Bangor Salmon Pool. Thomas named his earliest rods the Dirigo, for the motto of the state of Maine. *Dirigo:* "I lead." A local newspaper wrote, "Thomas, maker of the 'Dirigo' rods, is about the busiest man in the city. His shop is the gathering-place for all who have high-class repairing, and he can't get time to turn out his rods as fast as they are wanted." Within a couple of years, Thomas added a higher-grade model, the Special, which became the core of his success. The unspoken convention was that a gentleman used the Special, his guide the Dirigo.

The man had business acumen to burn. If you wanted a rod of a particular kind, Fred Thomas would send you one to try out. If you didn't like it, he would not only take it back but pay the return postage. If one of the big resort hotels, like the Mount Kineo House on Moosehead Lake, wanted to sponsor a contest for the biggest trout of the season, Fred Thomas would donate one of his rods as first prize. His advertisements were giddy masterpieces of high Edwardian prose. There was nothing in the world like fly-fishing, Fred Thomas said: "Its distinctive and sublimely infatuating element is the delightful sensation of electric thrill that comes through the titillation of the elbow by the vibratory connection of his hand and arm with a gamey fish." It's verging on the pornographic.

In 1902 Fred Thomas moved his shop across the river to Bangor and expanded his staff. But the most brilliant rod maker of all was missing from the team. Eustis Edwards had ditched his craft for the second time in six years. Again, his reasons can't be documented; they have to be inferred. Martin Keane's view was that Eustis had concluded that there wasn't enough of a business to support two men. But that didn't make sense to me, given the healthy state of Thomas's enterprise at the time. I preferred to think that Eustis went his own way precisely *because* the business was booming, and the pressure of keeping up with orders would once again threaten his desire to experiment, his idiosyncratic pursuit of perfection.

Turning his back on rod making again, Eustis started up a photography business in an upstairs studio next to the covered bridge over the Penobscot. The following year, 1902, he had a second son, whom he called Gene.

Among the papers that Stephen Morgan had found in his attic in Pilot were a set of photographs from the Brewer studio. I found them beautiful—conventional enough in their way, I suppose, but well framed and sensitively lit. There was a delicacy to them, a sense of deep affection for their subjects. There was a portrait of Eustis's father, William Scott Edwards, in profile, with a leonine head and a luxuriant Mark Twain mustache. Several shots of Eustis's wife, Bertha, a striking woman with large, shining eyes. Bertha holding Gene at the age of two or three, his blond hair cut in a severe pageboy.

Armed with these photographs, I drove the short distance from the Penobscot Salmon Club to the center of Brewer. The Edwards photographic studio was listed in the town directory for fifteen straight years, from 1901 to 1916. Surely there had to be some record of his work, if he was the only photographer in a town of five thousand people.

I called the Brewer town clerk and asked if I could look at the official records for the period. I found Eustis right away in the tax records, paying his poll tax regularly, declaring a piano valued at $150. Not a poor household, in other words. The town clerk brought out a set of massive leather-bound ledgers, in which every single council expenditure was listed in a neat copperplate hand. Every slaughter of a pig was recorded here, every cleaning of a cesspool, every burial of an insane pauper, everything down to the twenty-five-cent bounty paid for the disposal of a porcupine. But not a single word about Eustis Edwards.

I leafed through the records with mounting frustration. There had to be *something*, some commissioned portrait of the mayor, some picture of a civic parade, some photographic record of the great events of the time: the flood of 1902 that swept away the central span of the covered bridge, right next to the Edwards studio; the 1906 fire that destroyed the Rollins icehouse; the conflagration that consumed the *Annie Henderson* at its moorings on the Penobscot in the same year; the Great Fire that swept through Bangor in 1912. But there was nothing. Inexplicably the trail had gone cold again; the enigma of the man deepened.

But then, in 1916, the notation in the Bangor-Brewer register changed. For fifteen years, it had been "E. W. Edwards, photographer." Now, suddenly, it was "E. W. Edwards, photographer and mfr. of fishing rods." And his twenty-nine-year-old son Bill, until now listed as a chauffeur and mechanic, also appeared as "mfr. of fishing rods." Eustis had not only changed professions; in 1912 he had also moved house. He was now living at 8 Washington Street; and there on another page of the register was F. E. Thomas, 9 Washington Street. I walked the few short blocks over from the town hall to see how the two neighbors had lived.

The Thomas house was a handsome Victorian on a grassy rise,

painted yellow with a deep maroon trim. There was a For Sale sign in the yard, and some construction workers were busy on the wraparound porch. What was the asking price? I inquired. Ninety thousand, they said. I entertained a momentary fantasy of moving to Bangor.

Directly across the street, in striking contrast, the Edwards house was a modest affair without much character, built on an apparently haphazard floor plan that made it seem as if the separate parts had been built at different times. But somewhere in the house at 8 Washington Street, in a back room or a garden shed, with culms of tea-stick bamboo that he kept secret from Fred Thomas, Eustis Edwards had embarked on a series of experiments. In the course of these he would hit what Streamer had called "the magic spot," and so transform the craft of American rod making.

The Rod That Won the East

Lever and spring, flexibility and resilience, the greatest possible lightness in the hand. Eustis Edwards earned his living in one arena, but pursued his private obsessions in another. At the margins of his life as an obscure small-town photographer, Eustis continued to tinker with the tea stick. The idea was to take the organic properties of Tonkin bamboo—the vascular bundles of power fibers, the naturally retained moisture, the thermoplastic resins that cemented the plant cells together—and coax them to another level of functioning. Look at his rods as a forensic investigator, the way Streamer had, and you could see the relentless pursuit of a personal vision of perfection—which was the name Eustis Edwards would give his finest rods.

The secret turned out to be heat, by way of chemicals. "Being a photographer, of course," Streamer remarked to me one day, "Eustis would have had access to all kinds of acids, alkalis, other chemicals." To push the cane beyond its natural limits, he tried steam, ammonia, and then an open flame. It's possible that the use of fire was a matter of pragmatism as much as scientific experiment. Calcutta cane was what people knew; the token of their familiarity was the crisscrossing of dark burn marks that reflected the harvesters' efforts to remove insect larvae and straighten out the raw culms. One logical way of accommodating the customer's habit of mind was to imitate these marks by scorching the new Tonkin bamboo with a hot iron—which had the unforeseen but interesting result of altering the physical properties of the material. Apply the heat evenly to the core of the bamboo, as Eustis Edwards eventually did, and you achieved a transformation. In the process, he made rods that were shorter and lighter than the craft had ever seen. At the end of the nineteenth century, fly rods had customarily been nine or ten feet long. The self-appointed arbiter of these things, an opinionated blowhard named Dr. James Henshall, had decreed that "the lightest and 'withiest' fly rod" should weigh "from six to seven ounces." Now Edwards was experimenting with rods as short as seven feet that weighed barely three.

"A bamboo fly rod tests the physical extremes of natural raw material," Streamer went on. "It seems to do the impossible—it has to flex and rebound thousands of times without lasting effects. Plus it has to be strong enough to land a large fish. With Eustis's rods you see the finest line where natural material meets function; they test the limits of both. He knew that, and he was searching for something beyond the standards of his contemporaries. While they were competing and marketing and evolving slowly around him, he was off exploring on his own. And his intuitions turned out to be correct. Most rod makers today routinely show his influence—the heat treatment, the tapers—without even knowing it or giving him credit."

In the big yellow Victorian at 9 Washington Street, Fred Thomas knew nothing of this, I'm convinced. Again I had to rely on scraps of evidence, but what clinched it for me was a scribbled note I'd found among the Hawes family papers. Edwards, it seemed, had written to Hiram Hawes, his fellow Leonard alumnus, asking for some culms of bamboo so that he could build a rod for Abercrombie & Fitch, the tony New York outfitter. But why on earth would he do that? After all, Thomas was known as a businessman with a long-range view of things, and had stocked up on the supplies he would need for years of rod making. Wouldn't it have been logical, then, for Eustis to simply walk across the street to his "best friend's" house to get what he needed? The fact that he didn't do so persuaded me that his experiments were being conducted in secret.

Eustis's innovative use of heat had the effect of turning the bamboo a deep, dark brown, right to the core, and his neighbor and onetime partner soon began advertising rods of the same color. But Fred Thomas's "Mahogany" model only *looked* the same. "The Mahogany rod was just stained brown on the outside," Streamer said. "It took Thomas another year to figure out what Eustis had done, and then he copied the technique with his own Browntone model."

By 1916, Eustis Edwards was ready to go public with his breakthrough. And his elder son Bill joined him in his new rod shop, in a family succession that was replicated by all the graduates of the Leonard school at about this time. Eustis begat Bill, Fred Thomas anointed Leon, Hiram Hawes taught Merritt, and Ed Payne passed on his skills to Jim, whom he famously ordered never to play baseball so that his fingers could avoid harm and so work their magic. As indeed they did—Jim Payne made rods for fifty-three years without a break, from 1915 until his death in 1968, and they are widely regarded as the benchmark of consistent excellence. This laying on of hands, father to son, was astonishing, really, considering the unforgiving nature of the work and the marginal economic returns. But then you have to bear in mind that in the early part of the twentieth century the family business was still a cornerstone of the American economy.

Over the next two years, according to Martin Keane, Eustis and Bill turned out between a thousand and twelve hundred rods. Computing these figures, I found them a stretch. Depending on whom you ask, building a single bamboo fly rod is a matter of forty to sixty, even eighty, hours of skilled labor. Two men, two years: maybe two hundred rods, if they were driving themselves hard. A thousand rods: ten men at least. It would have been a business to equal Leonard's, in other words, and a direct rival to Fred Thomas.

I've only ever found one photograph of Eustis Edwards after he turned sixty. It shows a slightly built man, apparently younger than his years, with delicate features and round, thin-rimmed glasses that lend him a scholarly, even ascetic, demeanor. In 1918, Edwards found himself at something of a crossroads. Despite the fifteen-year hiatus, he was at the top of his profession. His reputation as an innovator was secure, and he had the satisfaction of seeing his influence take hold both in Thomas's work and in the rods coming out of the Leonard shop in Central Valley, which was now in the hands of old Hiram's nephew Reuben.

On a personal level, Eustis's life seemed to have reached the kind of tranquillity that men search for in middle age. His daughter Minnie had given him his first grandchild, and now Bill was about to produce a second. Eustis's younger son Gene, now a teenager, showed signs of having a craftsman's hands.

Yet everything about Eustis Edwards's career, from the pressures of the commercial marketplace to his own restless and perfectionist personality, would have made it clear to him that craftsmanship of this kind was hard to sustain. The making of high-quality bamboo fly rods is a brutal discipline, demanding the precision of a surgeon and the patience of a saint. The profit margins are slender. By 1918, with the exception of a few sentimental diehards who were still attached to their greenheart and lancewood, split bamboo was all there was. The big, bottom-feeding companies had developed mass-production techniques capable of churning out hundreds of thousands of rods that were cheap and crude but enough to satisfy the needs of the mass market. The boutique craftsman occupied a narrow and precarious niche.

The craft, in other words, did not—and *does* not—exist in a vacuum, but as part of a web of circumstances that can extend from the personal quirks of the craftsman through the larger forces of economic and societal change, even disease and war.

Eustis's father, William Scott Edwards, had spent the last year of his life at 8 Washington Street before his death in September 1918. It seemed an unremarkable event, a normal old man's death.

But then, as I studied the family genealogy that I had found in Pilot, Virginia, I noticed that one of Eustis's aunts had died on the very same day, and a second aunt only weeks earlier. And then in October 1918, even as Bill's son Scott was born, Eustis lost his daughter Minnie at the age of thirty-seven. This series of losses at first seemed a wicked set of coincidences. But then the penny dropped: Spanish flu.

Some said the virus was spread by German agents. But when the Spanish press published details of the epidemic (it was uncensored during wartime, unlike most of its European counterparts), the virus became known as "the Spanish Lady." In the United States, October 1918 was the deadliest month, with 195,000 of the total of 675,000 fatalities that occurred in the course of the epidemic. By the time World War I ended, the Spanish flu had taken an estimated 25 million lives worldwide—three times the number who had perished on the battlefields. Americans celebrated the armistice wearing face masks.

On top of the personal tragedies of the Edwards family came the turmoil of the postwar economy. War always stimulates the growth of technology and the production of certain strategic goods; but for the companies that benefit from wartime expansion, it also has a downside. When the conflict ends, these enterprises have to find something to do with their surplus capacity. This applies particularly to those that have specialized in armaments production.

The American arms industry had two iconic leaders. One was Samuel Colt's Patent Fire Arms Manufacturing Company; the other was the Winchester Repeating Arms Company. Both were located in the state of Connecticut, Colt in Hartford, Winchester in New Haven. Each had its signature weapon: Colt's .45-caliber handgun, the Peacemaker, and the Winchester 73, "the rifle that won the West." Connecticut, guns, and mechanical ingenuity had long been synonymous. Mark Twain's Connecticut Yankee, remember, was a foreman at Samuel Colt's "great arms factory" in Hartford before a blow on the head carried him off to King Arthur's court. The very idea of Connecticut as a seat of invention is summed up in the way Hank the Yankee introduces himself:

> *I am an American. I was born and reared in Hartford, in the state of Connecticut—anyway, just over the river, in the country. So I am a Yankee of the Yankees—and practical.... Why, I could make anything a body wanted—anything in the world, it didn't make any difference what; and if there wasn't any quick, new-fangled way to make a thing, I could invent one.*

You can hear a strong echo of Hank in Winchester's annual report for 1918, which said:

> *We have delivered to the Government substantial quantities of small arms and ammunition and have performed important engineering service in connection with the development of Government products and services.... The termination of Government contracts will find us with a considerable portion of our plant idle. The management is active at the present time investigating and developing new products and new lines of business.*

The following year, the company's directors unveiled the Winchester Plan. This was Winchester's retooling for peace, and it was a signal moment in the growth of American marketing—based on a strategy that nowadays we would call "vertical integration." Winchester announced that it would be buying up a wide range of companies—tool and die makers; companies that produced ice skates and pocketknives; clay pigeon and fishing reel manufacturers. These were all common, everyday products, hardware store standbys. But Winchester decided that something else was also

needed, something that would brand the company's name for social elites as well as for the mass market. It settled on something
that would represent the pinnacle of craftsmanship. Winchester
already had the gun that had won the West; now it wanted the
bamboo fly rod that would win the East.

On October 14, 1918, Eustis Edwards sold his small Maine rod-
making business to Winchester for $10,000—perhaps $125,000 in
current dollars. He agreed to "use his best endeavors in manufacturing fishing rods and instructing and training a working force
for the manufacture of fishing rods and in the development of the
machinery, equipment and tools therefore and such other duties as
may be assigned to him." For this Winchester would pay him an
annual salary of $3,000 for five years—not a fortune, by any
means, but the kind of financial security no boutique craftsman
could dream of. But the worrisome phrase in his contract was "instructing and training a working force." What that meant was that
Winchester intended to marry Edwards's individual craftsmanship with a mass-production scheme aimed at competing with the
bottom-feeders. I could only wonder what misgivings Eustis, who
had always been one to dance to his own drummer, may have had
about this arrangement.

Over the next forty years, the Edwards family traveled a good
deal, as Thoreau might have said, in and around Hamden, Connecticut. I went there one day, driving up the central artery of
Whitney Avenue, heading north from the neo-Gothic colleges of
Yale and the fieldstone and Italianate homes of the New Haven
periphery, looking for traces of Eustis Edwards in the Connecticut
suburbs.

I passed Hwang's Taekwondo on the left. After that, the Village
Shoppes, the Best Video, the Dry Cleanery, the Rascals Gym,
Margie's Beauty Salon. A Knights of Columbus bingo hall. A skin
and nail salon called Let's Face It. The Rainbow Cleaners ("Drop
your pants here!"). Inevitably there would be a hair salon in the

next minimall, and I took bets with myself about what it would be called. Mane Street, perhaps? The Yankee Clipper? Wrong. It was Shear Madness.

In the midst of this suburban sprawl, I found Filbert Street, the Edwards family's first home. It was a short, leafy cul-de-sac, backing onto a brushy, riffled section of the Mill River, just short of Lake Whitney. The Edwards home, number 40, was still standing, a solid, middle-class Cape-style home with a front porch and a well-tended lawn, nothing ostentatious. Just a musket shot away were the old dam and the industrial remains of Whitneyville.

Whitneyville, Whitney Avenue, Lake Whitney: you might say that Eli Whitney has left his mark on this piece of Connecticut suburbia. By the time Whitney came here in 1798, he was already famous for his invention of the cotton gin, which had revolutionized the plantation economy of the South. Incredibly, he had contrived to lose money on this enterprise, and he decided, as many have decided since, that making weapons for the government was a surer path to riches. The experiment in national independence was barely two decades old, and the United States saw enemies on all its frontiers—the British and French to the north, Spain to the south, hostile Indian tribes to the west. Congress, in a patriotic panic, appropriated the huge sum of $800,000 to arm the new republic. The only problem was procuring the weapons, since no one was yet able to manufacture them on a large scale. That was where Eli Whitney came in.

The man knew nothing about guns, but he was an inventive genius, and he recognized that waterpower was the key to his success. He wrote, "I am persuaded that machinery moved by water . . . would greatly diminish the labor and facilitate the Manufacture of this Article."

Whitney found his perfect site at the falls on the Mill River, in the shadow of the Sleeping Giant, one of the freakish upwellings of basalt traprock that march north from New Haven through the sedimentary beds of central Connecticut. There he built his dam, then his factory, and then the model manufacturing village of Whitneyville. After visiting Whitney's site, Timothy Dwight, the president of Yale, was impressed. "No position for a manufactory could be better," he wrote. "From the bleak winds of winter it is completely sheltered by the surrounding hills. . . . No place, perhaps, is more healthy; few are more romantic." And none, he might have added, was more profitable.

Eli Whitney wrote to President John Adams to say that his new factory could produce ten thousand stand of arms—a stand being a musket with its full accompaniment of bayonet, wiper, and screwdriver—for $13.40 apiece. The price was a little steep, but Whitney promised delivery in twenty-eight months. This sounded too good to be true, and it was. It took Whitney ten years in the end to fulfill his contract, but by the time he did so he had changed American society in profound ways. One of the first factories to develop machine tools that produced interchangeable parts, Whitneyville ushered in the era of mass production, and took the first large step toward creating what people would later call the military-industrial complex, stimulated by government procurements. Whitney's innovations on the Mill River also stratified American society in new ways, creating a source of tension between skilled individual craftsmen and assembly-line laborers. I couldn't help but wonder whether Eustis Edwards was familiar with this aspect of local history.

In 1855 or 1858 (I've seen both dates cited), long after old man Whitney had died, a local shirtmaker named Oliver Winchester took over Whitneyville and set up the New Haven Arms Company on the site. In the years that followed, Winchester gave the world the Henry Rifle, the design innovations of John Browning, and of course the Winchester 73. The labor to run Winchester's machines came from thousands of new immigrants who flooded into the New Haven area from all over Europe—but especially from Sweden, where the iron and steel industry had led directly to a local tradition of arms manufacturing.

The man behind Winchester's postwar expansion was a marketing genius named Louis K. Liggett. The source of Liggett's fame was his United Drug Company, and the chain of drugstores that he called "Rx for All"—or Rexall. Until 1900, American drugstores had been essentially mom-and-pop operations. But Louis Liggett dragged them, often kicking and screaming, into the twentieth century. The core principles of the operation were economies of scale, ruthlessness of competition, and an intense advertising campaign to brand the Rexall name. Now Liggett proposed to apply the same principles to the American hardware business.

Winchester's main problem in 1919 was carrying the costs of investment in new products as well as the financial drain of idle plant. But Liggett told the company there was no problem that couldn't be solved with a sufficient volume of sales. He targeted hardware stores in every town of more than fifty thousand people and offered them a deal they couldn't refuse. To keep prices down, Winchester would eliminate the middleman. Each Winchester franchise would be offered direct access to an identical set of product lines—cutlery, flashlights, and batteries; football helmets, roller skates, and baseball bats; hammers, pipe wrenches, and paintbrushes. A trade paper of the time gave this description:

> *Even the color scheme of the store plans will be standardized. The basic color of each front will be a uniform gray; the name of the owner will appear in red; other lettering will be gold against blue. The purpose of the gray basic color is to form a neutral framework for the standardized window displays, which will be in bright and glowing colors.*

All this was accompanied, the writer might have noted, by the instantly recognizable red logo that said *WINCHESTER* in slanting capital letters.

In the larger cities, meanwhile, Winchester would open stores under its own name. By the end of 1920, there were ten of these businesses, all of them high-end affairs and all of them in the Northeast. There was an immediate tension in this arrangement: it's safe to assume that a guy dropping into a hardware store in Sioux City or Idaho Falls probably wasn't much interested in a top-quality fly rod; by the same token, an affluent New Yorker visiting the Winchester store next door to Grand Central Station was unlikely to be looking for a pipe wrench. Recognizing this, the ten Northeastern stores quickly dropped the hardware and turned themselves into sporting goods emporia for gentlemen.

There were several such places in competition with one another in midtown Manhattan. Each was purveying a vision of upscale outdoor life; each showcased the handmade bamboo fly rod as its flagship product; and each offered the work of one of Hiram Leonard's master apprentices. Abercrombie & Fitch's twelve-story headquarters at Madison and Forty-fifth was the place to find a Hawes rod; if you wished, you could put one through its paces at the casting pool on the roof. Next door was Von Lengerke and Detmold, Fred Thomas's East Coast distributor. The Winchester store, just around the corner at 47 East Forty-second, gave pride of place to "Mr. E. W. Edwards, the foremost split bamboo rod expert in the country."

These establishments were the furthest thing from a small-town fishing tackle store you could imagine, and members of the snobbish Anglers' Club of New York loved them. "Many a time," read one article in the club's bulletin, "you have entered a cluttered tackle store, and across an awkward counter have poured your confidences into the drooping ear of an ex–hardware clerk whose chief aim in life is to sell you a gaudy plug bait or a clockwork reel." At the Winchester store, however, or at Abercrombie & Fitch, there *were* no counters; instead there were leather arm-chairs, a roaring fire, a private elevator to the gun room, and sales-clerks who looked like Herbert Hoover.

The rods that Eustis Edwards built during his time at Winchester were superb examples of the craftsman's art. This was when he made the 6166, the rod that had first won Streamer's heart. In time I managed to acquire a 6165 of my own, a model from the same series, whose fine tips, dark cane, and overall delicacy of action and aesthetics took my breath away. For sentimental reasons I took it fishing for the first time on Woodbury Creek, just above the falls, where Thomas, Edwards, and Loman Hawes had had their first rod shop.

Returning to the Central Valley area for the first time in a while, it was hard not to be reminded of the commercial pressures that had driven the three men to break away from the old Leonard operation. For Edwards's relationship with Winchester brought the same problems, only in a much more acute form. His contract was a classic Faustian bargain: in exchange for the freedom to make his own masterpieces, he had to train and oversee a mass-production workforce. What made this inherent conflict intolerable was a weak spot in Louis Liggett's theories of marketing. Winchester's decision to build cheap bamboo rods put the company in direct competition with high-volume producers such as the Montague Rod and Reel Company in Massachusetts and the Horrocks-Ibbotson Company of Utica, New York. But those competitors had years of experience; they could make cheap rods in their sleep. For Winchester, entering a tough marketplace, cost and quality were at cross-purposes. If Edwards insisted on quality control, Winchester rods became uncompetitive. If production costs were lowered, the quality declined.

You can sense Eustis, an old man now, straining to break free for one last flourish. Whether he actually tried to make rods under his own name or merely asked permission to do so, there's an amendment to his five-year contract, dated July 1923, that reads like a gag order. You're not a person, Winchester's lawyers are saying; you're a *brand.* You can have your name back if and when we part company; but until then, "Eustis W. Edwards" belongs to us. There's a kind of existential horror about losing the right to your own name, especially when it's synonymous with a vision of quality and integrity. Entering his late sixties, with his creative powers undiminished, Eustis saw his name used to sell junk, and there was nothing he could do about it. It must have made him heartsick. The only comfort was that the Winchester contract had barely fifteen months to run.

Eustis Edwards had six good years left, as it turned out. For almost half a century, he had struggled to balance the ideals of his craft with the realities of economic survival. He'd done so in almost every imaginable setting: as a Leonard acolyte and member of old Hiram's manufactory; as one of the elite "supergroup" with Thomas, Hawes, and Payne; as Fred Thomas's junior partner; as a secretive independent; as head of production for a huge industrial corporation with a bamboo sideline. At every stage he'd bucked the machine, balking at compromises, corporate pressures, and identity theft, turning his back on economic security for the independent pursuit of perfection. I think ultimately it was this, beyond the sheer beauty of his work, that made Eustis such a compelling figure to me.

In 1924, at the age of sixty-seven, he finally put the equation together. In the house on Filbert Street, in a furious yearlong burst of creative activity, Eustis made fifty rods that may have been his very finest. He called them the Perfection. "You can just sense all this pent-up frustration in him," Streamer said. "I think it was all about getting back his self-respect after the Winchester experience."

The following year, 1925, on a quiet street in the Mount

Carmel section of Hamden, a couple of miles from the family home, Eustis found a handsome mid-nineteenth-century building that was available for rent. The place had been built by a local family of philanthropists, the Dickermans, to serve as a pioneering private school for girls, the Mount Carmel Young Ladies' Female Seminary. Later it had been a home for Protestant orphans. Now Eustis rented the place, converting the upper floor to a rod shop and storing his supplies of bamboo in a room downstairs.

Eustis and his younger son Gene got the new company on its feet; then, in 1927, Bill quit his auto repair job in Bangor and came to Connecticut to join them. By now, E. W. Edwards & Sons had a staff of six. It was a full-fledged "production company," like Leonard's but on a smaller scale, with Eustis in sole creative control and a clear division of labor below him—one man to work the beveler, another to glue up the "sticks," another to apply the varnish, and so on. They were helped out by a twelve-year-old Swedish-American kid named Clarence Carlson, whose father had joined the wave of immigration to New Haven to work in the Winchester factory. Clarence stopped by after school every day to sweep the floors, for which Eustis paid him a dime. The boy always rode a Samson bike to work, so Eustis gave him a nickname that stuck—"Sam."

After all the years of experimentation, Eustis narrowed his output to three models—in ascending order of quality, the Mount Carmel, the Special, and the Deluxe. They were gorgeous rods, the culms of *Arundinaria amabilis* heat-treated to a deep caramel color, and they were a commercial success. The company even seems to have ridden out the early years of the Depression—the explanation being, I suppose, that there is a market for luxury goods even in the harshest of economic times.

You can see the Edwards influence in a number of other fine Connecticut craftsmen who emerged around this time. One was a cantankerous, redheaded perfectionist named Harold "Pinky" Gillum, who worked forty miles away in Danbury, refused to advertise his rods, and liked to say that any client acquiring one was "buying two weeks of a man's life." Another, up in West Hartford, was Henry Russell Sedgwick.

I first encountered one of Sedgwick's rods on a visit to the American Museum of Fly Fishing in Manchester, Vermont. It was one of the most beautiful pieces of bamboo I'd ever seen, with intricate silk signature wraps of gold and black and exquisitely tooled metalwork. H.R., as I'd suspected, turned out to be one of the famous New England Sedgwick family, which arrived in Boston in 1629, at about the same time as the Edwards and the Leonards. The Sedgwicks went on to produce two generals (Robert and John); a railroad tycoon (Frederick); a president of the U.S. Senate (Theodore); a distinguished geologist (Adam); a novelist (Catherine); and, much later, an actress from the Andy Warhol studio (Edie) and a minor movie star (Kyra).

H.R. was born in 1868, the son of John Russell Sedgwick and Henrietta Jorelman. John Sedgwick had a pioneer streak. He and Henrietta spent years living in a one-room cabin in deepest Illinois, sixteen miles from the nearest railroad, where John hunted and farmed. The family genealogist, Hubert M. Sedgwick, observed that "it was not comfortable for his wife to be left alone." Her discomfort one day consisted of little Charlie dying while John was out searching for timber. On another occasion, she looked out the window of the cabin to see prairie wolves digging up the grave of an unnamed third child, who had died at birth. On other uncomfortable days, she lay in bed, racked with fever; hid out in the dugout during tornadoes, and encountered rattlesnakes coiled in her vegetable garden. John returned home often enough for her to conceive two more children. Eventually even John seems to have noticed that the cabin was not comfortable for his wife and moved the family back to West Hartford, where Henrietta produced another five children, including twin boys. They named one of them Henry Russell.

H.R. seems to have inherited some of his father's genes. In

1898, at thirty, he headed to the Yukon to join the great gold rush. He hunted and fished for salmon in the Alaskan wilderness. According to the family genealogist, "After reaching the headwater of the Yukon, like thousands of other venturesome spirits, he cut out logs and sawed boards with a whipsaw, constructed a serviceable boat 25 feet long, in which he traveled about 2,500 miles to St. Michael, where he traded his boat for a bottle of whiskey, there being no market at that end of the route for boats." After these adventures, H. R. Sedgwick came back to Connecticut, where he became a champion trapshooter and built beautiful and delicate fly rods for wealthy Hartford businessmen.

This digression has a purpose. You'd think that a craft as specialized and distinctive as bamboo fly rod making would attract a certain consistent temperament. But I think it was Sedgwick who first made me realize that this singular brand of perfectionism cut across all personality types. As I met more and more contemporary rod makers, I was struck by their diversity. I found that they included carpenters and machinists, college professors, extreme sport fanatics, and Zen Buddhists; there were some who fished and others, amazingly, who didn't; there were quiet men and wild men, and H. R. Sedgwick definitely seemed to fall into the latter category. I'd like to have met him.

Eustis Edwards's younger son Gene was married in the summer of 1931 and left at the end of June for a honeymoon in Maine. From a letter he wrote his mother, it's clear that the family hadn't been back to Maine in the twelve years since the move to Connecticut. Gene and his new wife, Liz, looked up old friends in Brewer and Bangor, rented a cabin on Phillips Lake, wondered at the huge new paper mill in Bucksport, dined on Penobscot salmon, and finished their trip by driving over to Lake Umbagog on the New Hampshire border, where the clanking, hissing, leaky steamer

Union had once ferried tourists across to Middle Dam and the Angler's Retreat. Gene ended his letter with a postscript: "PS, I never felt better in my life."

But soon after Gene's return to Mount Carmel, his father was taken gravely ill. On New Year's Eve of 1931, Eustis died at the age of seventy-four.

In a sense, you can see his life as having a happy ending. After decades of frustration, he had finally succeeded in breaking free of the institutions that had cramped his quest for perfection. For the last six years of his life, he had exercised full creative control over his work; his business had done well; and his two sons seemed set to take up their father's craft.

Yet in another sense, you can see Eustis's death as another way station in the bamboo rod maker's struggle to balance perfectionism with economic security. Even as he lay dying, corporate suitors came sniffing round his bedside, and with their father gone, it seems that Gene and Bill were unable to resist their blandishments. The decision they eventually made would come close to crippling the family's reputation—and it would also explain why, at the beginning of my own search for perfection, I had been able to afford a rod made by Eustis Edwards.

PART TWO

Fathers and Sons

Eustis Edwards
in Brewer, Maine, 1902.

"Very good. Exquisitely worked. You've crafted a jewel, my boy. Perfect for a courtesan or a priest to pluck after supper, or polish, Sundays after mass. In other words, this violin will never bear my name." (He smashes the violin.)
—*Luthier Nicolo Bussotti*
in François Gérard's
The Red Violin *(1998)*

CHAPTER 7

Decline and Fall

In 1888, a year before the breakup of Hiram Leonard's super-group, a former crinoline-hoop maker named Everett Horton walked into a bank in Bristol, Connecticut, and asked to see the manager. To the man's dismay, Horton showed him a telescoping tubular steel fishing rod concealed in his trouser leg. "Why are you hiding a fishing rod in your pants?" the bank manager asked, logically enough. "So you can sneak off fishing whenever you like," Horton replied, "even on a Sunday." The bank manager still looked skeptical. "Trust me," Horton said. "It will make both our fortunes." And it did.

Forty-three years later, in 1931, the Horton Manufacturing Company was still mass-producing tens of thousands of its founder's patented steel rods. They were horrible things that managed to be both heavy and fragile at the same time, but they were cheap and popular, and presumably still allowed their owners to elude the priest's attention on the Sabbath. But steel rods weren't all that Horton made. The local economy had taken off in the mid-1800s, when Bristol, thanks to inventors like Eli Terry, became the largest clockmaking center in the country. Clockmaking called for a range of skilled artisans—foundrymen, engravers, pattern makers, machinists, cabinetmakers—and those were both desirable and transferable skills. By the time the Depression struck, Everett Horton's company was making a wide variety of everyday products, and so was the town. Bristol was now a busy industrial center with a population of thirty thousand, with dozens of factories and mills lining, and befouling, the once pretty Pequabuck River.

This was all a long way from the bucolic setting of Mount Carmel, twenty miles to the south, but improbably it was where Gene and Bill Edwards ended up after their father's death. It's not clear whether the half brothers had decided to put the family business up for sale or whether Horton took the initiative. With the company floundering in the third year of the Depression, it may have seen either an opportunity to add cachet to its unromantic product lines or an opportunity for profit as Eustis Edwards lay dying. Whatever the motives, two weeks before his death Horton took out an option to buy the Edwards business for $18,000—a decent increase in the company's value since Eustis had sold it to Winchester thirteen years earlier.

Whatever benefit the Edwards family derived from this arrangement, however, it was erased by two events—one a hard financial knock, the other a calamity—in the space of nine months. When Horton finally exercised its option in March 1932, the deal was a travesty of what had been promised. The purchase price of $18,000 had dwindled to a cash payment of $4,000, a twelve-month promissory note for $1,000, and then another five annual payouts of $1,000—contingent on sales. Worst of all, the finished fly rods in the Mount Carmel workshop, which Horton had valued as high as $34 apiece, were now snapped up for a quarter of that amount. Again, it's hard to say whether this was a matter of price gouging on Horton's part or simply a reflection of the dismal business climate of the Depression.

The financial reverse was bad enough, but what came next was worse. On the freezing night of December 19, 1932, Sam Carlson, the boy with the bike who had swept the floors at E. W. Edwards & Sons, had finished a game of basketball at the Y in New Haven and taken the trolley home. As he walked uphill past the old girls' seminary, he became aware of a faint smell of smoke. He thought nothing of it and went to bed. But then, around midnight, he was awakened by the clanging bell of a fire truck. The sky was lit by the flames rising from the Edwards rod shop. The damage was estimated at $5,000.

You couldn't dream up a more bitter parable of the vulnerabilities of the bamboo rod maker. With its stacks of raw bamboo, pots of volatile varnish, blowtorches to flame the cane, and in this case a potbellied stove to keep the place warm on a glacial winter night, every rod shop was an accident waiting to happen. Fires were an occupational hazard, and the Edwards shop was neither the first nor the last to burn. And then the Bristol deal, coming only months before, was a cruel reminder—worse than William Mills's takeover of Leonard, worse than the sale to Winchester—of the power of larger market forces to control and constrict the rod maker's craft.

The two half brothers couldn't have been more different in temperament. Gene had converted to Christian Science, his wife's religion. He was known as a kind and generous man, but there was something somber about him; he worried a lot about money. Bill, despite his long face and gaunt features, was more easygoing. ("He drinks," his new sister-in-law commented disapprovingly, although that should probably be taken with a grain of salt, since she banned even sauerkraut from the house as an alcohol risk.) Between the lines of my research I kept finding small hints of conflict between the two men, and the move to Bristol must have exaggerated their differences. Gene had put in years of apprenticeship with his father, and by some accounts had been sent back to Bangor for a spell to study under Fred Thomas; Bill had less experience of rod making but was arguably an equally gifted craftsman—and certainly the more experimental of the two. Gene retained the right to make higher-end rods under the Edwards name; Bill got the runts of the litter, supervising production of a line of Bristol rods that were designated by their cost in dollars, which made them sound rather like fighter planes. The best of them was the F-18; the worst was the F-5, which was designed to compete with the cheapest mass-production companies. The move to Bristol kept the family afloat at a time when one-quarter of the American workforce was without a job, but it must have been a galling comedown—recall that Eustis Edwards's finest handmade rods for Winchester had sold for $60 fifteen years earlier.

The best thing you can say about the Bristol deal was that it allowed the brothers—Gene in particular—a little more freedom than Winchester had allowed their father. Meanwhile, rods made in the Bristol factory were shipped off to individual craftsmen who were suffering from the Depression, like Paul Young in Detroit, who later emerged as a rod maker of rare ability. Unmarked Bristol rods were also sold to a variety of dealers as far away as Denver and Seattle. Even large department stores got into the act—Marshall Field's in Chicago, Macy's in New York. But the biggest contract of all rekindled the relationship between the Edwards family and the state (not to mention the *idea*) of Maine.

If the idea of Maine had first been marketed by Fly Rod Crosby, its apotheosis came at the hands of Leon Leonwood Bean. In New York, Abercrombie & Fitch was still packaging the idea of the affluent, sophisticated sportsman and adventurer. Bean sold a less pretentious, but ultimately more lucrative, image of Maine that grew directly out of Crosbyland, the turn-of-the-century fishing and hunting camps of the Rangeley Lakes and the western mountains. Like Crosby, L. L. Bean—and the outfits you bought from him—promised "wilderness with all the comforts."

Bean made the transition from small-town dry goods salesman to national marketing wizard in 1911, when he invented his famous rubber-bottomed, leather-topped boots. Twenty-five years later, his company had grown to a million-dollar business and was sending out a 108-page mail-order catalog twice a year. In the process, L. L. Bean broadened its reach. The catalog was now marketing more than an image of Maine; it was selling an idea of Nature—

with a capital *N.* This was a step beyond what Abercrombie & Fitch had done. The New York–based outfitter had always been reticent about marketing; its business was based on the notion that the well-heeled customer would know how to find his way to A&F and, once there, would find all the accoutrements a gentleman needed for his outdoor activities. Bean aggressively sold a line of clothing and sporting equipment that was equal parts sport and preppie. Images of the company's founder in the north woods— "L.L. with dead moose, L.L. and dead bear, L.L. and dead deer," as a biographer put it—were interleaved with pictures of models wearing chinos and tweed jackets. "To this day," the same author wrote in 1984, "the largest possible proportion of L. L. Bean clothing to ordinary gear is seen at a Harvard class reunion picnic, or any given day at Bennington College."

Bean himself didn't spend too much time with the tedious, hands-on business of running his growing empire; he was much too busy hunting or fishing for brook trout or salmon. In the late 1930s, the top-of-the-line item in the Bean catalog was the 1199 Dry-Fly Rod, made by Gene Edwards. The advertising copy said, "Mr. Bean personally used it for both trolling and casting and says it is the best Rod he ever tested regardless of price."

For Gene, the relationship with Bean seems to have been more prosaic; it was just part of the Horton factory's ceaseless demand for higher output. Eustis Edwards had been dead for almost a decade now, and the memory of his work began to blur. Were Edwards rods tools for the elite or for the masses? Did the name stand for meticulous handcrafting or the grinding output of a factory in a beaten-down industrial town? Was a particular Edwards rod made by Gene? By Bill? By father and sons working together? By Eustis himself (or, as some people still called him, Billy)? Or by some anonymous laborer on the Bristol production line? Time, the Depression, and economic compromises had all combined to erode the family's reputation.

· · ·

The two half brothers struggled to stay true, each in his own way, to their father's creative legacy. In the first fly rods that Gene made after Eustis's death in 1931, you can see a conscious desire to emulate his father's style. Early Gene, late Eustis—even Streamer, who had handled as many of the family's rods as anyone I knew, said he sometimes had a hard time telling them apart. But the continuities of style began to fray under the commercial pressures of the Bristol years. The drudgery went on until early 1942, when Horton finally turned over its entire plant to war production and put its inventory of bamboo into deep storage. Gene took a job closer to home as a machinist with High Standard, a Swedish-owned gun manufacturer in New Haven, where he crossed paths again with Sam Carlson, the boy who had swept the floors in the old Edwards shop. Sam was now in his late twenties, and High Standard was employing him as a skilled toolmaker.

Bill Edwards danced to an entirely different drummer. Gene, for all his undoubted skill as a craftsman, was a temperamental conservative and no innovator. But Bill inherited his father's restless, experimental streak. When Eustis discovered how to apply heat in a way that transformed the inherent properties of bamboo, he had changed the course of rod making. Bill came up with something that was every bit as radical, even if it was ultimately not as influential.

Bill Edwards quit Horton in 1939 and set up his own shop with his son Scott. This arrangement didn't last long: Scott volunteered after Pearl Harbor, opted for a career in the military, and broke the family tradition of rod making in the third generation. In those three years, however, Bill drew on some elementary principles of engineering to design something entirely new—a rod that was made from four strips of bamboo, not six.

"Entirely new" isn't strictly accurate, so perhaps I should modify that a little. As Fred Thomas pointed out when he heard of Bill's innovation, a four-sided rod was something that Hiram

Leonard had experimented with in his earliest days in Bangor. But
Leonard was just trying to imitate the appearance of the wooden
fly rods that were standard equipment in the 1870s, shaving off
the corners of the four strips of bamboo to make a rod that was
perfectly round in cross section. But he sacrificed a lot of the bamboo's critical power fibers in the process. If Leonard had been con-
tent to stick with four ninety-degree angles, he might have made
the technical breakthrough that Bill Edwards achieved almost seventy years later.

The physics work something like this. A hexagonal rod has an
inclination to flex in different directions; if you're an indifferent
caster, as I am, you're likely to introduce torque into your casting
stroke, and that will translate into inaccuracy. A four-sided rod—
or a Quadrate, as Bill Edwards called it—has a greater resistance
to lateral stress. When the bamboo fibers are compressed by the
act of casting, the energy is channeled into a vertical plane, and
the result, at least in theory, is greater accuracy. With broader flat
surfaces, a Quadrate rod will also give you a greater concentration
of power fibers. The rods are also downright beautiful. Varnish is
not only the last cosmetic touch on a fly rod; it is also one of the
most complex and skilled operations involved, and rod makers
have traditionally mixed their varnishes according to formulas as
arcane and secretive as those of Stradivarius or Guarneri. In the
hands of a master varnisher, the broader rod surfaces of the
Quadrate gleam and reflect light and bring out the grain and natural coloration of the bamboo.

When I bought my first Edwards Quadrate, I was blown away. I
acquired it from a rod maker I had come to know in Massachusetts.
He was a professor of environmental studies at Amherst and his
work often took him to Russia. He'd used the rod to fish for salmon
in Siberia, and almost from the moment he'd sold it to me I could
tell he regretted its loss. It was a nine-foot rod, and I took it out several times on bigger rivers like the Housatonic in Connecticut.

I was amazed by its power—it could throw a line seventy feet with little effort—and entranced by the beauty of its appearance, the way that the varnish accentuated the rich chestnut tones of the flamed bamboo and the contrasting yellow-brown of the nodes. But in the end the rod was too heavy for my hand, and I sold it back to my Massachusetts friend. He seemed relieved, and so, frankly, was I.

At about the same time, I found an eight-foot Quadrate I could afford. Relative to its weight it had the same kind of power and accuracy, and I found it just as beautiful. But most important, I could fish it all day without discomfort, and its length meant that it was adaptable to all sorts of conditions, from smaller wild trout streams to the big, Western-style water of the Housatonic. The rod came in a traveling case of fine belting leather and, within that, an aluminum tube of smaller diameter. The tube bore a rectangular silver label:

> **W. E. EDWARDS & SON**
> **HIGH GRADE FISHING TACKLE**
> **3321 Whitney Ave.**
> **Mt. Carmel, Conn.**

I found Bill's old shop on the east side of Whitney Avenue, backing onto the Mill River, the pretty trout stream that Eli Whitney had once dammed to provide power to his arms factory. A little way to the north, at 3820, was the unprepossessing cement-block building that Gene Edwards had rented after World War II. Gene's old rod shop was tucked in between a doughnut shop and Aunt Chilada's Mexican eatery. The building was locked up, and there was an aging, yellowed For Rent sign in the window.

Behind Bill Edwards's place, I heard the sudden roar of a chain saw and went round back to investigate. A slight figure was darting backing and forth in the yard, cutting up tree limbs that had blown down in a storm. He told me his name was David; he was from Taiwan. He'd never heard of Bill Edwards, never knew that a famous bamboo fly rod maker once lived here. David ran a business called Mercury Travel; before that the place had been the Sandalwood gift shop; before that a Century 21 real estate brokerage.

I went to the trunk of my car, showed him my Quadrate, showed him the tube. He squinted at it, a little suspicious at first. Then he read the label: 3321. He looked up at his front door: 3321. He broke into a broad grin. I wasn't trying to put something over on him.

"What's more," I told him, "the bamboo in this rod came from China—the PRC, I mean, not Taiwan—from a certain valley in Guangdong Province."

His eyes narrowed at this. "How much you say this rod is worth?" he asked.

"I don't know. Eight hundred, maybe a thousand dollars."

His eyes widened again. I could see the wheels turning in his head. Cost of raw material; cost of Chinese labor; cost of shipping.

"Why you got to send this bamboo out of China? Why not get Chinese workmen make it into fishing rods right there? Very cheap. Maybe we could export to United States, make a great business."

"Well," I said, "if only it were that easy. People have tried it. But that's a long story."

The wheels stopped turning. "Well, anyway," he said, "you want to find out more about this Edwards fellow, maybe you try the sports shop across the street. Have a nice day."

The place was called Mulligan's. It was full of noise: telephones ringing, the whiz and zing of skate blades being sharpened on a wheel. Teenage kids, fathers and small sons, were examining racks of golf clubs, baseball bats, and hockey sticks. Behind the counter was a middle-aged man with a beard and long white hair that fell across his shoulders. "I know this is a strange question," I said to him, "but I was wondering if maybe you knew anything about the old Edwards rod shop across the street." This had the definite feel of a wild-goose chase.

"Can't say I do," the man replied. "But my partner sure does. Hey, Ray!"

A heavyset man of about my own age, with a thick black beard and piercing eyes, came over to join us. "Ray Gambordella Jr.," he introduced himself, extending a hand. "My father was Bill Edwards's chief rod maker." He turned to his white-bearded partner: "Hey, fetch me down those rod blanks up on the shelf."

"Look at these," he said, turning to me. "Two-piece, seven-and-a-half-foot F. E. Thomas blanks. These are from when my dad and Sam Carlson bought out the Edwards name in the fifties, when Bill Edwards retired to Florida, and then they went up to Maine and bought up the remaining stock of the Thomas Company when it went under. They bought the business with a rubber check. Times were hard. I got a room full of this stuff—blanks and rods and Quadrates by the dozen, saltwater Quads, and God knows what."

Whoa, wait a minute, I thought: Sam Carlson bought up Edwards? And Thomas? Let's not get ahead of ourselves here. "Tell me about your dad," I said, trying to collect my thoughts.

Ray Gambordella Jr. grinned. "My dad was a hell of a fisherman," he said. "He just loved to fish and fish and fish. He could cast an entire fly line with his bare hands, without a rod. Plus he was a great tournament fly caster." Just like Hiram Hawes, I thought.

I glanced uneasily at my watch. I was here on a whim and hadn't left myself enough time to pursue this conversation. In the lot outside, I'd left my car parked next to a 1931 Ford, with "Mulligan's" painted on its gleaming coachwork. "Just look at that," Ray said. "I wish to God I'd lived in those times, when people appreciated craftsmanship." He waved in the other direction, indicating an aluminum-and-vinyl-sided building. "Now look at that," he said. "That stuff won't last a hundred years. Hell, it won't last twenty years. It'll just fall down, and no one will remember it. No one appreciates quality anymore.

"Come back another time!" Ray yelled as I backed out of the lot. "I'll get an old fishing buddy of my dad's to come over, and you can ask him all the questions you want."

Back in New York the next day, an extraordinary thing happened, a small piece of serendipity. There are a few dealers in bamboo fly rods scattered around the country, and by this time I was subscribing to most of their catalogs. Occasionally I'd buy a lower-priced Edwards rod, and with time I mastered the art of trading up, so that I'd put together a small collection. But I'd never seen a rod by Ray Gambordella—indeed, until my trip to Mount Carmel the previous day, I'd never even *heard* of Ray Gambordella. But here at the top of the list from a dealer I knew in California was a six-foot bamboo rod signed "R. Gamby." The price was reasonable, so I snapped it up. As soon as the UPS man delivered it a few days later, I called Ray Gambordella Jr. to schedule my follow-up visit.

"R. Gamby, number 17," Ray said, beaming as he read the India ink inscription on the rod shaft and turned the rod slowly in his hands. "God, yes, I remember these. This one's part of a batch of twenty-five rods my dad made in the 1970s. We sold them to some guy over on the Connecticut River who went up to Maine. We made them from old Thomas blanks. My sister and I helped work on these after my dad taught us to glue the strips." He held the rod a little closer, peering appraisingly at the silk wraps. "See, these aren't quite right," he said, pointing at some tiny imperfection. "We were just learning."

"Let me take a look at that," said a voice over my shoulder. The accent could only be described, at the risk of stereotyping, as Connecticut Italian. "Here's my card," the man said by way of introduction as I turned around. The card said: *Andrew E. Fucci. Division Manager, Kasco Pet Foods.* "Call me Edgie," he said. "Everyone else does." So I did. He was a spry, birdlike little man of eighty or so, and the name suited him.

"This is my dad's friend I was telling you about," Ray said.

"Will you look at this rod?" Edgie said gleefully. "His dad had the greatest hands, the greatest feel. With Ray's dad, the rods were personalized. It wasn't that he just made a rod and sold it; you'd come in and say, 'I want a seven-foot rod for the dry fly,' and he'd say, 'No problem,' and he'd do it."

He handed the Gambordella rod back to me and went on, "I always thought Bill Edwards made the best rods that were ever made. Here, take a look at this one. Every five, six, seven years, someone comes up and wants to see an Edwards rod, so I get this one out to show 'em." Edgie cackled and passed me an aluminum tube. Inside was the smallest fly rod I'd ever seen. Bill Edwards catalogs that I'd seen listed rods as short as six feet. This one was four feet four inches. It was battered and worn. It was lovely. Written on the shaft, in the same rounded, yellow-white ink that was on the shaft of my own Quadrate, was "Edgie."

"Bill Edwards made this for me," he said. "Two tips, two different weights. I never knew Bill to fish, you know, but Ray's dad . . . whoa, he was a great fisherman."

"Yeah." Ray nodded. "My dad cast his rods up and down the East Coast, won a million trophies."

"He was a nice man, Bill Edwards. He was a quiet man, a very stable personality. There used to be some laughter in his workshop."

"Yeah," Ray agreed. "I never heard my dad say a bad word about him."

. . .

But I had to bring the conversation back to where Ray and I had left off last time. What he'd said then had stunned me. The friendship between Eustis Edwards and Fred Thomas went back to the early 1880s; then they'd worked together briefly in Maine at the turn of the century, and had been neighbors for the better part of two decades. But as far as I could tell, Eustis's move to Connecticut in 1919 had been the end of it. Now Ray was saying that the relationship between the two families had been brought full circle, and that the person responsible had been Sam Carlson, the boy who'd swept the floors.

As I pieced the story together, it became clear that it was a far from simple one, that the decline of the craft of bamboo fly rod making after World War II was the result of many different factors. I thought it no exaggeration to say that it had elements of tragedy.

Until the war, the F. E. Thomas rod had been a full-blown rival to Leonard, which continued to prosper in Central Valley. Fred himself had died in 1938. For forty years, his obituary said, the Thomas rod had been "built upon honor from the best obtainable bamboo and with such care and accuracy that none could be constructed more perfectly from a human standpoint." At the time of Fred's death there were twelve skilled craftsman in the Thomas shop on Baptist Hill in Bangor, and between them they were making four or five hundred rods a year. Even after the old man died, the business continued to chug along under his son Leon, but many people will tell you that the quality was never quite the same. You can ascribe this to Leon's failings, as some do, or you can ascribe it to the larger forces that swirled around him, the fact that the craftsman's life is lived at the mercy of external circumstances. I prefer the second of these explanations.

After 1918, the combination of war, technology, and economics had taken Eustis Edwards into his five-year contract with Winchester; after 1945, the same combination brought the Edwards family, the Thomas business, and the whole craft of bamboo fly rod making to their knees.

As soon as the conflict was over, soldiers flocked home from the battlefields of Europe and the Pacific, and tens of thousands who stopped over in occupied Japan brought back cheap, locally made fly rods, bearing names like Mermaid, Pearl, Seahorse, and West Point—not to mention Nippon Fishing Tackle, the rod that had set me off on my odyssey in the first place. In themselves, these Japanese rods were a relatively trivial factor in the decline of the craft in the United States, more a garish symptom than a cause of change; the real crisis of bamboo rod making was rooted in the profound social upheavals that followed the war.

The troops came home to a college education under the G.I. Bill; they moved to the suburbs; postwar affluence gave them homes stuffed with labor-saving gadgets and garages filled with shiny new automobiles; new paved highways took those automobiles to formerly wild and remote parts of the country. The Maine woods, like the great national parks of the West, were suddenly aswarm with vacationers and weekend tourists, and their rivers were elbow-to-elbow with fishermen. In the process, the human relationship to the natural outdoor world changed, perhaps forever. Like everything else, nature—and the things you did there, things like fishing—started to become a commodity to be advertised and sold. And there was no longer just L. L. Bean, but mail-order catalogs by the dozen to sell you the clothing and the tools you needed to play in the great American landscape.

Aldo Leopold, who was an avid fly fisher and hunter and probably the greatest environmental writer of the midcentury, saw clearly what was happening. In his 1949 classic, *A Sand County Almanac*, he wrote:

> *Your true modern is separated from the land by many middlemen, and by innumerable physical gadgets.... The gadgeteer, otherwise known as the sporting-goods dealer... has draped the American outdoors man with an infinity of con-*

traptions, all offered as aids to self-reliance, hardihood, wood-craft, or marksmanship, but too often functioning as substitutes for them. Gadgets fill the pockets, they dangle from neck and belt. The overflow fills the auto-trunk, and also the trailer. Each item of outdoor equipment grows lighter and often better, but the aggregate poundage becomes tonnage.

You can see the spinning reel, and the advertising blitz that accompanied it, as the paradigmatic gadget of postwar recreation. The cult of fly-fishing had always been based on a certain amount of pretension: it's an arcane skill with an accompanying set of social protocols, virtual Masonic rituals; ergo, only educated gentlemen are equipped to do it. Oh, and by the way, the tools it requires—the *good* ones, that is—cost a small fortune. The spinning reel, by contrast, is a cheap, simple device that can take almost infinite abuse. Put your index finger on the bail; toss the line a country mile; catch a fish. Anyone can master it; millions did. "I hate this whole spinning business," wrote Edward Ringwood Hewitt, one of the pillars of the old Catskills fly-fishing aristocracy. "It will absolutely ruin all fishing in trout streams—I'd outlaw it if I could." But it was hard not to see the old fly-fishing snobs as having been hoist by their own petard.

If the spin-fishing craze was the first body blow to the bamboo fly rod, faraway politics were the second. Both the Japanese occupation of Hong Kong and the Chinese civil war had interrupted supplies of the bamboo rod maker's sole source of raw material. Although shipments resumed after the war, the ongoing conflict disrupted planting, harvesting, and quality controls in the Sui River Valley. Then, in October 1949, Mao Zedong stood before Tiananmen Gate in Beijing and declared the victory of his peasant revolution; within fourteen months the United States had slapped an embargo on all Chinese exports, and that was the end of the trade in Tonkin cane.

The third and most serious reverse that the rod maker suffered was rooted in technological change. The war unleashed a wave of new practical applications for the latest advances in physics and chemistry. It gave us synthetic fibers to wear, plastics to build with, DDT to spray on our fields and forests, inorganic fertilizers to boost our crop yields. It took decades for us to understand that these things wreaked havoc with the environment, but no time at all for them to ignite a revolution in popular tastes. After 1950, the market was flooded with synthetic materials—first fiberglass and later graphite—that were an outgrowth of wartime military technologies and could do many of the same things bamboo could do, if less romantically. At first these new materials were exotic luxuries, but as their popularity grew prices dropped, and by the late 1950s, 97 percent of the fishing rods that Americans were buying were made of fiberglass.

Ray Gambordella's face clouded over when he reached this part of the story. "You couldn't make a living making bamboo rods in the fifties," he said with a grunt of disgust. "When Caldor's opened up in Hamden Plaza in 1957, all that mattered was what was cheapest. Not quality. They had fiberglass rods there for ten bucks, and no one wanted to pay fifty anymore for an Edwards bamboo Quadrate. I remember my dad with bundles of rods on the dining room table after fiberglass came in. Twenty dollars, take any one you want. We had tag sales."

What the consumer lost in this process was craftsmanship, a sense of history, a connection to the organic. What he gained was money saved. For most, it was no contest.

CHAPTER 8

The Price of Perfection

Here are some of the phrases that rod historians, dealers, and collectors had used when I asked them about Sam Carlson: "dean of American fly rod makers" ... "greatest living bamboo craftsman" ... "living legend" ... "last direct link to the old Leonard tradition."

Those weren't the first words on Ray Gambordella's lips. But if there was a tinge of bitterness in his voice, it seemed to have less to do with any questioning of Sam's skills and integrity than with the fact that his renown was so intimately tied up with Ray Sr.'s decline into anonymity.

In buying the old Thomas Rod Company, Sam and Ray had demonstrated a breathtakingly bad sense of timing. They began their partnership in the mid-1950s, just as the China embargo and the new miracle invention of fiberglass were tearing the heart out of their craft. Ray always seemed to be broke; Sam provided a little seed capital, borrowed from his father. They ran the business for a while right here in Hamden, Ray Jr. said, then briefly moved to Essex, at the mouth of the Connecticut River, reasoning that the saltwater angling trade might boost their moribund sales. Ray had worked with Bill Edwards for years; Sam's association with the family went back to his childhood, although he'd spent more of his working life as a skilled machinist and toolmaker in the weapons and aircraft industries than in rod making.

In many ways it was a marriage made in hell. Temperamentally, the men were radical opposites. Ray was a dynamo and a salesman; Sam was an obsessive perfectionist.

"Not to belittle Sam," Edgie said, "but he didn't have any knowledge of building a rod back then. But he did know how to make a rod look like a piece of jewelry."

Ray nodded in agreement. "My father was the master of the taper," he said. "He didn't care about cosmetics, or fancy fittings. He just cared about making a rod that fished well. Sam's rods were beautiful, but he'd make six rods a year and it would drive my dad nuts. Six rods, and they'd have orders for a hundred."

"Ray's father had a production schedule," Edgie went on. "They were fine rods, but he'd say, 'Let's get 'em outta here.' See, we were around these rods all the time, so we didn't think that much about them. Eisenhower bought a Quadrate rod from Bill Edwards. Gary Cooper. But to us, heck, it was just a fishing rod. Freshwater, saltwater, whatever. Throw it in the back of the car or the station wagon. See, you've got to understand the old Yankee craftsman in his own way. He worked out of a basket."

He paused, then said, "I'd tell you more, but I don't think there's any more to tell. All the old company records are gone."

"I just have a few old papers of my dad's left," Ray said, handing me a slim folder. There were Edwards Quadrate and F. E. Thomas catalogs from the 1940s, creased and torn photographs of Bill Edwards stooped over his beveler, newspaper clippings showing Ray's father knee-deep in the Mill River, holding up a stringer of brook trout and smiling. He had an open, ingenuous face, with those black-rimmed Walter Cronkite glasses that men used to wear in the sixties. A faded purple silk medal ribbon from a fly-casting tournament. Handwritten order forms and inventories of stock. A note from H. R. Sedgwick of Hartford with a secret arsenic-based formula for oxidizing ferrules. That one pleased me, because it confirmed the ties I'd suspected between Sedgwick and the Edwards family.

"Here's the pictures from the trip to Maine," Edgie said with a smile, "when they bought up the Thomas operation. Your dad spent the weekend up there with Leon Thomas and his wife,

I remember. Caught a million salmon and there's a million pictures."

"Look," Ray said, "here's the receipt from the cabins they stayed in. Moosehead Lake Highlands, Greenville, Maine, May 24, 1958."

They'd retraced Thoreau's journey, in other words, the trip to Greenville a hundred years earlier when he'd shared a stagecoach with Hiram Leonard.

"Nasty Maine weather," Ray said. "Look at those oilskins. Two boats, two days, eight dollars a day, an outboard at three dollars a day. The whole two days cost them sixty bucks."

Edgie picked up one of the small, square black-and-white photos. It was the kind that had deckled edges, the kind that were popular at the same time as the Walter Cronkite glasses. Ray Gambordella was holding up a trophy brook trout, a Maine squaretail of about four pounds.

"There's your dad with a nice fish," Edgie said.

"Sam didn't go on that trip, of course," Ray said. "He'd paid for the Thomas business with that rubber check. Got the money from his dad."

"Where's Sam now?" I asked.

"Oh," Ray answered, "last I heard he was living in a trailer house up in New Hampshire."

A double-wide on a secondary highway in rural New Hampshire is not where you'd expect to find a living legend. But that was where I found Sam Carlson. He was standing in front of the house when I turned in to his driveway one sultry afternoon in July. Behind him, the Stars and Stripes hung limply from a flagpole. Sam was wearing stained olive green work pants, low-cut brown boots, a checked shirt, and a baseball cap. He was an old man, in his mid-eighties now, with rheumy eyes and jowls that were beginning to sag. But he was still building bamboo fly rods. We shook hands and went into his workshop.

Words like "legend" and "dean" and "master" were not the only ones I'd heard applied to Sam Carlson. I'd also heard people use epithets like "difficult" and "withdrawn." But after we'd chatted for a few minutes those terms made no sense to me. I found Sam modest and diffident, and I wondered if some of the unkind things I'd heard had something to do with the scarcity of Carlson rods, the colossal prices they commanded at auction, and the frustration of those who'd like to own one but couldn't afford it. Not that Sam saw any of the income from the secondary market himself, as you could tell from his peeling trailer home and the cramped, jumbled workshop in the shed out back.

"That's Bill Edwards's stool you're sitting on there," he said as he eased himself in beside me at the workbench. I gave a start, half expecting a medium to join us. The workshop was like the storage room of a favorite museum: all those things you've fantasized about but that are never put on public display. There were whole rods, and parts of rods, and glued-up sections, one of them test-wrapped in silks that were all the colors of the rainbow. There were jewelers' loupes and micrometers and spools of thread and sections of nickel silver tubing for making ferrules. A few of the rods were six-strip bamboo, from the early days of working with the old Thomas stock, but most were four-sided. After Bill Edwards retired, Sam had become the principal exponent of the Quadrate idiom.

All his people were from Sweden, he told me. With his wife, Verna, and his brother-in-law, Sam had gone over there once to trace his family's roots in an old iron-making town that had turned to the manufacture of armaments. Industries like Winchester had attracted thousands of Swedes to New Haven—it's still the biggest Swedish community in the country, in fact—and Sam said he had been touring for sixty years with the Apollo Singing Society, which was part of the American Union of Swedish Singers. In fact, he told me a little bashfully, he'd won many awards for his solo tenor recordings. There was something in the way he said this that made me think he was more proud of his accomplishments as a singer than as a rod maker.

I asked Sam how he'd come by his craftsman's hands. It was mainly on account of his father, he said. "My dad was a tool-maker," he said, "and he came to work for Winchester." The Carlsons moved to Mount Carmel in 1919, the year Eustis Edwards began his five-year stint with Winchester. "After that," Sam went on, "my people went to work for a well-known artist named Bancel LaFarge. The LaFarges had a place up on Tuckernuck, which was an adjacent island to Nantucket. I don't know what happened to that job, but my pop went back into the toolmaking game, between toolmaking and carpentry. After that we moved to a place called Dickerman Hill. Ben Dickerman was a local Yankee; he owned this property that was once a girls' school, and we moved in almost next door."

The old school, of course, was where Eustis Edwards had opened his rod shop in 1925.

"So being in the neighborhood, I went nosing around," Sam went on. "And Gene Edwards kind of took me under his wing. Those two rooms upstairs, I swept them for a dime apiece every day after school. In summertime they put me to work polishing reel seats and the like. They couldn't do that today, of course, not with the child labor laws." He closed his eyes for a moment and smiled. "I can still smell the pungent odors of that place, you know."

Sam reached over to a crowded corner of his workbench and pulled down a set of rod blanks that were waiting to be wrapped and varnished. The six strips of bamboo were bound tightly with fine string to hold them secure until the glue set firmly.

"See, this is what a glued stick looks like," he said. "The guys in the Edwards shop would bundle this stuff in big mounds and I'd sit there and cut the thread off. By the hour."

Was that when he'd first thought of becoming a rod maker? I asked.

"I'd have to say no, not really. I was only interested in the twenty cents a day I got out of it. I didn't fish much as a kid either."

He thought about this for a moment, then said, "It occurs to me to say here that most of the people that have fiddled around with fishing rods, to make their own, did it because they were interested in fishing. But I was never really interested in it that much, to have done what I did in the rod game. And I wish I'd never seen it, to be perfectly honest with you. I could have had a better family life, although my wife and I were married fifty-eight years yesterday. And our kids suffered because of the rod business."

Sam fell silent, and as if on cue, Verna Carlson came in. She had materialized at my shoulder without a sound; there was a taciturn, inscrutable quality about her. She brought us colored plastic glasses of iced tea that was thick with sugar. The glasses were cool and damp with condensation in the heat of the afternoon. "Skoal," Sam said, still looking a little abashed, as if he'd been caught talking out of turn.

He put his glass down and rubbed his eyes. "People will say about a rod maker, 'He made great rods'—not talking about myself here. But you know, Jim Payne—he was subsidized. The Thomas people made a lot of rods, but then Leon Thomas, at the end, from what I understand, he just drank his way out of the thing. And even Eustis Edwards, when you come right down to it, of course he was in and out with all the other famous people in the rod game when they worked with Leonard, then with Thomas and Payne and all those ventures. But then after Winchester, he was only on his own for another six years. And in 1931 he was dead. Now, you can't really call that a successful-type business."

Sam reached into a drawer and handed me a yellowed clipping from the *New Haven Register*. The headline said, "Flash Fire in School Building." From the way he recounted the story, he seemed almost to feel personally responsible for the destruction of the Edwards rod shop, as if it never would have burned if he hadn't fallen asleep that night.

"Did they lose all the bamboo?" I asked.

Sam wasn't sure. "The cane was stored downstairs, so maybe not. They apparently salvaged two bevelers, although it's hard for me to see how that happened, because they were on the second floor and the fire was upstairs."

But in midsentence he seemed to pause at an inconsistency in his memory. He got up from his stool and walked over to a dusty corner of the workshop. He said he wanted to find some parts—"sticks," he called them—that Eustis Edwards had crafted, to show me the difference in cane work between father and sons. He emerged from the corner with an armload of unfinished rod sections wrapped in a dense bundle. "These are Eustis cuts," he said, sitting down again and placing them in my hands. "They were left out in the backyard after the fire. See how they're only singed a little at the ends? I've had those since 1932." The sticks carried the faint, resilient smell of old smoke down through the years.

Sam lost touch with the Edwards boys when he went to high school, then ran into Gene again during the war, in the High Standard arms factory. "Gene did production work," he recalled, "running the milling machine or something of the sort. I was in the tool room downstairs. Then, when the war ended, Gene approached me and said he was going back into the rod business, and would I join him? Apparently Horton was going to give him all the old Bristol stocks of cane. Gene said that he had two daughters, no son, and I would be more or less the heir to the business." He stopped and shook his head with a frown. "Just how that was to come about I wouldn't know."

I'd heard lots of stories by this time of the Leonards and the Paynes, the Thomases and the Edwardses. They'd made it all sound so seamless, the secret knowledge handed down like Torah scrolls through a continuous lineage that ran from father to son, from founder to apprentice-heir. But Sam told a different story, one of fits and starts, of hard work and declining returns, of a hand-to-mouth existence filled with frustrations and blind alleys.

He stayed with Gene Edwards for five years, he went on, from 1946 to 1951. "I did all his assembly work," he said. "I mean, I was a novice when you come right down to it. I took over the glueing after old Bert Van Hennick left, all the reel seats, made all the ferrules. Gene did most of the repair work and looked after customers." After that, it was another five years of jumping around from pillar to post, relying on his toolmaking skills to put food on the table. During that time, Ray Gambordella took Sam's place for a while. Gene tried to evade the China embargo by working with American bamboo that he got from Louisiana, but it was ugly gray stuff and no substitute for the real thing. He made spinning rods, trying to adapt to the new craze. He taught himself how to make rods from the new miracle material, fiberglass. But none of it worked, and in 1955 the Gene Edwards rod shop finally went down the tubes.

I'd heard the rest of Gene's story from his daughter Barbara, whom I'd tracked down in Florida. The collapse of his business led to a nervous breakdown, she'd told me. That came on top of the lung disease he'd contracted during the war, when he'd worked with asbestos at High Standard without a protective mask. He'd checked in to a Christian Science nursing home in Boston, where his faith had pulled him through without medical intervention.

Afterward, Gene did this and that. He ran to the bank quite a bit. He talked about going into business with Ted Williams, the Boston Red Sox slugger who ended up in not only the Baseball Hall of Fame but also the Fishing Hall of Fame. He went out to

Minneapolis for a spell to make lures for the Paul Bunyan Bait Company, but the brutal winter climate led to a bout of emphysema that almost killed him. Finally in 1958 he moved into an apartment in Bronxville, New York, and rode the train into Manhattan every day to work for Abercrombie & Fitch, doing rod repairs. Gene had made rods for A&F for years, hustling for business during the lean winter months, and he seemed to have been happy with the new job. He made friends with Gadabout Gaddis, who hosted a popular television show called *The Flying Fisherman,* and with Helen Shaw, who was known as "the Greta Garbo of Fly-Tying." He met other famous people at A&F—Perry Como, Jonathan Winters. When people asked him which customer he'd most like to serve, he said Jackie Kennedy.

Gene retired in 1967 and bought a little place on Long Island Sound. He fretted about Vietnam and falling dominoes in Southeast Asia. He puttered around the sound in a little boat catching bluefish. He liked to fish with Jewish people, he said, because they didn't drink or use foul language. One of his fishing buddies had a blue number from Auschwitz tattooed on his arm. In the wintertime Gene had a trailer home in Florida, near Cape Canaveral. He sat outside on a lawn chair and watched them put the first man on the moon.

"When Gene went out," Sam said, "I bought that wood lathe over there and this old Atlas lathe over here from him for a hundred bucks. It was thirdhand when Gene got it, and I put it in shape. So I had acquired those two machines, but I couldn't do anything with them. I lived in a building up on Sleeping Giant Drive in Hamden that had neither basement nor attic. So I stored the lathes in a little utility room and went back to work."

"Where was that?" I asked.

"Oh, I worked in many, many places from '51 to '56. Marlin

Firearms, where I worked in R&D as a model maker. O. F. Mossberg, another gunmaker, in the same capacity. A long spell with Pratt & Whitney Aircraft. Then Ray began to go down; he was just losing it. Nobody ever gave Ray a break. He was a good rod man, and it's unfortunate what happened to him. He was pretty much in turmoil because he'd come into the business at just the wrong time. Plus the guy just didn't have enough money in the bank. When he finally gave up, he was paying for Bill Edwards's rod business on the five-year plan.

"So Ray sold me what he had for fifteen hundred dollars in mid-December 1956. It was what I call a bunch of hooks, lines, and sinkers. He had two bevelers, and fortunately I got the better one. Everything seemed to happen at the same time. My mother had just passed away, and I had to see my father to get the money. So then I foolishly went to my foreman at Pratt & Whitney to ask for a leave of absence, to see if I could get my business started."

A look of self-disgust crossed his face. "I can laugh about it now—it was ridiculous, a company as big as that. Leave of absence? Huh! You're either in or you're out. So I quit and started this thing here. I started my rod business on January 1, 1957. And here I am still." This was said more in sorrow than satisfaction. "If I didn't have the toolmaking trade, I'd be out of this. That's what subsidized it, the toolmaking."

Sam remained silent for a long time after this, apparently trying to make sense of what had happened to him. At last he resumed his story.

"After Ray sold out to me, he went back to working as a salesman for a while. He could have sold refrigerators to the Eskimos, you know. When Bill Edwards finally sold up and moved to Florida, he offered me the chance to move into the shop at 3321 Whitney Avenue, but Verna said, 'Naah, you live over your business, people can come and bother you any hour of the day or night.' Not that I would have had the backing to buy the business anyway.

"Now, Ray was a pretty shrewd guy, no dummy like me. It was while we were in Essex that he heard that the Thomas Rod Company was for sale. He was going to go up there to Maine and buy it, and be my competitor. Trouble was, Thomas was a massive business compared to what Ray was doing, and Ray had no money. As a matter of fact, he borrowed money from me to go up there. It sounds ridiculous, but Ray told me when he got back that Leon Thomas wouldn't sell it to him because Ray didn't have an operating shop of his own. So it came to pass that I was sort of drawn into the deal. 'You buy it, Sam.' "

He paused, then looked up and sighed. "I'm not going to comment further on what I think about that," he said. "But it did happen. That was the summer of 1958, and Ray left me the following year, April of 1959."

The workshop was growing humid and stuffy in the afternoon heat, and Sam swatted at a mosquito on his arm. "I'm sorry about these," he said distractedly. "They get bad in here at this time of year." He looked suddenly perplexed, as if unsure of how to proceed. There was a kind of bewilderment in the face of a string of bad decisions, in which he seemed, oddly, to have been a passive bystander rather than an active participant.

"You must have acquired a lot of stuff in the Thomas deal," I ventured, as much to break the awkward silence as anything. "I mean, Thomas was a serious enterprise."

"Oh man," Sam groaned. "I still have most of what I acquired upstairs. I haven't really made a lot of rods since then. Plus I also had some of Gene's cane, and that was on top of what I had when I was already in business back in '57. And then one day when Bill Edwards was still living at 3321, he got a postcard in the mail. Sidney Herskowitz, auctioneer, New York City. Selling off the contents of Nat Uslan's place." Uslan, I knew, had been another well-known rod maker of the time, and his specialty was *five*-sided rods, so the contents of his workshop were the last thing in the world Sam needed.

"Since Bill was out of the rod business, he gave the card to me. Well, I got three hundred and two pounds of nickel silver tubing from Uslan, plus all these cabinets full of stuff. Some of it I've sold, some of it was junk. And there was also a carload of sticks, but they weren't any good."

Another lousy decision, as baffling to Sam as all the rest.

"My dad used to come and work with me," he continued. "He kept himself busy, making ferrules for me, making tooling out of wood. He was a good mechanic. Then he died in '72. So since then I've been kind of hanging on. After I moved up here to New Hampshire in 1977, I was having a tough time of it. I actually had to remortgage my house to meet the payments on the Thomas business. I was really not doing very good."

He stopped again and waved ineffectually at another mosquito. Then he gave a sardonic laugh and went on talking about the bitter economics of what he called the rod game.

"Now, I think there has to be a little bit of personality involved," he said. "I know a guy out in Michigan, Bob Summers, this guy must work thirty hours a day, nine days a week. Me, I come in here, I do this, I do that. It looks like I'm tinkering, but I'm not tinkering. Tell you the truth, I've no idea how long it takes to make a rod. Some people will tell you a week, sixty hours, eighty hours. Of course, you can run four strips of bamboo through the beveler in about sixty seconds, and it only takes another couple of minutes to glue them up. But the ferrule work, for instance—nobody thinks about the time that goes into the design; you have to refine it and reject it and modify it before you spend time on the rod itself. Anyway, look at me—I've been teetering between part-time jobs. Whenever I had a full-time job this just took a backseat."

"But people call you the greatest living American rod maker," I said lamely.

For the first time, Sam seemed irritated by something I'd said.

"That's a lot of crap," he said impatiently. "I look at it this way. A bamboo fly rod has to fall between certain parameters or it's no good. So Joe Doaks or Sam Carlson or Harry somebody-or-other builds one that falls within those parameters, he does a good job and people can say he's the best. I mean, my rods sell at auction for *astronomical* numbers, probably because people think I'm *dead*. There has to be a reason, I guess. I'm not a fisherman, so what can I say about rod actions? I did inherit some of my thoughts from Ray. He knew fishing rods, there's no question about that. He was a good rod mechanic, and fast as lightning. Where I'm kind of picky, you know? Fussy. Ray was the kind of guy, if he dropped a file on the floor while he was working, he'd pick it up when he needed it. If I dropped it, I'd pick it up *then*, see."

He still seemed a little annoyed by my question. "I developed a lot of rods after Ray left, different tapers and stuff. But I only had a *feel* they were right. I don't fish at all, you know. To me, fishing in a stream is impossible. I just don't see how anyone can do it. But I knew people who fished and I'd say, 'Take this and cast it,' to see if it had that uncanny feel that was right." Now he looked embarrassed, as if he was sounding churlish, and said, "Anyway, apparently I turn out a fairly good product, and apparently a good fishing stick, which is important, you know." His voice trailed off.

I said, "One thing you have a great reputation for is your varnish work. Your rods have a finish like a sheet of glass." I wasn't flattering him; it was true.

Sam conceded this point with a certain reluctance. "It's true that apparently my varnish job was extraordinary. But come and I'll show you my varnish room, it's full of junk now. People talk about dust-proof rooms, my God. There's nothing special about it. I'm just lucky."

I'd talked to rod makers who guarded their varnish rooms as if they were air-locked decontamination chambers. I'd heard about one classic rod maker who had an unwelcome visitor one morning while he was varnishing; he'd made the man sit there all day, motionless, so he wouldn't stir up any dust. But Sam's legendary varnish room was just a tiny cubicle the size of a shower stall, with an upright cylindrical aluminum tank for dipping the rod sections. All around it, as Sam had promised, a bunch of junk. No climate control, no humidifier, no dust screens, not even a door.

Back at the workbench again, I asked Sam if he had any idea how many rods he'd made in his career.

"Tell you the truth, I haven't a clue. But I guess maybe we could figure it out." He rooted around in the bric-a-brac on the workbench until he found a dog-eared order book with penciled notations. "Well," he said, squinting at his notes, "in 1960 it looks like I made seven rods. Another seven in 1961. Twenty-three rods in 1962. Nineteen sixty-three, eighteen. Nineteen in 1964." Later, I would ask a close friend of Sam's the same question. Three hundred and seventy-five rods, he estimated—the lifetime output of the man they called America's greatest rod maker.

I asked Sam if he'd ever thought of passing on his rod-making skills to the next generation, as Eustis Edwards and Ed Payne and Fred Thomas had done.

"I've got a son, Rich, who's an auto mechanic," Sam replied. "He's in his fifties now. He was working for his in-laws down in Hamden and not doing real well, and that's when we started talking about the rod game. He was going to come in, and we were going to have a good old time. He had the mechanical ability, no doubt about it. But it never got real serious. It became clear that Rich wouldn't move up here. He was broke, and I wasn't much better. So he got a job with the Hamden school system, as a custodian. He says he wishes he'd been able to do the rod thing, but he made the right decision. I told him, 'This is not it for you, like it's not been it for me. You'll never be able to make up for what you've lost in your lifetime.' "

The early evening shadows were growing longer and Sam was

going deeper into himself, to a place that I didn't necessarily want to take him. But he seemed to want to unburden himself.

"I told Rich, my poor father was running around with the money all those years, just subsidizing me. By the time he died, he had nothing. He was living on his social security because I had wiped him out. It was not with any malice aforethought: I figured we're gonna make it here, get Pop his money back. But it didn't happen. I very often feel badly about that. But I can't go back. None of us can."

There was a long silence now. I couldn't think of anything to say, so I changed the subject to ask if he'd kept in touch with the Edwards brothers.

"Not really," he said. "Bill died in Jensen Beach, Florida, in 1980, at the age of ninety-three. His son Scott never went back into the rod game; he made a career for himself in the military. Gene had died much earlier than that, in 1973, even though he was much younger than his brother. We still hear from his daughter Barbara at Christmas, but that's all."

I stood up to go. As we walked out into the shadows of Sam's yard, his mood seemed to lift once more. He gave me a firm handshake and both of us agreed that we should meet again. I wanted to do that; I'd liked Sam a lot, and his story had moved me. But I wondered if there was much more that he'd want to tell. I felt a sadness as I drove away, as if Sam's story had been a kind of requiem, not only for a single life but for a whole American craft.

PART THREE

Renaissance Men

Rod sections by Per Brandin.

*Trout fishing regarded as bait for catching
men, for the saving of both body and soul,
is important, and deserves all the expense
and care bestowed on it.*
                                    —John Muir,
                    Our National Parks *(1902)*

*Genius is nothing other than a great
aptitude for patience.*
        —Georges Louis Leclerc de Buffon
                                (1707–1788)

CHAPTER 9

Chairman Mao's Fly Rod

And that was that, supposedly. For almost half a century, fifty years of chronic ambivalence, bad decisions, and precarious bank accounts, Sam Carlson had struggled to make a go of the rod game. He knew that he had gone back into it at the worst possible moment, abandoning a secure and specialized trade to gather up the remnants of the Thomas and Edwards rod shops even as the obituaries for bamboo were being written. Economics, the China embargo, changing public tastes, the passion for new synthetic materials and gadgetry: even the most passionate devotees of the handcrafted fly rod seemed to accept that it had become the buggy whip of the age. In 1958, Jim Payne—in most people's view the most gifted graduate of the school of Leonard—had written sorrowfully to a client and friend in Massachusetts:

This departure from quality workmanship reflects the changing pattern of our present way of life. The real old hand craftsmen are passing out, and the younger generation haven't the incentive to learn hand work, primarily because the remuneration is less, due to low production as compared to the machine age.

The closure of the China market was the final blow, Payne wrote in a later letter to the same correspondent.

The bamboo rod makers are faced today with the problem of getting prime bamboo, as you may or may not know that there has not been any bamboo coming from China since 1950, and the prospects don't seem to improve, and it just seems that this kind of bamboo does not grow in any other part of the world, so what the future holds for the Bamboo [sic] rod is anyone's guess, possibly they will be made in Japan.

"Prime" was the salient word here, because ironically there was both too much bamboo and too little. When the old mass-production companies folded in the mid-1950s they left behind vast quantities of unused cane, whole freight cars bulging with the stuff. Some of it found its way to individuals struggling to keep the craft alive, but it was second-rate, fifty-cent-a-culm bamboo for the most part, that had been imported to make factory rods, not masterpieces. Other rod makers, having convinced themselves that their work was obsolete, had destroyed irreplaceable stocks of pre-embargo cane.

Harold Demarest had managed to squeeze out one final shipment of high-quality Tonkin cane from China at the very moment Mao Zedong's Communists were raising their banners over Tiananmen Square. As Demarest's airplane touched down at Hong Kong's Kai Tak Airport, he looked out the window and saw two dozen DC-3s lined up on the tarmac, the fleeing remnants of Chenault's Nationalist Chinese Air Arm. Demarest's Hong Kong suppliers reminded him that the price he was paying for this last batch of bamboo had to take into account the payoffs they'd been forced to make to the pirates who infested the Pearl River delta.

Edwards was gone; so were Thomas and Hawes. Of the old Maine crew, the other founding giants of the craft, only Payne and Leonard soldiered on. But in July 1964, the Leonard plant in Central Valley burned down, and in April 1968 Jim Payne complained of feeling unwell, walked out of his dilapidated shop in Highland Mills after fifty-three years of building wondrous fly rods day in and day out, and never came back. Within a month he was dead. Since the death of his father, Ed, in 1914, the Payne shop had turned out as many as ten thousand rods, perhaps as many as fourteen thousand. But production had declined steadily since the fifties, and even though he was the best, Jim Payne died poor, like most great rod makers. They laid him to rest in the Cemetery of the Highlands, on a hillside above Woodbury Creek, close to the graves of Hiram Leonard, Hiram Hawes, and Eustis Edwards. A friend remembered Payne as "an old-fashioned New Englander, as honest as anyone can get. His whole philosophy was based on perfection."

After picking through the charred rubble of their shop, the folks at Leonard called on Sam Carlson, begging for fresh supplies of bamboo. He told them to take their pick; after all, it appeared that the survival of the craft was at stake, and Sam had more cane than he would ever need. There was talk of him taking over at Leonard, and then rumors that he was buying up the Payne business. But after his acquisition of Thomas and Edwards, that would have been one bad decision too many. Besides, Verna would as soon have packed up and settled in Baghdad as move to New York.

Had there been any other means, I wondered, of gathering together the fragments of the old Maine-Catskills craft tradition? Had there been anyone else but Sam to keep the thing alive? When I asked around, people mentioned survivors from the old days at Leonard and Payne, gifted rod makers who had opened workshops—one-man affairs for the most part—in various obscure corners of the Northeast, where they had settled like widely scattered spores. They operated with apparent disregard for economic logic: one rod maker in deepest Pennsylvania, a couple in upstate New York someplace, a pair of small enterprises in Massachusetts. People spoke their names with reverence: Walt Carpenter, Ron Kusse, Bob Taylor, Marc Aroner, Tom Maxwell.

But these craftsmen seemed, as I say, to be *survivors,* and what

I was searching for was not so much keepers of the flame as con-
duits to a new generation, people who would build a better mouse-
trap, one adapted to changing tastes and economic circumstances.

When I framed the question that way, I got different answers.
Three names in particular came up repeatedly: one was a lifestyle
marketing genius, one was a legendary explorer from *National
Geographic*, and the third was someone with a household name,
though it was one that startled me in this unfamiliar context.

I'd often thought how strange it must be to be born the son of a famous father or, stranger yet, to be somebody *junior*. How odd to be
christened Hank Williams, or Sammy Davis, or Martin Luther
King. Or in this case, Hoagy Carmichael. Hoagy *B*. Carmichael, to
be precise (the *B* standing for Bix, that being his father's tribute to
his bosom friend the great jazzman Bix Beiderbecke).

I tracked down Hoagy Carmichael Jr. in a cramped eighth-
floor office on Forty-seventh Street, in the heart of Manhattan's
theater district. The walls were covered with memorabilia from
his father's career. Above his desk, inevitably, was a poster from the
1944 movie *To Have and Have Not*—Hoagy Sr. as the piano player,
Walter Brennan as the alcoholic ship's mate, and a sultry nineteen-
year-old named Lauren Bacall who's about to teach Humphrey
Bogart how to whistle.

Though there wasn't a close physical resemblance between father and son, Hoagy Bix had the same gift of appearing effort-
lessly relaxed. His voice was an easy, melodious drawl. He was, in
other words, the very model of urbanity.

A small sign at the entrance to his office said "Hoagy and Bix."
I asked him about the "and." He told me that it was the name of a
musical based on his father's life and music. He'd been trying to
breathe life into the idea for many years. There had been a staged
version on the lawn of Hugh Hefner's mansion in Los Angeles a

decade ago, but by all accounts it had been a bit of a flop. In those days the project had been called *The Stardust Road;* since then it had mutated into *Hoagy and Bix.* The heart of the thing was to be the great songs—"Stardust," "Hong Kong Blues," "Georgia on My Mind"—but finding the right narrative structure had proved to be more of a problem. Most recently the British playwright Peter Nichols, the author of *A Day in the Death of Joe Egg,* had been drafted to work on the book.

As a young man, the last thing on Hoagy's mind had been to act as the agent of a bamboo fly rod renaissance. His childhood had been spent among Hollywood royalty. I asked him if he'd liked to go fishing as a kid; he laughed. I asked if his father had fished; he laughed more loudly. "I mean, I fished under the covers, reading *Field and Stream* by flashlight. It was all in my head." He reflected on this for a moment, then added, "Which is all that fishing is, actually—it's all in your imagination."

While he was in college, Hoagy worked for Burt Lancaster at Columbia Pictures and Universal. He came to New York in 1962, at the age of twenty-four, and worked for a couple of brokerage firms on Wall Street. This was a miserable experience, so he went to Boston and got a job as a producer for the local public television station, WGBH. After that he moved to the Pittsburgh PBS affiliate, WQED, where he produced *Mister Rogers' Neighborhood* for several years. Between times, he managed his father's extensive catalog; he played in a jazz band; he replaced Mary Rodgers, the daughter of Richard Rodgers, as president of Amsong, an organization that works to extend copyright protection for songwriters and their heirs. And in the middle of all this he was bitten by the fly-fishing bug.

It happened on the way back from Expo '67, he said, the World's Fair in Montreal, where he'd gone with a particularly memorable girlfriend. They'd stopped off in Manchester, Vermont, where the Orvis Company had its headquarters. He'd spent ten or eleven days fly-fishing on the nearby Battenkill, a notoriously tough and moody river, and caught one fish. But that was enough.

Like my friend Streamer, and like so many other aspiring rod makers, Hoagy had started off with a kit rod from Orvis—all the component parts, ready to be put together by the hobbyist. He took it fishing on the sacred streams of the Catskills—the Beaverkill, the Willowemoc, the Neversink—that were the cultural and historical touchstones of American fly-fishing. He joined the Anglers' Club of New York, and hung out at the Tuscarora Club in the Catskills. This was a very WASPy place, known among other things for a poem that had been composed for one of its annual dinners at the Harvard Club. The poem began:

> Saint Peter stood at Heaven's gate,
> All souls' claims to adjudicate,
> Saying to some souls, "Enter in!"
> "Go to Hell," to others, "you are steeped in sin."
> When up from earth, with a great hubbub,
> Came all the members of the Tuscarora Club.
> The angel Gabriel, peering out,
> Said, "What the Devil is this noise about?"
> "Gabe," said Peter, "There's always lots of noise
> At any get-together of the Tuscarora boys—
> Those are anglers, and they all tell lies
> About the trout that got away, their fierceness and their size.
> They want to enter Heaven, for our brooks are full of trout,
> But I won't have any liars, and I'll keep the whole gang out;
> No liars enter Heaven, and I'll most distinctly tell
> The whole dang Tuscarora Club, it has to go to Hell."

One day in 1969, Hoagy Carmichael joined a group of club members who were testing out some bamboo fly rods. "I had my best rod with me," he recalled. "It was my Orvis kit rod, which I had struggled to put together, and I showed it off quite proudly." Standing nearby was an austere-looking elderly gentleman named Everett Garrison, who had also brought some rods he'd made. Hoagy examined one, "and it was, oh wow . . . now we're talking."

Garrison had been tinkering with fly rods since the early 1920s, thanks to his friendship with a neighbor in Yonkers, New York, Dr. George Parker Holden, the author of a well-known instructional book called *The Idyl* [*sic*] *of the Split-Bamboo*. Garrison was an engineer by training, but he'd been laid off from his job with the New York Central Railroad at the height of the Depression and at that point turned his attention seriously to making bamboo rods. He'd become a close friend of Jim Payne's. As an engineer, he was fascinated by the physical properties of the raw material, and he was obsessed with the form and function of a rod rather than its cosmetics. He used a slide rule to compute the mathematical formulas for his tapers; he designed a hand-planing form of unprecedented precision.

To guarantee the consistency of the power fibers, all six strips of Garrison's rods had to be planed from the same culm of bamboo; if a single piece was nicked by the blade or otherwise compromised, all six had to be junked. Not infrequently entire rods were tossed into the garbage. This was something the great rod makers of the past had rarely had the luxury of doing, tyrannized as they were by the pressures of the marketplace. In a sense Garrison's hand-planing was a throwback to the earliest days of bamboo rod making in the 1870s, before Loman Hawes and Hiram Leonard had invented their revolutionary beveling machine.

Hoagy Carmichael was captivated by Garrison, and it seems the feeling was mutual. Hoagy charmed his way into the old man's basement workshop in Ossining, New York. "Mr. Garrison had a reputation for not letting anyone downstairs," he said, "but he abrogated that rule for me." In the summer of 1973, Hoagy persuaded the Anglers' Club to fund a short film on Garrison's work.

"What a God-given opportunity," the club's president wrote, "to preserve for all time a record of the techniques and skills ... [of] the last of the great custom rod-builders of the famous Eastern school." But the intent seemed to be to preserve an archival memory of the craft, rather than to find a reason for its renewal.

Garrison thought and talked like an engineer, and he'd once tried without much success to put his theories down on paper. "I'm leaving out the mathematics in the interest of clearness," he'd written by way of introduction, but then he'd started off,

> In a "couple" composed of an area A at a distance h above a neutral axis and an equal area A at an equal distance h below the axis, the moment of inertia of the couple would be A times h^2 plus A times h^2 or two times A times h^2, thus making it evident that this balanced couple is symmetrical about the neutral axis.

This wasn't exactly calculated to make the principles of rod making accessible to the great unwashed. So Hoagy told him, "Just tell me what you're doing as you're doing it, Garry."

Hoagy gave me a copy of his film to take home. The print was a little grainy, the colors muddy, the titles done in a swirling orange 1970s font that looked as if it belonged on the cover of the *Whole Earth Catalog* or an album by the Captain and Tennille. Everett Garrison walks down a darkened flight of basement steps, sits down in the shadows at a worn workbench, turns on a light. Guitar music plays. Garrison has iron gray hair clipped short, a gray toothbrush mustache, and heavy-rimmed glasses. He wears a check shirt, buttoned up at the neck, sleeves rolled down. He speaks in a grave and somber monotone, with occasional flashes of tinder-dry humor. The workbench sequences, shot for the most part in extreme close-up, are interspersed with scenes of Garrison fishing a trout pool on the Neversink beneath a tumbling waterfall, laying out a long, lovely fly line as he reminisces about the time in 1913 when a college engineering professor demonstrated to him the principles of wave linear motion.

Garrison takes a culm of preembargo cane from a ceiling rack; he aligns the reel seat on the finished rod. In between he demonstrates, by one count, eighty-four separate steps in the construction of a bamboo fly rod. Many people, I suppose, would find this as exciting as watching paint dry. But it was hard for me not to feel a kind of awe for the old man, and I liked the film for the methodical clarity with which it captured the details of his craft. Perhaps, just conceivably, even a lesser mortal could actually make one of these things.

As Hoagy got to know Garrison better, he also immersed himself in the work of other master craftsmen. He flew out to the Midwest to meet the great Michigan rod maker Lyle Dickerson. He spent more time up in Manchester, Vermont, getting to know the Orvis Company's president, Leigh Perkins, and its chief rod maker, Wes Jordan, and generally making a pest of himself. And he hung around the reconstituted Leonard shop in Central Valley, New York, where the grand old company had clawed its way back, at least temporarily, from the traumatic 1964 fire.

"There was a whole new cadre of guys showing up at Leonard in the late sixties," Hoagy said. He rolled his eyes and grinned. "I remember seeing guys up there making rods listening to Blood, Sweat and Tears. God knows what they were smoking."

Jim Frank knew what they were smoking, for the good reason that he was probably one of those smoking it. It so happened that I'd come to know Jim just a few months earlier. It was at one of the shows I'd begun to frequent, at a Holiday Inn just outside of Boston, and someone had pointed him out to me as a former Leonard craftsman and a devotee of Eustis Edwards.

I couldn't think right away who Jim Frank reminded me of. At first I thought it was the actor Woody Harrelson. Then I thought it was more like the Aerosmith guitarist, Joe Perry. Either way, it was the face of a man who had had some adventures in his life, though it turned out that the wildness in his eyes concealed a shrewd and knowing intelligence and a fork-bending amount of talent. I had the same disconcerting feeling I'd had before, that this highly specialized craft could embrace such a diverse set of personalities: the urbane son of a famous songwriter; an austere engineer with a sport jacket and a slide rule; and a man who looked as if he was coming off twenty dissipated years playing guitar in a heavy-metal band.

Jim and I chatted briefly at the show, and he showed me a couple of rods he'd made. He was living temporarily in New Hampshire (most of Jim's homes had this temporary quality, I would learn), and a few weeks later I stopped off to see him on the way back from a trip to Maine.

Jim Frank had grown up in Seattle in a middle-class family of fly fishermen, learning to handle a fly rod when he was five years old. When he was eleven his father took him to meet the great Jim Payne, an encounter that had clearly left its mark. "He scared me," Jim said. "By all accounts he was a taskmaster of unbelievable sternness, but still, the experience, wow . . . Do I wish? Oh yeah, do I wish . . . can you imagine?"

As a rebellious teenager, Jim slammed the door once too often and his father packed him off to a construction job in Alaska, lying about his age so that he could get the kid a union card. Jim passed his journey test at seventeen, then flirted with the idea of a career in pro baseball. Just like Loman Hawes, we laughed.

Jim was a catcher, and a good one—good enough to get a try-out with the Los Angeles Dodgers. He went to camp, two days a week for six weeks, in Spokane, Washington, where the Dodgers had their Triple-A farm team. It was a jolt. You'd been a super-star—high school, statewide, American Legion ball—and suddenly *everyone* was a superstar. You were playing with solid career pros, people like Ron Cey and Steve Garvey, and younger and better talents were waiting to take their place.

"All you have to do is look at it," Jim said. "There's like, what, twenty-eight hundred jobs, year after year, and there's *millions* of really excellent baseball players." He grinned. "There were these two kids from Venezuela, pretty hot prospects, playing second and short. And I'd be behind the plate, and I'd be saying, 'That one's getting through,' and then all of a sudden... *fwhffft! fwhffft!*"—he mimed a lightning-fast double play—"and I'd be going, '*Oh my Lord*'... because they were off the scale. I was *astounded* by these guys. And you know what?" He paused for dramatic effect. "*They didn't make it!* Never went to the major leagues."

"But it sounds as if the experience taught you a lot," I said.

Jim laughed wryly. "Oh yeah, it was an interesting little lesson. I'm watching guys make the impossible look normal. The lesson is right there in front of your face. How good *are* you? And personally, I think that every person that comes up against *Well, this is as good as you're going to get* learns something." He gestured at his workbench, making the obvious comparison.

"So anyway, the coaches were saying to me, 'It's a bus-league thing for you, you know? The best that's going to happen is thirty-five thousand dollars and ride the buses.' And I knew I could make more than that in Alaska, bending nails."

Which is pretty much what Jim did. Kodiak, Anchorage, the islands, building schools and churches, making union scale. Marriage, a baby. They were hippies; it was the early seventies. Santa Cruz, California, hanging out on the beach and pounding nails to feed the family; a job in a shake mill on the Olympic Peninsula; a spell rebuilding an old hunting camp on Lake Talon in northern Ontario. "And that was when I cooked up the big idea," Jim cackled. "It's August of '72, I'm sitting there at the table, the job's done, it's the end of summer, and my wife is looking at me, and she's like, *'What now, hotshot?'* And I say, 'Well, you know what, I always wanted to learn how to make bamboo rods.' "

"And presumably she thought you were crazy?" I said.

He thought about this for a moment. "Well, it was more like, 'Hmmm, well, I don't know what that means. But sure, let's go find out.' "

So they drove across the country in their Volvo wagon, and like Hoagy Carmichael, the first stop on their pilgrimage was Manchester, Vermont, where Jim summoned up the gall to talk to Wes Jordan, who had recently retired after thirty years as the Orvis Company's chief rod maker. Jordan was friendly enough, but he didn't offer Jim much encouragement; he told him that the rodmaking business was moribund. There was very little bamboo coming in from China, and Orvis's rods were being made up by a supplier in England. But of course there was always Leonard, he said.

"Leonard!" Jim exclaimed. "I was what, twenty-two, twentythree? I was deep in ridiculous ignorance."

But like any good hippie, Jim didn't let realism stand in his way. The rebuilt Leonard shop in Central Valley was being run now by a gifted craftsman by the name of Ted Simroe, and Jim secured an introduction. They talked for fifteen minutes, no more.

"So what do you do?" Simroe asked.

"Carpenter."

"How come you want to make bamboo rods?"

"Uh, just curious."

"Well, have you got any objection to being an employee?"

"Uh, no. That's good."

And the next thing Jim Frank knew, there he was standing face-to-face with the Leonard beveler.

"How did you feel?" I asked, the obvious eleven-o'clock-news question, the image too surreal for words. "Were you walking around saying, 'God, I'm in the presence of history'?"

"God, no. It was a gizmo, you know? To me, it was like, 'I've got to figure this thing out. Because it's me or the machine.' "

Hap Mills, the last of the family to own Leonard, said to Jim one day, "Don't you feel a duty to the bamboo?"

Jim said, "No, I'm just trying to keep all my fingers on my hand."

But inevitably the sense of history crept up on him. "After about three months, you figure out that there's this line of people, and they've been doing this for a hundred years. All that cumulative knowledge of the craft, it starts to build up on you and you say, 'Holy shit, this is something to live up to. Don't blow it.' "

Under Simroe's careful tutelage, Jim learned every facet of the craft—finding out how ferrules were made by observing the master metalworker Tom Bailey, who had come over to Leonard after the death of Jim Payne; learning how to apply the silk windings and the final varnish from the legendary Ethel Clawson, who was pushing eighty and had been with Leonard for more than half a century—until at last he felt able to put it all together.

There were plenty of storm clouds hovering in the background—the Mills family was in the process of divesting itself of Leonard after more than ninety years, and the company was entering a period of ever-changing ownership and financial woes that grew steadily worse until it was seized by the IRS for nonpayment of taxes and shut down for good in 1985. But none of that mattered to Jim Frank. The Leonard shop was turning out twenty fly rods a week, and it was *fun*.

"It was, like, clearly the coolest job I ever had in my life," Jim said, "and I was making seven dollars an hour. When I could have gone to the carpentry union and made $18.56, you know?" His eyes danced with pleasure at the memory, setting the stage for his dramatic finale.

"OK, here's my perfect example," he said. "It's 1975 and I'm running the beveler, right? And into the shop comes"—pause—

"Everett Garrison. Now, I've got blond hair this long, it's in a single braid, tied back. And the tattoos. And I'm running the Leonard beveler. And Everett Garrison sits in a chair. Hoagy Carmichael's in the office with Ted. And Garrison sits in the chair and watches me bevel. For like an hour. And I'm *twenty...five...years...old.* And he's asking me questions. And I'm going, *'Whoa. Wh-o-o-o-o-o-a-a-a-a-h-h-h-h-h...'* And through the whole thing, you could see on his face what he was thinking. Greatest fly rods on the planet, and they're being made by a bunch of freakin' hippies! You could open any drawer and there's a bag of pot. Every Friday at two-thirty, if your work is done, you stop and draw straws, the guy with the short straw goes to get the Miller, and you play darts and clean the shop and drink beer until four, OK? It's a bunch of kids, laughing, pulling tricks on each other, tying their stool to your belt so you get up to do something and . . . it's just endless fun making fly rods in this place, and, you know what, they're *fabulous freakin' fly rods!*"

Meanwhile, in Washington, D.C., Beijing, and Manchester, Vermont, change was in the air. The C. F. Orvis Company was more than a hundred years old now, and for much of the middle part of the century it had fallen on hard times. By 1940 Orvis was down to two employees, and it survived World War II only on the strength of a contract to make bamboo ski poles for the Pentagon.

In 1965, however, an entrepreneur and outdoor sports enthusiast named Leigh Perkins had bought Orvis for $400,000. Perkins was a great admirer of a young Arkansas businessman named Sam Walton, who had recently opened the first in a chain of stores he would call Wal-Mart. Looking over his new acquisition, Perkins saw two things that he felt were the key to reviving the hidebound old Vermont company without sacrificing its sense of tradition. Indeed, both of the things that Perkins focused on had been central to the vision of its founder. The first was mail order (Orvis had been sending out catalogs longer than anyone, since before the Civil War), and the second was the bamboo fly rod.

"From what I could discover," Perkins wrote in his autobiography,

> no company had ever made much money in the fly rod business.... But there was more and more interest in the sporting life—in recreation and leisure—and everybody knew that. My plan for growing the business was to put together a catalog of all the trappings that an upscale outdoorsman country lover needed and desired.... What we were creating and selling was, for lack of a better word, a lifestyle...a kind of Americanized version of elegant, English country living.

Fly-fishing would be the cornerstone of this fantasy lifestyle, and the fine bamboo fly rod would be Orvis's signature product. As Charles F. Orvis himself had written a hundred years earlier, "The rod, of course, is of the first importance in an outfit, as very much depends on its perfection." *Perfection:* there was that word again.

Orvis began to create and then sell this lifestyle world at a time when Ralph Lauren was still Ralph Lifshitz. L. L. Bean had kicked things off years earlier, of course, using the rubber-bottomed boot as the first step in selling the idea of Maine. And other companies were picking up on the same principle—Carroll Reed had started off with skis and Lands' End with sailing hardware, and each now used the magic of mail order to construct its own idealized, branded universe. But no one did it better than Orvis. Once you'd created the brand, there was no limit to the merchandise you could hang on it—everything, in Orvis's case, from dog baskets and hearth rugs to Lucite toilet seats with salmon flies embedded in them. The fact that this was the 1970s also did no harm, since the modern environmental movement was astir, much of it staked out by affluent Northeasterners bent on preserving their own particular slice of paradise. To reach buyers like these, Leigh Perkins placed his ads in all the best upscale publications—*Vogue, Harper's Bazaar, Esquire,* and, of course, the *The New Yorker*.

It was all very reminiscent of the late 1800s, when Fly Rod Crosby had enticed sports, tourists, and nascent conservationists to the Maine woods with her promise of "wilderness with all the comforts." But this time around the scale and sophistication of the marketing effort were infinitely greater. The earlier generation had belonged to Abercrombie & Fitch; that proud and stuffy old company had sold rods made by Eustis Edwards, Hiram Hawes, and Jim Payne, and had outfitted the likes of Teddy Roosevelt. But A&F was no match for Orvis. Leigh Perkins had begun to build his mail-order empire by exchanging lists with A&F, L. L. Bean, and his other competitors. "After a couple of years," he wrote, "Abercrombie decided to stop trading lists with us. Their explanation was that we were doing better than they were. The reason was that they were locked into a retail mentality and put items in their catalog only when they wouldn't move in their stores." You can't help but feel Perkins's contempt for the weaker opponent: A&F had started off with a huge competitive advantage in defining outdoor tastes, but "they didn't know how to handle the new world of mail order." The lost war with Orvis was the start of Abercrombie & Fitch's long decline, which ended only with its rebirth a quarter of a century later, as a logo to be branded across the chests of skimpily dressed, anorexic teenage girls.

Now, this was all well and good, but the bamboo fly rod could be the company's flagship product only if Orvis could get hold of the bamboo. And like everyone else during the China embargo, it couldn't. Perkins wanted Orvis to produce fifteen hundred rods a year, more than Leonard was making, but at one point the company had only thirty usable culms of cane on hand. Desperate rod makers had always done their best to evade the embargo; there were stories of people smuggling Tonkin cane into the country through Canada, concealed inside Oriental rugs. Perkins worked out a deal with suppliers in Scotland and France: if they would cut the raw bamboo into strips and subject it to heat treatment, then presumably Orvis could say it was importing manufactured parts, not raw materials, and that would be enough to skirt the restrictions imposed by the embargo. Er, *no*, actually, said some stern men from the FBI and the Office of Foreign Assets Control: that counted as *processing*, not *manufacturing*, and therefore still fell under the heading of trading with the enemy.

This was the kind of dispute that can end up making a lot of lawyers very rich, but fortunately the question became academic in 1972 when Nixon and Kissinger took it into their heads to go to China. ("Only good thing Richard Nixon ever did for me," Hoagy Carmichael had quipped.) Yet it was naïve to think that the machinery of the China trade could be switched on again overnight. Mao's Cultural Revolution was still in full swing, and like the rest of the country, the bamboo-growing areas of rural Guangdong Province were in chaos. It would take something else, someone with the right political connections, to force the door open. Someone like Luis Marden.

At sixty, Marden (who had actually been born Annibale Luigi Paragallo) was chief of foreign correspondents for *National Geographic* magazine. He was a Renaissance man, an iconic figure in his field: pilot, sailor, photographer, fossil hunter, deep-sea diver, science fiction buff, wine connoisseur, fly fisherman, and amateur bamboo rod maker (inspired, as Everett Garrison had been, by the writings of George Parker Holden). Marden had given his name to a previously unknown species of orchid (*Epistephium mardeni*) and a lobster parasite (*Dolobrotus mardeni*). Most famously, in 1957 he had dived in the dangerous waters off Pitcairn Island (ignoring the concerns of the locals, who warned him, "Man, you gwen be dead as a hatchet!") and found the remains of the H.M.S. *Bounty*.

Now, in 1974, Luis Marden proposed to write a *National Geographic* feature on bamboo, taking advantage of Nixon's opening to China to visit the cane-growing districts of the Sui River Valley. He would be the first representative of the magazine to visit China since 1949, and the first foreigner to reach the bamboo plantations since Floyd Alonzo McClure of the Smithsonian had visited in 1925, falling in love with the tea stick and later giving it its name, *Arundinaria amabilis*. Marden was just as entranced as McClure had been by the beauty of the plant, and the Chinese landscape in which it thrived. He wrote:

> *In the opalescent light perspective vanished, turning the riverscape into a two-dimensional ink painting. Through the slanting brush-strokes of rain, the ranks of green-black bamboos faded to gray and silver in receding planes to the vanishing point. Far downstream, against a bamboo-feathered promontory on the left bank, were three fishermen in umbrella-shaped bamboo hats, two standing, one hunched amidships, on a motionless bamboo raft.*

Back in Washington, Luis Marden offered to help Leigh Perkins solve his cane supply problem. He gathered together a group for lunch—himself, Perkins, Hoagy Carmichael, the bamboo importer Charles Demarest, assorted Chinese officials—and by the time the last toasts had been drunk Perkins and Demarest had the visas they needed to attend the 1975 Guangzhou trade fair. Marden suggested to Perkins that the wheels of business might be further greased if Orvis were to make a presentation rod for Chairman Mao.

The American party stayed four days at the Dongfang Hotel (the name means "The East Is Red"), where they met the Chinese cane growers, drank more toasts, and handed over the Chairman's fly rod. The growers had been a little hazy about what exactly these round-eyes were using their bamboo for, so Leigh Perkins offered them a demonstration. He went outside to the hotel's goldfish pond, rigged up a line, and began casting. "No, no!" a Chinese official protested. "Those are the Chairman's fish." Perkins said, "Look, no hook! No hook!"

There is no record of whether the Orvis fly rod ever reached Chairman Mao. "Fly-fishing," Perkins wrote later, "probably wasn't a very proletarian sort of thing."

CHAPTER 10

Trade Secrets

Sam Carlson, forever picking things up and putting them down again, once famously took nineteen years to complete the restoration of a rod that someone had left off in his shop. Streamer hadn't kept my Eustis Edwards Perfection that long, but still it had been a while. In the intervening months, his father, the portrait painter, had died, leaving behind a studio full of work to be organized and cataloged; there was endless work to be done on the house he'd built; and his growing reputation as one of the best of the younger generation of craftsmen was creating a steady backlog of orders for new rods. But one day he called to say that my rod—the first Edwards I'd owned—was done. I drove up to northwest Connecticut to collect it.

Repairs and restorations like this had been Streamer's entrée into the world of full-time rod making—a story I'd heard from several other craftsmen. For many, in fact, the income from restoration work is the critical margin that allows them to persist with their craft. People have always patched up worn-out and broken rods, of course. But the restoration business today is much more than a means of extending a rod's useful life as a fishing tool. That's called *refinishing*, not *restoration*, and rod makers are jealous of the distinction.

Authenticity is everything in restoration; the work has to match the original in every way. It's another facet of the quest for perfection. If Eustis Edwards used royal purple silk, you use royal purple silk. Use burgundy, and in some indefinable way you've betrayed the spirit of the man who made the rod. You've also diminished its market value.

Ideally you use original components for a restoration job, and sometimes, if you're lucky, you can stumble on stuff that's been gathering dust in someone's basement since one of the old rod shops closed down half a century ago.

"I ran into a funny old guy years ago," Streamer recalled, "who carried all these boxes around in his van. I think they'd come originally from someone who'd worked with Gene Edwards. Enough blanks to make up six or seven rods, nickel silver ferrules, winding checks, snake eyes, and then another box that was filled with real agate guides." (Semiprecious agate rings, set into the first—or "stripping"—guide as a means of reducing friction on the fly line, are one indicator of the finest bamboo rods.)

"I said, 'What do you want for all this?' and he said, 'Oh, I'll take seventy-five bucks for the lot.' I couldn't get my wallet out fast enough."

After that, a kind of informal barter system kicked in, of a sort that's common among rod makers. Streamer traded a batch of more than a thousand tungsten snake guides for some culms of bamboo; his trading partner then found another rod maker who was looking for guides and who offered an old lathe in return.

Building a new fly rod and restoring an old one may be closely related skills, but they take you into entirely different mental zones, Streamer said. It's hard to jump from one to the other. "Making one of my own rods is more like carpentry," he explained; "it's mechanical, very methodical. I lay everything out and do it in order. But if I'm restoring a vintage rod, I work very slowly. It's not so much *concentration on* what I'm doing, it's more *absorption in* what I'm doing. With a restoration, I get transported; I know I'm touching a piece of history."

I asked Streamer how many Eustis Edwards rods he'd worked on over the years. About thirty, he said, and my Perfection, like all of them, had offered its own small history lessons and forensic opportunities, its own ways of edging a little closer to the ghost in the Edwards machine. I remembered how he'd begun the job by dismantling the rod's broken butt section, discovering in the process how Eustis had hollowed out its bamboo core for the sake of lightness. Then, rather than build me a replacement section from scratch, he'd tracked down an Edwards blank that was a close match for the original. He'd stripped off the old varnish and the ugly nylon thread, whose colors and patterns had borne no relation to what Edwards had intended. Then he showed me how he'd replicated the original design, using a magnifying lens to reveal the slight discoloration of the cane—the "ghosting"—left by the old silk, as well as the microscopic nicks in the enamel surface of the bamboo that showed where Edwards had trimmed off the tag ends of thread with a razor blade. "That was one of Eustis's little idiosyncracies," Streamer said.

He left the best until last. "Look at this," he said, pointing to the silk wraps at the ferrule. The silk was gold, but embedded within it was the minutest stripe of deep purple. As the varnish on a rod ages and contracts, and the bamboo flexes with use, a small crack will appear in the ferrule wrap; it's inevitable. When that happens, water can seep into the crack, and water is the mortal enemy of bamboo that is unprotected by varnish. Streamer explained, "Eustis would occasionally do that little series of purple, no more than three turns of thread, to help camouflage the line. No one else will do that in a restoration; I'm the only one." He looked up at me. His expression was somewhere between "I'm really proud of that" and "You think I'm crazy, don't you?"

I held the rod to the light, admiring the tiny grace note under the glistening sheen of varnish. "That's the toughest thing for me, the finish," Streamer went on. This surprised me, because he has a great reputation for his varnish work, which makes his rods look as if they were encased in shimmering glass. But varnish, since the days of Stradivarius and the other great Italian luthiers, has always demanded a special degree of skill. The consistency has to be right, the temperature has to be right, the varnish must defy the forces of gravity as it sets. Some rod makers apply the varnish with fine sable brushes; others use their fingertips; some, borrowing from a technique that is depicted in Hoagy Carmichael's film of Garrison, suspend each rod section in a vertical dip tank and then withdraw it from its varnish bath at a carefully regulated speed. Sam Carlson did it this way; so does Streamer.

"I mean, I lay on what I consider to be the perfect finish," he continued; "it comes out of the tube, it looks gorgeous, and I come back the next day and it's sunken and lopsided. There are guys who must hit them with seventeen, eighteen coats of varnish and sand them flat between each coat. Everybody seems to love my finishes, although sometimes a client will ask to take a rod when I know it isn't ready to go out the door."

"You want it to be perfect," I said.

He looked dubious. "*Perfect* . . . well, I see it more as a matter of solving problems. I guess that's something I learned from cabinet-making. I don't care who you are, I don't care what kind of materials you're working with, *something always happens*. And then you have to solve the problem without having to scrap the project. I mean, no rod is ever perfect. You get as close as is reasonable, and then you move on to the next step." And every perfectionist, I thought, will have his own definition of "reasonable."

Like the Garrison movie, like the end of the China embargo, like the packaging of the Orvis lifestyle, this sense of honoring an American tradition—while at the same time feeding the appetite of collectors and investors—was an important part of the renaissance of rod making in the 1970s.

The ball started rolling as early as 1968, several people told me, on the day Jim Payne died. Abercrombie & Fitch may have been losing its battle with Orvis to define the image of sophisticated country living, but it was still the only retail outlet for the work of Payne, the greatest of the old Maine-Catskill school. When news came of the old man's death, discreet clerks scuttled around the racks crossing out the $175 price tag and jacking up the price of a Payne by $50 or $75. Despite the hike, the rods were snapped up immediately. Some say the buyers were speculators; others that they were apostles of the true church; perhaps they were both.

They were also part of a defensive reaction against technological innovation. In 1965, the Royal Aircraft Establishment in Farnborough, England, announced that it had developed an extremely stiff carbon fiber (commonly referred to in the United States as graphite, though it has nothing to do with the lead in your pencil). Golf-club makers were the first to see the recreational potential of the new ultralight synthetic, with companies like Callaway promising that graphite could add fifty yards to your drive. Weekend duffers looked into their mirrors and saw Jack Nicklaus. Rod manufacturers quickly jumped on the bandwagon, and graphite rods, which cast farther and faster, drew hundreds of thousands of newcomers into the ancient art of fly-fishing.

The manufacture of a graphite rod was the antithesis of handcrafting an organic material with a hundred-year history. There seemed something coldhearted, even malevolent, about the process of embedding carbon fibers in an epoxy resin matrix and rolling it to shape around a steel mandrel. It even sounds ugly when you describe it.

In its impact, this second technological revolution was very different from the first. In the 1950s, fiberglass had killed off most of the old-style production shops; the Edwards brothers were its emblematic casualties. Graphite, by contrast, helped to spark a traditionalist backlash from bamboo addicts. It's when something is in the process of dying that it struggles most fiercely to be reborn.

Within a year of Payne's death, a couple of important things happened. First of all, Orvis financed the creation of the American Museum of Fly Fishing in Manchester, Vermont, to which Leigh Perkins made the initial donations. At about the same time, a Connecticut real estate agent named Martin Keane—who would later publish the seminal history of the craft, *Classic Rods and Rodmakers*—decided to offer his personal collection for sale. "This collection was started when no one else was interested," Keane wrote in his prospectus. "I soon realized that I was actually the first person to witness the unfolding of fifty to a hundred years of America's accumulated dormant tackle. Here indeed was the physical evidence of the evolution of America's proud sporting heritage."

Keane had assembled a group of almost a hundred classic rods by the masters of the craft, as well as dozens of reels. His asking price was $280,000—an astonishing sum in those days. Keane had acquired nothing but the best: if he found a finer specimen of a particular rod, the old one had to go. Among the highlights of his personal museum was the rod that Eustis Edwards had reserved for his own use; it was one of the fifty Perfection models he had built in 1924 after his contract with Winchester ended—a twin, in other words, to the rod that Streamer had just finished restoring for me.

Keane refused to split up his collection; it had to be sold intact. And he made a further stipulation: the buyer would have to provide "a signed statement that the collection will physically remain in the United States." What Perkins and Keane were doing, each in his own way, was to enshrine the idea that the bamboo fly rod was a distinctively *American* artifact, worthy of reverence and preservation.

Part historian, part businessman, Keane was also shrewd enough to recognize that these pieces of American heritage were also rarities. Pinky Gillum, the cantankerous Connecticut craftsman who had learned his skills by watching Eustis Edwards, had built fewer than 2,000 rods in his lifetime. Lyle Dickerson of Michigan had made about 1,350. Hiram Hawes and his son Merritt had produced 1,100 between them. Garrison made about 650 rods, Sam Carlson barely half that number. Needless to say, stressing this scarcity did no harm in the marketplace that Keane was instrumental in creating. His catalogs became famous for their purple prose—Keane's best offerings were always "deeply joyous creations" or "uniquely lovely aristocrats," or had "subtle and elusive tapers that respond to your every whim"—and with the aid of language like that, fly rods by the likes of Gillum and Garrison began to fetch five-figure sums. People went scurrying to their attics, hoping that Grandpa's old fishing rod would bring in a quick fortune.

Those who flocked to the new secondary market were an eclectic bunch, a cross section of the American male population. According to one online survey I read, bamboo rod collectors were biologists and geologists, park rangers and state troopers, farriers and firefighters. There were supermarket managers, school principals, and funeral home directors. There were beach lifeguards and diplomats. There was an ammo dealer from Omaha and a commercial lobsterman from Maine. There was a B-777 pilot for United Airlines out of Chicago; a Titan-4B rocket engineer in California; a man who operated a pornographic Web site in Manhattan; another who did R&D for Heinz ketchup. For most of them, Marty Keane's next catalog was something they anticipated like a kid waiting for Santa to come down the chimney.

When I first began to buy bamboo rods, I'd sometimes stop by to visit Marty at his home in the Berkshire Hills of Massachusetts. It was obvious that the rod business had afforded him a handsome living. There was a Mercedes at the end of the long private driveway and another in the garage. Picture windows looked out over a pretty garden, a waterfall, and a trout stream. It was impossible not to be struck by the irony. This was what the secondary market brought you; as Marty himself had the grace to acknowledge, no rod maker had ever lived like this.

Sometimes I'd go there to buy; sometimes to sell; sometimes just to listen to Marty's war stories of the great rod makers he'd known. I'd invariably find him surrounded by uncased rods, a large glass of red wine by his elbow, an inch of cigarette ash hanging from his fingers, a smell of varnish and tung oil and old poplin all around him. Business was thriving, he'd tell me; as soon as his catalog hit the mailboxes, judges would call from their chambers during court recesses; cardiologists would hit the phones between triple and quadruple bypass surgeries. The last time I dropped by, Marty was trying to price a fly reel of 1890s vintage. It was a lovely thing, with engraved mother-of-pearl side plates—$8,500, Marty thought. He knew he could get twice as much from a Japanese client, but patriotism said no. You had to keep these things in the country.

Hoagy Carmichael, too, was attentive to the growth of the new secondary market and as a sideline began to restore and resell rods by the old masters. His life, in fact, had taken a number of surprising turns since the Garrison movie, each of them drawing him deeper into the world of the bamboo fly rod.

When Everett Garrison fell terminally ill in 1974, Hoagy wondered if the documentary alone was enough of a testament. It had conveyed many things: respect for the old man and the tradition he embodied, a sense that the craft of rod making could be made both logical and accessible to the layperson. But film has its limitations as a medium. Now Hoagy looked down at the old man's gnarled fingers on the counterpane and wondered about his duty to them. "Garry," he said, "let's see if we can write a book." He laughed in disbelief as he remembered the conversation thirty years later. "Of course, I had no idea then how many people would end up reading it."

A Master's Guide to Building a Bamboo Fly Rod changed everything. What had been secret was now placed in the public domain. For a hundred years, the craft had been defined by a central conflict: the driven individual's striving for perfection versus the unrelenting pressures of the commercial marketplace. Master your art or put food on the table. Right brain and left brain permanently at war with each other. Eustis Edwards's life story.

Because it was ultimately a business, and because the essence of business is competition, rod makers' proprietary designs had always been closely guarded secrets. That's why the bevelers were kept behind locked doors.

At the same time, from Leonard on, rod makers had arrived at their designs, their tapers, by a process of trial and error. But Garrison's whole approach was that of an engineer; there wasn't an empirical bone in the man's body. He had computed his tapers with his slide rule, calculating how energy could be transmitted through the medium of bamboo with the greatest possible speed and efficiency. His designs could be communicated—you might say they could *only* be communicated—through mathematical formulas on the page.

"It was hard for me to learn that stuff," Hoagy admitted. "Getting all that math into the book, that was maybe the hardest thing I'd ever done." But once it *was* done, something fundamental had changed. Now you could not only build your own bamboo fly rod; you could build your own Garrison. And over time, hundreds, perhaps thousands, did.

Hoagy was one of them. The idea of making rods himself had never occurred to him until Garrison died. But then, he said, "I thought, well, OK. I looked around and there was nobody else coming down those stairs. I felt as if I owed it to him, to use what he'd given me."

And so Hoagy Carmichael, Hollywood princeling–cum–stockbroker–cum–jazz musician–cum–documentary filmmaker, went to night school to learn how to run a lathe. "I remember the first day they showed us how to grind tools," he said. "It scared us half to death."

But he buckled down to learning the fundamentals, and in the process found unsuspected reserves of perfectionism within himself. "I have a critical eye," he told me, "and my standards are my own standards, which I guess are pretty high. I'm careful. And I decided I wanted to become a complete rod maker, make everything that Garry made. Only better."

I asked him the same question I'd asked Streamer: what was the most difficult part of the process? He didn't hesitate for a second: it was the planing, he said. That was the hardest thing—fiendishly so at times—but also, when it all came together, the most rewarding.

"There are times in hand-planing," he said, "when everything is tuned right, and I can hand-plane bamboo as if it was the easiest thing in the world. You can feel it, you can *hear* it." He made a sound that was between a *whizzzz* and a *zzzzippp*.

"There would be times when I was almost dancing a jig, I was so thrilled because I was getting things *just right*! It was coming off with these perfect curls, from the very beginning to the very end of the strip. And I knew I was taking three-quarters of a thou each time, just *perfectly*! The other stuff . . . anybody could do that. That's not difficult work. It starts and ends with the bamboo."

I asked Hoagy how many rods he'd made in the thirty years since Garrison's death. He answered precisely: 104. They're regarded as masterpieces; no one who owns a Carmichael would ever part with it.

But of course, not every craftsman who propped a copy of the book on his workbench produced a masterpiece. "My educated guess," Hoagy went on, "is that before the book there were maybe twenty guys making rods. At the risk of giving the book too much credit, I suspect it was the thing that gave the impetus, that kick-started the revival of bamboo. Because now you could do it yourself. Carmichael or somebody could sell you the tools. You could buy the planes at the hardware store. You could diddle around and get a little shop together. You have no idea how many books I've

signed since the rod revival began. I've met hundreds of rod makers who have used the book, I mean *hundreds.*"

"That must be a great feeling," I said.

"Well," he answered, "I've had that supreme pleasure of seeing a man actually buy one, go out and do stuff, and then walk in
and hand me a rod and say, 'I made this from that book.' "

Some of those rods were good; some weren't. To Hoagy it
didn't seem to matter. He said, "I respect anybody who takes the
time and signs his name to one. Because the name stays there.
We're all nothing, really, at the end of our days, so you want to
leave a few things behind, you know?"

But actually to make a *living* at this. Not just as a hobby, not just to
diddle around, in Hoagy's phrase. To have the kind of mental discipline it takes to go into that zone every day, one rod after another
after another, in sufficient numbers to pay the bills and feed the
family. To be like Streamer, in other words. What did *that* take?

There were twenty people out there making bamboo fly rods
when his book came out in 1977, Hoagy had said. Today that number is in the high hundreds at least, and it's a safe bet that every
last one of them owns a copy of *A Master's Guide.* The purists still
insist on hand-planing their rods from start to finish, as Garrison
did. But the majority, like Streamer, use some kind of machinery,
either hand-powered or power-driven, to "rough bevel" the bamboo strips before picking up the plane. One or two traditionalists
have even kept the old masters' bevelers, those steel-and-wood be-
hemoths, oiled and running.

It's hard to say how many contemporary rod makers pursue the
craft as a full-time occupation or as a substantial sideline—let's say,
for the sake of argument, that that means making more than a
dozen rods a year, advertising and selling them commercially, perhaps maintaining a Web site. Maybe a couple hundred. With only a

handful of exceptions, which we'll get to in a moment, these are one-man operations. I was surprised to discover how far they'd spread from the original centers of the craft in the Northeast. A few rod makers still operate in Maine. New York State and Pennsylvania are traditional strongholds. But these days the greatest numbers may be in the West, in states like California, Colorado, and Oregon. You'll even find rod makers in unlikely places such as Louisiana and North Dakota, hundreds of miles from the nearest trout stream.

Kick-started by the Garrison book, and nurtured in the last ten years or so by the Internet, this new generation of craftsmen has evolved a subculture that is intensely democratic and, as such, at times fiercely contentious. They'll argue back and forward for weeks in their online forums and chat rooms, sometimes sharing tips, sometimes quibbling interminably about glues and router bits and different ways to flatten the nodes in a piece of bamboo. One person will say that no further design innovations are possible: the old masters of the Leonard school dotted every last *i* and crossed every last *t*. Bullshit, another will respond; the new computer-controlled woodworking equipment opens up a whole new world of possibilities.

Politically, too, they're all over the place. There are Zen Buddhists and Southern Baptists, militant liberals and Neanderthal conservatives, though on balance I think you'd have to say the center of gravity was slightly to the right of center. The flag gets waved a lot in their online forums and chat rooms; even if there are upstart rod makers these days in Europe, Asia, and Latin America, this is still viewed as an intrinsically American craft.

In one sense, the craft has been democratized because it has little alternative. Though there's always room for new tricks and tweaks—new high-tech adhesives, new varnishing techniques, personal "interpretations" of a classic design—the era of jealously guarded trade secrets is long gone. The heart of the bamboo fly rod will always be the taper, and the door that Hoagy cracked by publishing Garrison's formulas has now swung wide open. If you regard the classic tapers of the past as the last word, they're now just a mouse click away, in the form of charts and graphs. For that reason, most contemporary rod makers focus their efforts on reproductions, much as luthiers will offer you a Gibson Stradivarius or furniture makers will copy a Chippendale ribbon-back chair. Visit a rod maker's Web site and you'll find lots of Payne 198 clones, Leonard 50-DF clones, Dickerson 7613 clones.

As I got to know more and more rod makers, I'd invariably start by asking them the same question: *What in God's name makes you do this?* Then I'd ask, *How many hours does it take you to make a rod? How many can you make in a year? How much can you sell them for? How many rods do you have to make*—what's the sweat equity, in other words—*before you're good enough to persuade someone to shell out good money for one?* Then we'd crunch the numbers together, and I'd shake my head while they rolled their eyes and looked sheepish. Assuming your goals in life included survival and sanity, full-time bamboo fly rod making seemed to be as quixotic an idea in the new age of the solitary craftsman as it had been in the old days when Eustis Edwards was trying to break free from the straitjacket of corporate ownership.

"Someone told me that behind every great rod maker is a wife with a job," I remarked to Streamer one day as we were sitting around in his shop drinking scotch at the end of the afternoon.

"Well," he said, "I've heard a wife with a job or a wife who walked out on him." He paused and grinned. "I've had one of each." At the time, his second wife, Suzy, was commuting sixty miles to Stamford, Connecticut, each day for a job with Swiss Bank. Her real passion in life, though, had been acting, he told me. "She was a child actress, and she'd love to be doing that, but . . ." He left the thought unfinished, then went on, "So, yeah, I owe some of it to her, and I give her credit for going out and producing regular income. At the same time, because I built the house myself, the mortgage isn't that much. And then there's some Yankee in me that came from my dad, about dealing with expenses and not having too much debt."

Even so, the math just didn't add up for me. Browsing through one of the online forums, I'd come across a West Coast rod maker's calculations of the economics of the business, the most detailed breakdown I'd seen. His hypothetical craftsman was producing fifty rods a year and charging $1,500 apiece. Of this, what he called the direct manufacturing costs—everything from the raw bamboo to the amortized costs of major tools—accounted for about $300. Add in the manufacturing overhead—utilities, shipping, excise taxes, and so forth—and you're lopping off another $200. For administrative costs—health insurance, advertising and promotion, phone bills—deduct another $150. So for each rod, this hypothetical maker was actually clearing $850. Multiply that by fifty, allow for the odd sick day, and we're talking about a pretax income of around $40,000.

But wait a second, I thought. Making even that kind of a living depended on some very high-end assumptions. Each rod represents forty or sixty hours of skilled and disciplined work, in some cases as much as a hundred; it's a rare craftsman who can do this fifty times a year. And then $1,500 is a price threshold to which few makers can aspire. Streamer's goal was to make twenty-five or thirty rods a year, and as a young craftsman still building his reputation he was reluctant to charge more than $1,000 apiece. His restoration work, the odd guiding job, casting lessons for local schools—these things helped.

Even so, I couldn't make it compute. But then, rod makers seem to approach the subject of economics with a kind of gallows humor. It's like the old joke about wine, one said. *Q: What does it take to make a million dollars as a winemaker? A: A vineyard—and two million dollars.*

CHAPTER 11

Zen and the Art of Rod Making

One day I was chatting with Joe Garman, a legendary collector, now in his eighties, who had known most of the great midcentury rod makers from Jim Payne on down. When I mentioned Streamer's work, and how much praise it was garnering, the first thing Joe asked was how much his rods were selling for. When I told him, he frowned and said, "You tell your friend Bill Abrams, and this is coming from an eighty-year-old, to jack his prices up."

"But isn't that a catch-22?" I argued. "If you price them too high, aren't people going to say, 'Who the hell does this guy think he is, charging that kind of money before he's established a reputation?'"

"Naah," said Joe, with a dismissive wave of his hand. "If he comes out at thirteen hundred, fifteen hundred, no one's going to say that. Let me tell you a story. When I ran a clothing store, we used to mark everything down for two sales a year. Used to give stuff away, just to get rid of it. One time I had some nice sport coats, $79.50, which was a lot of money back then. So Washington's Birthday I marked them down, $29.95. Couldn't sell 'em. Not a one. Three weeks later, I ran an ad—same sport coats, marked down to $69.95. And *then* I sold 'em."

It was a mundane example, I suppose, but it was clear that Joe was making a larger point about the bizarre relationship our culture has chosen to establish between the price we pay for something and the value we assign to it. The marketing axiom that higher price equals higher value affects not just a specialized object like a bamboo fly rod, but everything to which we attach monetary value in an affluent society, be it a sport coat or a Jackson

Pollock. The axiom applies particularly to luxury goods, and when you can stop in at your local Wal-Mart and pick up a perfectly serviceable Chinese-made graphite fly rod for less than fifty bucks, I suppose a fifteen-hundred-dollar handmade fishing rod must qualify as a luxury item by anyone's standards.

The price = value axiom goes all the way back to Thorstein Veblen, of course. It's more than a hundred years since Veblen coined the idea of the "conspicuous consumption of valuable goods," which he saw as "a means of reputability to the gentleman of leisure." The Harvard economist Juliet Schor, reflecting on the new fad for luxury goods that began with the economic boom of the 1980s, prefers the term "competitive consumption." And in recent years, the cultural commentator James Twitchell has written, luxury spending in the United States has been growing at four times the rate of spending overall. Each social group, Twitchell says, "has its own luxury markers—positional goods, in marketing jargon." The bamboo fly rod would seem to be an excellent example.

These notions clearly resonated with Streamer when I asked him about his clientele, and why they chose to buy a bamboo fly rod. "Certainly there are guys who see it more as being a social statement than something they want to do personally," he said. "There's one client I'm making a rod for now—he's a well-known chairman of the board, major corporation, who really has no idea why he's getting a bamboo rod, other than the fact that he knows he can fish with it, and it's really nice, and he can afford to spend whatever he wants to spend."

Beyond the bamboo fly rod, you could make a case that the sport of fly-fishing as a whole has become a positional marker, a sign of both affluence and good taste. In TV commercials and upscale magazines, the iconography of fly-fishing is used to sell everything from sport utility vehicles and real estate and prescription drugs to investment brokerages. Many outfitters and resorts have made corporate fly-fishing retreats the mainstay of their business, with the trout stream functioning as a kind of aquatic golf course. Fly-fishing is a large part of what draws dot-com-billionaire environmentalists to build new mansions in Aspen, Jackson Hole, and Montana's Bitterroot Valley, what entices affluent ecotourists to Patagonia and Siberia, changing the face of places that not so long ago were trackless wilderness. Twitchell again: "Commercialized luxury has colonized much of the space once held as sacred."

The idea of luxury, Twitchell argues, is always socially constructed; what we crave is not so much the object itself as its "attributed meaning." And that meaning is largely created after the object has parted company with its manufacturer; it's the result of packaging, advertising, and branding. Taken together, these things make up the *story* of the object, and that's what ultimately sells it, since storytelling is the basic organizing principle of human society.

Yet I wondered about this. I could see easily enough how it applied to blue jeans, for example, where the thirty-dollar Levis I've always worn and the three-hundred-dollar luxury brands that my teenagers are taught to aspire to—True Religion, Chip & Pepper, Seven for All Mankind—probably roll off the same Chinese production lines and are indistinguishable in quality, set apart from one another only by their labels. But a bamboo fly rod? Did Twitchell's theory of storytelling really apply to that?

The difference, I thought, was that the bamboo fly rod is *intrinsically* a luxury object, its price a necessary reflection of all those hours of perfectionist labor. And it really *does* have a story to tell—an authentic one, that is, and not just the invention of some marketing guru. I don't want to sound naïve here: even in more innocent times, branding was always part of the game. I had only to think of the marriage of mutual convenience between Eustis Edwards and Abercrombie & Fitch. Eustis's name benefited from the stamp of approval of a retailer whose brand signified class and prestige; A&F's image benefited, too, from its association with the solitary craftsman of genius. You can imagine the A&F salesman, in his Herbert Hoover celluloid collar, taking the client aside and murmuring discreetly, "Well, of course, sir, it's an *Edwards.*"

A contemporary rod maker, it seemed to me, had to experience a certain amount of schizophrenia, having one foot in the values of the past and one in the values of the present. In *doing* his work, he's a remnant of the old producer culture, his skills defined by self-discipline, self-reliance, and self-respect. But in *selling* his work, he's forced to operate by the rules of the new consumer culture. The language that rod makers used on their Web sites—how they told the *story* of their rods, how they created their *brand,* if you like—often reflected that tension, honoring the history while flattering the client. One typical site, for example, invited you to "own a piece of angling tradition." Another offered "one of the most perfectly designed and executed triumphs of human artisanship." A third wooed you with the promise of "premium handcrafted bamboo fly rods, created for the discriminating angler." Fresh from reading Twitchell, I recognized "premium" (applied to the object) and "discriminating" (applied to the buyer) as two of the more loaded words in the luxury marketer's lexicon.

Streamer had chosen to tell a different and, it seemed to me, a less calculating story. One distinctive feature of his Web site was an autobiographical sketch in which he talked about his father and touched on the importance of appreciating history. I took to visiting the site—www.housatonicrods.com—for the pleasure of seeing his photographs of that beautiful Connecticut trout stream as it changed with the seasons. They conveyed something he'd often implied when we'd talked—that a sense of place, of landscape, was important to his craft. And then, on one visit to the Web site, I noticed that Streamer had raised his prices—close to the level that Joe Garman had suggested and high enough, I hoped, to stave off poverty.

A fifteen-hundred-dollar fishing rod might seem a major ex-travagance, but I'd learned by now that there were a handful of rod makers whose work fetched twice as much. These were the true elite of the craft, and in my personal pursuit of perfection, they were next on the list.

I hadn't realized just how contentious a group rod makers could be until I started asking them to name the five greatest contemporary practitioners of the craft. As soon as a name was added to the list, someone else would voice a criticism. X's cosmetics were crude; Y hadn't put enough thought into his tapers; Z's rods were inconsistent. The only one on whom there seemed to be a virtual consensus was a rod maker in Shelburne Falls, Massachusetts, named Per Brandin. Since I was looking at Web sites, I looked at his. The first sentence said: "My intent in building cane rods is simply to make the finest rod that can be made, both in terms of craftsmanship and performance." You couldn't say it plainer than that.

Yet the more I learned about Per Brandin, the clearer it be-came that he wasn't just a superlative craftsman. There seemed to be a kind of restless intelligence at work; he was someone pushing and refining this peculiarly American craft in peculiarly American ways. He had drawn on impeccable models from the past like Jim Payne and Bill Edwards; and he had learned from impeccable mentors like Hoagy Carmichael and Sam Carlson. He was fully, almost *academically*, versed in tradition, yet at the same time he was a technical innovator, fiercely experimental. His roots were in Maine and the Catskills, where the craft had been born, but his vi-sion had leapfrogged to the West Coast, a leap that transforms all things American. I came to think of him as the intellectual among rod makers.

Shelburne Falls is a pretty New England village, best known for its pedestrian Bridge of Flowers, which spans the Deerfield

River. I found Per Brandin at home in an imposing Victorian at the edge of town, which reminded me a little of Fred Thomas's old house in Brewer, Maine. He was a man of about my own age, early fifties perhaps. There was something ascetic about his appearance—balding, with a close-cropped, graying beard and a bright, intense expression. He hobbled away from the door on crutches, his leg imprisoned in a Bledsoe brace. He'd only recently bought the house, and within days of moving here from California he'd fallen down a steep flight of stairs and shattered his shin bone just below the knee. The consequence of this accident was six months without being able to make a rod—in other words, six months without any income. In his most productive year, he had made about thirty-five rods; this year, he said, he'd be lucky to complete five. Another vignette of the unforgiving economics of rod making.

Per came into the craft in the usual way—which is to say, circuitously. As the name implies, he was born in Sweden, but his family moved to the United States when he was six. From his teens on, all he dreamed about was fishing—reading old copies of *Outdoor Life* and *Field and Stream* in the basement of the local library, haunting the trout streams of the Catskills where American fly-fishing had taken root. In the fly shops in small Catskills towns like Roscoe and Phoenicia, he'd finger the rods on the rack and learn the makers' names—Leonard, Payne, Orvis—magnetized by their mystique but too shy to ask if he could try them out. He drove a cab eighty hours a week, saving enough money to buy bamboo fly rods. It seemed out of the question, however, to make these magical things for a living. For the bread and butter of his career, Per decided on photography.

He went into the next room and brought back some boxes of prints. They were all black-and-white. I liked them. The most recent ones were images of water. No landscape around it, no horizon to give depth and perspective—simply patterns on the surface of water, broken riffles, swirling back eddies, foam lines and slicks. The earlier work was entirely different, its subject matter, editorial attitude, and black-edged framing all classic 1970s. There were broken urban landscapes and portraits of working-class people who looked alternately beaten down and smoldering with anger.

Per gave a wry laugh. "I wanted to be the great American artist-photographer, you know, the next Robert Frank. What was always cool to me was to reveal and show the truth."

"Now, there's a quaint, old-fashioned notion," I said.

"That's always the way I do something, it's just something that interests me. I was just so arrogant. . . ."

He smiled, seeming to imply that this wasn't entirely a criticism. Then he looked up at me, as if gauging my reaction. In the course of a couple of visits to Per I saw this expression often. There were times when his manner was quiet and cerebral, others when he could be funny and profane. But the whole time there was a composure, a self-possession about him that I suppose some people would take for arrogance, though I didn't perceive it that way.

"Anyway," he went on, "the biggest thing I was involved with was a thing called the Long Island Project, which was back in the late seventies. It was a conceptual project, basically looking at post–World War Two suburbanization. A lot of work, wonderful people, lots of shows. And it was quite successful. I mean, the Bibliothèque Nationale in Paris bought my work, the Neue Sammlung in Munich."

"So you weren't doing the Eustis Edwards thing," I said, "making a living with a photographer's studio, shooting weddings and family portraits?"

He gave a sardonic smile. "Well, you say 'making a living.' Making my living was earning three thousand bucks a year. The stuff that interested me about photography had no commercial application. And then I got married, and Ronald Reagan got elected, and I started doing commercial work, a lot of tabletop stuff, book covers, catalogs. Basically stuff that I hated."

"So instead you went off and made fish poles."

"Well, you know, I really just fell into it. I just ran into the right people at the right time."

Of these right people, the rightest was Hoagy Carmichael Jr.

The two men were near neighbors in Westchester County, New York, and after Hoagy published his book on Everett Garrison, Per was one of the first to come to him for advice. "I don't know that he had done any work yet," Hoagy had told me, "but I could see he had the hands, he had the intelligence, and he was keen as hell. If I had one achievement in this game, it would be whatever I did to move Per Brandin along. Because I think he's the greatest rod maker alive. Just as I think Jim Payne was the single greatest rod maker who ever lived."

Like Hoagy, Per assembled his first bamboo rod from a kit he bought from Orvis. After that he handled and fished as many rods as he could get his hands on, measuring them with his ever-present micrometer, plotting their tapers on graph paper. "I just wanted to know what makes a bamboo rod tick," he said. There was a driven, obsessive quality to all this self-education. Per was always asking questions, said Len Codella, a well-known rod dealer who knew him in the late 1970s, when he was first bitten by the bamboo bug. Then Codella stopped and refined the thought. "No, not so much asking questions," he said, "more like *challenging* you all the time. I said to him, 'Per, you're a pain in the ass.' " A beat. " 'But I like you.' "

By now Per Brandin had become a superb, self-taught fly caster, and the more rods he tried, the more critical he became of them—even of the makers he most admired. He fished lots of Leonards but found something wanting in them, something that wasn't quite right. After the disastrous 1964 fire, the company hadn't tried to reconstitute the old Leonard tapers. Per said he found that hard to comprehend; it had taken almost a century of trial and error to perfect those classic designs. With the newer Leonard rods there seemed to be too much bamboo in the butt of the rod, too little in the tip. Jim Frank had described these as "fabulous freakin' fly rods"; Per begged to disagree.

He was more intrigued by the Quadrate, the four-sided rod that Eustis Edwards's son Bill had developed in the late 1930s. It was different, and Per was always interested in doing things that were different. On a theoretical level, too, the design appealed to him— four flats of bamboo rather than six gave you a higher density of the critical power fibers, and that translated into greater strength and stiffness for the same amount of cane. Per compared the effect to the torque of a long-stroke piston engine. Yet he thought Bill Edwards's tapers left a lot to be desired; perhaps he could figure out how to improve on them. He asked Hoagy where he could turn for advice on building his own Quadrates. Sam Carlson's your man, Hoagy said, and gave Per his phone number.

So Per Brandin, who had built a grand total of one rod from an Orvis kit, headed up to New Hampshire to meet the dean of rod makers, the living legend, the last direct link to the taproot of the craft. Telling me this part of the story, Per seemed for the first time a little abashed at his own bumptiousness. He said, "I remember telling Sam in that first meeting, 'I've really looked at all this stuff, hex rods and square rods, and it seems to me that this square rod would be stronger and better.' This is *Sam Carlson*, right, and I'm like this young fucking whippersnapper! And Sam just goes"—Per hooded his eyes and affected a sardonic growl— " 'Oh yeah?' "

Even so, Sam took a shine to the young man, much as Len Codella had. This was curious, because Sam was not known for passing on the knowledge he'd acquired in half a century in the rod game. What seemed to break the ice was their common language. There was even a family connection between the Brandins and the Carlsons through the Nordic Glee Club, they discovered, and it might have been enough to bring the two men together even without Hoagy's involvement.

"Per and Sam were kind of close," a mutual friend said. "When they first met each other, they'd break into Swedish. They'd be looking around and snickering, and probably a good part of it was that nobody would have a clue what they were talking about."

Actually, calling Dana Gray a "mutual friend" is to do him an injustice. As I would soon learn, Dana was a big part of Sam's life and an important link in the chain that kept the old rod-making tradition alive.

I'd met Dana a few times at shows. On one occasion he'd been with Sam; another time I'd bought a grand old Leonard Catskill rod from him, one of his flawless restoration jobs. In background, appearance, manner, and approach to the craft, Per and Dana could hardly have been more dissimilar. Yet there was a deep mutual respect and affection in the way each spoke about the other.

Dana was Massachusetts born and bred, with a strong Boston accent. Stocky in build, with a thick, dark mustache, he always looked to me as if he belonged on the Red Sox bench circa mid-1980s, sitting between Dwight Evans and Bill Buckner perhaps— even though the cleft in his chin was pure Don Mattingly.

It turned out that Dana also had deep roots in the Rangeley Lakes of Maine, and as far as the bamboo fly rod was concerned, that was as deep as roots could go. The Grays had owned a small family camp just a few miles from the old Angler's Retreat at Middle Dam, and we swapped stories of the big brook trout and landlocked salmon we'd caught there on the Rapid River. He'd been fishing the river for more than thirty years; I'd been there once. So the better part of the stories were his.

Surprisingly for someone with a camp in the Rangeleys, Dana's father didn't fish, didn't hunt, but he was good with his hands. Much like Sam Carlson and his toolmaker father, Dana thought that was where he'd acquired his own do-it-yourself attitude. "I was always pretty good at taking stuff apart and putting it back together again," he told me. He worked for a spell as a mechanic in a garage, as Bill Edwards once had. In the sixties and early seventies, the era of the Detroit muscle car, he and his friends would race on the streets. If your ride needed fixing, you'd bring it to Dana.

From auto repairs he moved into construction and carpentry. The world of joinery—mortise and tenon, dovetail and rabbet—fascinated him, and as a fly fisherman it was a short step for him from there to picking up Hoagy's book. "I just thought it was like a magical feat," he said. "In fact I still get a kick out of showing people who don't know anything about rods that there's actually six strips packed together there, and they just look at you and say, 'How do you take a piece of bamboo and sand it down so it's got six sides to it?' "

Somewhere along the line, Dana told his future wife that that was what he'd like to do: build bamboo fly rods. She seems to have reacted in much the same way as Jim Frank's wife had. Raised eyebrows.

Then, sometime in the mid-1980s, Dana bumped into Sam Carlson at one of the shows. They struck up a conversation and discovered that they were neighbors, living ten miles apart. Drive up sometime and visit, Sam said.

"Was he actually looking for a protégé?" I asked.

"Oh no," Dana said emphatically. "He had no interest in that."

On this point both Per and Dana agreed. If the details of his craft remained arcane, that was just fine with Sam. For one thing, his business was precarious and he had no desire to encourage competitors. But from my own conversations with Sam I thought there was also a more generous impulse at work—he didn't want to see others make the same bitter mistake he thought he'd made himself.

Per certainly had never considered himself to be Sam's apprentice. But he did get in the door where others had tried and failed. Perhaps it was the Swedish that led Sam to make an exception in Per's case, perhaps it was the signs of the young man's exceptional talent, or perhaps it was just Per's sheer persistence. Either way, Per learned a lot. The most important thing Sam taught him was how to make Quadrate ferrules. This is no mean challenge: it requires a high degree of metalworking skill to tease the nickel silver progressively from a square to a round cross section and ensure that the energy still flows smoothly from one section of the rod to the next. But Sam showed Per how it was done. Other than that, Per said, "he just let me hang around and pester him, to the point where I could see for myself how something was done."

Dana Gray, meanwhile, began to drive the ten miles to Greenville, New Hampshire, on a regular basis. He helped Sam rebuild a shed that had collapsed under the weight of a blizzard. He hung around in the rod shop, did menial jobs, observed Sam at the bench. Sam wasn't an aesthete or a theorist or a philosopher, and he didn't think of himself as a teacher. But he was happy enough for Dana to sit there and watch him work. Like his mentor—and quite unlike Per Brandin—Dana wasn't much interested in theoretical talk about tapers, which Sam thought was a lot of hogwash. What he focused on was the patient, hands-on labor. When I asked Dana what he thought made a great bamboo fly rod, he thought for a moment and then said, "Well, that's kind of an abstract thing, but you could sum it up by watching the way that Sam built one. Every little step, every little stage in the rod's development, has to be absolutely perfect, or it doesn't move on."

Gradually Dana won the old man's confidence, became trusted enough to do a small repair, glue up a set of blanks, put on some silk wraps, until at last he moved up the ladder to the higher-end skills of the craft: straightening strips, flaming cane, building ferrules. Whether or not Sam had ever wanted an apprentice, he now seemed to have one. He had also acquired, in a sense, a surro-gate son.

When Per Brandin heard that the relationship had flowered to this extent, he couldn't have been happier. "I said, '*Great,*' because I couldn't think of a better person. I mean, there's a lot of people I wouldn't have wanted to see there. But Dana, I just trust him a thousand percent. Total integrity. Just a really good, solid guy."

Per, meanwhile, was headed west. His wife was from California and wanted to go back to school; both of them were tired of New York. In the winter of 1989 they moved to the San Francisco Bay Area.

Soon after they arrived, Per developed a passion for tai chi, for the unique discipline it provided, and for the clear parallels he saw between the tai chi sword and the bamboo fly rod. He explained, "With a fly rod you don't want any gaps in the energy leaving your feet, moving through your body, leaving your hand, going through the rod. You have this sense of connection. If there's a break any-where, it's jarring, it's uncomfortable, it gets in the way."

Tai chi was all about this command of energy. He said, "If I'm pushing with my teacher—and I'm nowhere near as good as he is—sometimes I'll have an interruption, I'll have a little pullback, which creates a gap in the energy. And he is so good, his body is so tuned, that he'll automatically fill that gap and throw me against the wall. *Boom!*" He smiled.

Per set up shop just outside Berkeley, in El Cerrito, with an-other gifted craftsman named Mario Wojnicki, and the two of them continued to push the envelope of bamboo rod design. This meant, paradoxically, going back to first principles. If bamboo has a single drawback compared to synthetic materials, it's weight. In the heyday of Calcutta cane in the nineteenth century, fly rods had customarily been ten or eleven feet long, and a rod that length could easily weigh seven or eight ounces. That may not sound like much, but try fishing with it all day. The human wrist just isn't built for that kind of repetitive stress.

Hiram Leonard and his star pupils had experimented with a variety of weight-loss remedies. For their casting tournaments in Central Park in the 1880s, Leonard and his nephew Hiram Hawes had proved that you could build a nine-foot rod that weighed less than four and a half ounces and use it to cast unprecedented distances. As Streamer had discovered in restoring my Perfection, Eustis Edwards had made crude attempts to reduce the heft of his rods by hollowing out part of the butt section. But Eustis's main innovation was to make rods that were shorter, and by the late teens he and Hawes were both building revolutionary rods that were only seven feet long and weighed as little as three ounces. Those tiny wands were beautifully suited for the small streams of the Catskills, but until the rod-making renaissance of the 1970s they remained a minority taste.

In the West they remained virtually unknown. There may be cultural reasons for that, perhaps obscurely rooted in Western machismo: remember that critics of the time had derided Leonard's lightweight tournament creations as "effeminate toy rods." But there were also sounder practical considerations: Western rivers (and Western trout) are generally bigger than those in the East. If you're fishing for steelhead, for example—the large migratory rainbow trout of the California coast and the Pacific Northwest— you may need to cast your fly eighty, ninety, even a hundred feet to reach the water where the fish are lying. You can't do that with a seven-foot rod.

Also, it's easy to forget today that until at least the middle of the twentieth century, Eastern and Western cultural habits and tastes developed in relative isolation from each other. More than any other craftsman, it was Per Brandin who married the two, enlarging the old Maine-Catskills tradition to encompass ideas from the other coast. His basic conception of a fly rod was drawn from Bill Edwards and Sam Carlson; his tapers were derived from Jim Payne's, modified somewhat to suit the contours of the Quadrate; but his technical fingerprint came primarily from two Californian innovators: a San Francisco machinist named Lew Stoner and a former peach orchard operator called Edwin Courtney Powell.

Working independently of each other, and apparently oblivious to the rod-making history of the Northeast, Stoner and Powell arrived at the same epiphany almost simultaneously. In the same year, 1933, each of them registered a patent for a revolutionary new approach to rod design. Per explained to me their basic insight: if the problem was that more bamboo equaled more weight, then the solution was obviously less bamboo. And if the power fibers, the part that actually did the work, were on the outside of the rod, then why not remove the interior core of the bamboo, which was basically nothing but deadweight?

The result, in cross section, was not the closed hexagon of the classic bamboo fly rod. Marty Keane put it well: if you were to split open an E. C. Powell rod, you would see a structure very much like that of bamboo itself. "He built them like hollow cylinders," Keane wrote, "with solid spacers at strategic points to add cohesive strength to the unit without loss of power or delicacy, just like the culms from which the rod strips were split." Lew Stoner further refined the principle, patenting a technique that he called "hollow fluting," which involved gouging small oval channels from the bamboo at intervals that could be varied at will.

In conception, the idea sounds simple enough. In execution, it's anything but. If the essence of genius is, as Leclerc suggested, "a great aptitude for patience," then hollow building pushes the definition to extreme limits, as well as adding even more hours of labor—and thus of cost—to an already laborious process. There's also the tricky matter of how to assemble the sections once they've been hollowed out. Making a regular rod involves sticking together the adjacent flat surfaces of four or six equilateral triangles, each of which may be as narrow as one-fortieth of an inch at the tip. However, if the apex of each triangle is removed, well . . . my fingers hurt just thinking about it.

Per and others talked to me a lot about glue at this point, the most mundane of subjects but one that's vital to the rod maker. Since my intimacy with hardware stores is basically limited to buying lightbulbs, batteries, and the occasional can of paint, I'm not sure I followed all the technical arcana. But the gist of it was that all these technical feats had been made possible by epoxy resins and other modern adhesives; the water-soluble hide and fish glues that the old masters had used wouldn't have done the job. It struck me as a little ironic that it should have been the revolution in synthetics that helped to sustain and deepen the tradition in organics.

Since the halcyon days in Central Park, tournament casting had all but disappeared in the East, but in California in the 1930s it was still alive and thriving. E. C. Powell had been a championship caster, and had come up with most of his technical innovations with the demands of the tournament in mind. Many of his initial designs were so fragile, in fact, putting so much stress on the properties of the raw material, that they lasted for only one or two sessions of competition before they fell apart.

For Per Brandin, with his passion for technical performance, this kind of competitive casting was a natural fit, and in the Bay Area he found the perfect venue in the Golden Gate Angling and Casting Club, one of the last places where the activity still had a following.

"Sounds pretty snooty," I said, thinking of Cora Leonard and her Gordon tartan silk waist.

"Not at all," Per replied. "It's a very public thing. Membership is open to anyone who wants to pay eighty bucks a year, and it's in Golden Gate Park. It was actually built by the Works Project Administration back in the thirties, and it's owned by the City of San Francisco."

"So is it mainly set up for tournaments?" I asked.

"Not really," he answered. "The tournament casting is in decline—there are some new people coming in, but most of the tournament casters are older. So there are casting demonstrations, casting lessons, casting symposia."

"What was the longest cast you ever made?"

"A hundred and fifty-nine feet, though that was with graphite, not bamboo."

Fifty-three yards: more than half a city block. Why would anyone need to cast a fly that far? My expression must have betrayed my thoughts, because Per said, "If you ever saw it, well . . . it kind of relates to fishing and it kind of doesn't. There's a pure tournament mode. And at a certain point it becomes totally abstracted from fishing. In fact there's one really good caster at the Golden Gate Club who doesn't fish at all. He's German. We call him the *Überkaster*."

I had a hard time getting my brain around this. A fishing rod was a tool, and the purpose of the tool was to catch fish. Now we had a fishing rod that wasn't for fishing. It was like a Zen koan, and that was probably no accident in view of what I knew about Per from our first meeting.

We'd been sitting talking about what made a great fly rod. Per was saying, "It's the balance of a lot of different things. You can't teach it and you can't copy it, and a lot of people wouldn't know what the hell I'm talking about when I say that. But if you have any sense of aesthetics, you know when it has a sort of *presence* to it. There's a woman I know in Hollywood, California, who's a very famous violin restorer. Her company is one of the best in the world. I was visiting her shop one day and she brought out a really good violin. It might have been a Guarneri, or maybe it was one or two levels below a Guarneri. And she said, 'Just look at the scroll!' And you look at it, and you go, 'My God!' It's like the guy is in there. You can tell. It's the presence."

At about this point in the conversation, the doorbell rang. I'd asked a friend to join us, another Massachusetts rod maker named Rick Taupier, who'd been wanting to meet Per. Rick teaches environmental studies at Amherst and is another Carlson-Edwards fanatic. Rick, in fact, was the person who had sold me my first ever Edwards Quadrate. He's also an expert on the Kalmuk, a tribe of nomadic Mongolian Buddhists, and the conversation quickly took a turn in that direction.

"You know," Rick said, "when I left college I ran off to become a Buddhist monk. I stuck with it for quite a while, not enough to become a monk but long enough that I could read and write passable Tibetan. But then I decided that the social life was not quite up to my needs."

We all laughed at this.

Rick continued, "But I often think about making fly rods and achieving some kind of harmony. I don't know that I'll ever get good enough to put all the pieces together. But when people ask me what I'm trying to achieve when I'm fly-fishing, I reply that it has almost nothing to do with catching fish. It has to do with harmony."

Harmony was the key, we all agreed—not that this was something you could ever define. You just knew it when you sensed its presence. Hiram Hawes had it, Per said, "and Jim Payne and Ed Payne, they might not have said it this way, but I think that's what they were after, too."

"And so did Eustis Edwards," I said.

"There's a Buddhist text called *The Questions of Milinda*," Per went on. "Two thousand years ago, the Greek king Menander goes to India and meets a Buddhist sage called Nagasena. And one of the things Nagasena talks about is the horse cart. What is it that makes the horse cart a horse cart? Is it the wheel? Is it the hub? Is it the spoke? Is it the seat? Is it the kind of wood? And then at the end he says—and this is the interesting part—is it all those things taken together?

"And you know what?" He looked up at us, his eyes twinkling. "It isn't that either."

CHAPTER 12

Brad Pitt's Waders

As Per Brandin saw it, most roads in American culture lead eventually to the West. And to fly fishermen in general, all roads lead to Montana. I would go there next, I decided, in search of a legendary rod maker named Glenn Brackett. I didn't suspect at the time that the trip would turn out to be a parable of American demographics and the global economy.

It was Per who had first suggested that I should talk to Glenn Brackett—the two of them had been friends for thirty years. The more I considered the idea, the more reasons I found for seeking him out. First of all, he was renowned as a craftsman of uncommon skill; when I'd asked others for their "top five" lists of the best living rod makers, the names of Per Brandin and Glenn Brackett had often been spoken in the same breath. Second, as I thought about all the ways in which rod makers had struggled for more than a century to reconcile their craft with economic reality, Glenn appeared to have carved out a model that was unique. He was the head of a four-man bamboo shop that was part of a much larger whole—the R. L. Winston Rod Company, a corporation that had been in existence for more than seventy-five years and now made most of its money from manufacturing graphite fly rods. And third, Glenn was reputed to be a man of rare modesty and charisma, someone who opened his shop to any aspiring rod maker willing to make the pilgrimage to Twin Bridges, Montana, asking for advice. Glenn Brackett was Yoda.

It was dark when I flew into Missoula. I picked up a rental car at the airport, checked into a cheap motel on the edge of town, and lay down on the bed to consult the tourist literature I'd been given by the clerk at the Avis desk. Most of the brochures were embellished with quotations from Norman Maclean's famous novella *A River Runs Through It.* The line they seemed to like best was the one about there being no clear line between religion and fly-fishing.

I found it particularly instructive to browse through a magazine called *Big Sky Journal,* a publication so glossy and heavy that I had to prop myself on the pillow and use both hands to hold it up. On every page, another trout. I'd read somewhere that sport fishing contributes almost $300 million a year to Montana's economy, and gorgeous images of fly-fishing and gigantic trout were being used here to sell everything from log homes, interior design studios, and exclusive resorts to Coldwell Banker, the American Bank of Montana, and Sotheby's International Realty. These were places that were busy putting the "nouveau" in "riche." There were private clubs and gated communities and "rustic cabins" the size of Madison Square Garden. You could fly-fish until you were weak at the knees at the Club at Spanish Peaks, the Monterra Condos at Whitefish, and Aspen Pointe at Hillcrest. Why were these places always the something *at* somewhere? I wondered. And come to that, why did "point" have that *e* on the end? Did that mean you had to pronounce it *pwahnt,* in the French manner?

Three hundred million a year. That would probably cover a down payment on some of the real estate in the *Big Sky Journal.* What could I look for with the money I'd saved on the motel? Mountain Meadows Ranch, $5.5 million. Chickenfeed. Here was one for $7.5 million, and another for $9.8. Ten, ten six. The meter ticked steadily upward as I turned the pages: $14.5 million, $15.5 million, and finally, there it was, Shangri-La—a residence "reminiscent of an exclusive European resort accented with walnut, stone, marble, copper, and glass," together with a ranch manager's quarters, a separate handcrafted log home, a custom indoor horse arena, several private lakes, a personal fish hatchery, and seventeen thousand acres. Oh, and an airstrip. A steal at $25.9 million.

This is the new reality of the Rocky Mountain West. For most of the twentieth century the economy of states like Montana was sustained by ranching, mining, and logging. Now it was sustained by beauty, and the desire of wealthy outsiders, West Coast people for the most part, to enjoy it. Later in the week I met an architect in Missoula who told me, "Three-quarters of my clients are from California, and all of them fly-fish. It's the single biggest reason they come here."

These were not, generally speaking, people who wanted to hole up in a cabin in the wilderness and fight off grizzlies. That kind of life was reserved for people who were bitter about their displacement, about the loss of well-paying blue-collar jobs. I recalled that the Bitterroot Valley, south of Missoula, had been the epicenter of the militia eruptions of the 1990s, and that the Unabomber had found the solitude he craved in a cabin in the upper reaches of the Big Blackfoot River.

Early the next morning I left town by way of Hellgate Canyon, taking a left turn off I-90 at the Milltown Dam in Bonner to see something of the Big Blackfoot. This was the river that Norman Maclean had written about, and I wondered idly if I'd spot any of the places I remembered from the book—places like the sandbar where the narrator's obnoxious brother-in-law and Big Rawhide, his "fishing whore," acquired the epic sunburn (hers across buttocks that are tattooed with the word LOVE) that takes up ten of the finest, funniest, best-written pages in all of literature.

The Blackfoot was Norman Maclean's river, and in a less literal sense it was Robert Redford's. Fly fishermen display a certain amount of ambivalence when you ask them about Redford's 1992 movie version of *A River Runs Through It.* Undeniably the movie accounted for much of the growth of fly-fishing chic in the 1990s, and for a fair portion of Montana chic, too. But anglers aren't sure whether they altogether approve of the boom in their sport. It's a sort of cross between Groucho Marx's "I don't want to belong to any club that will accept me as a member" and Yogi Berra's "Nobody goes there anymore. It's too crowded."

When Redford set out to film Maclean's story of two fly-fishing brothers and their Scottish Presbyterian minister father, he found that the Blackfoot no longer offered the kind of landscapes that the book had celebrated. Plans were afoot to build a huge cyanide heap-leach gold mine on the headwaters of the Blackfoot, and much of the river valley was a patchwork of clear-cuts, most of them there by the grace of the Plum Creek Timber Company. So Redford filmed instead in the canyon of the Gallatin River, two hundred miles or more to the southeast.

I'd always respected the movie for its faithfulness to the spirit, if not the exact plotline, of Maclean's story. But the choice of the Gallatin was one of the many small, harmless infidelities that made it more Hollywood Montana than the real thing. Nineteen-twenties Missoula was rendered by the present-day town of Livingston, tricked out with dirt streets and fake storefronts. The twenty-two-inch rainbow trout that Brad Pitt catches was actually a contraption of lead and fiberglass, nicknamed "Fernando." The movements of a hooked trout underwater were imitated by attaching to the fly line a quart-size milk carton part filled with rocks. Brad Pitt looked very fetching in waders, and even learned to use a fly rod for the movie, but its celebrated "shadowcasting" scene was the work of a professional fly caster named Jason Borger. And the rod that he used was made of graphite, though, in the most subtle of these small deceptions, it was made in hexagonal form to imitate the appearance of bamboo.

Although we'd arranged to meet in Twin Bridges, Glenn Brackett had told me that he'd recently moved forty miles away to Butte, the onetime center of the Montana (and world) copper industry, and I took a second detour from the interstate to look at the old Anaconda smelter stack, a 565-foot-tall tower that is the largest freestanding brick structure in the world. The Butte-Anaconda area is one vast complex of federal Superfund sites, and the smelter stack seemed to me a thing of singular malevolence. A great brute finger atop a gargantuan heap of mine tailings, black streaked with orange, it brought to mind nothing so much as Isengard, the dark tower in Tolkien's *Lord of the Rings* where the evil wizard Saruman forges his engines of war.

I couldn't wait to put the thing behind me, so I struck out on a dirt road that twisted across a huge, empty landscape of fragrant sagebrush and occasional knots of cattle—the Montana of my imagination. I drove for an hour or so. Then, on the plain below me, edged by the sawtooth peaks of the Ruby Mountains, I saw a cluster of buildings and a water tower that said "Twin Bridges."

In a town of four hundred people, Winston's corporate headquarters on South Main Street was not hard to find. The company had just celebrated its seventy-fifth anniversary and dozens of the company's dark green graphite rods were arranged on the walls of the entrance lobby. The showcases were part sales display, part museum exhibit, part religious reliquary. The receptionist invited me to look around and handed me a copy of the seventy-fifth-anniversary catalog. On the cover, in the same characteristic flowing italic script I'd seen in many of the real estate ads in the *Big Sky Journal,* was the single word "uncompromising." We were deep in the world of branding here.

The whole affair was a mix of nostalgic Americana and New West affluence. A black-and-white anniversary poster showed the main street of Twin Bridges. There was an old car in the foreground and banks of cirrus clouds in the big Montana sky. Arranged around the poster there were memorabilia to burn—or as the display copy put it, "quality accessories for the discerning Winston customer." There were four T-shirt designs and four grades of baseball cap. There were tote bags and coffee mugs and a sixteen-ounce Nalgene water bottle, all with the Winston logo.

There was trout-themed furniture and there were trout-themed knickknacks. There were hand-carved trout; you could even order a custom carving for $30 an inch—an expensive proposition in a place where twenty-inch fish are commonplace. But the centerpiece of the display was Winston's seventy-fifth-anniversary bamboo rod, priced for the discerning customer at $3,900.

Despite this, the receptionist told me that I was in the wrong place to find Glenn Brackett. She gave me directions to the bamboo rod shop. I drove a mile and crossed into another world.

The rod shop turned out to be a nondescript cinder-block building tucked away at the back of an empty parking lot. Its interior was dim and cool against the warmth of the day. Glenn Brackett, a small, slightly built man in his mid-sixties with twinkling eyes and a thick tangle of white beard, was showing a three-thousand-dollar fly rod to two women from New Jersey who were staying as guests on a nearby ranch. "Take it with you," he was saying. "Try it out for a couple of days." The women winced and looked at each other in disbelief, and I had to admit I'd never known a rod maker to make that kind of offer to a pair of strangers. Glenn put the sections of the rod in their cloth bag and threw it on the floor, hard. The women looked at each other some more. Then he picked up the bag by one end and whacked it against the workbench. They flinched. "Can't do that with graphite," he said. "Don't worry—it won't break. They'll cry out if they're hurting."

He took the bag, one hand at each end, and presented it formally to one of the women. "Here," he said. "Bring it back when you're done. And remember, it's alive, it's alive, it's alive. That's the word."

When they had gone, I remarked that the incident would leave the two women with a good story to tell when they got back to New Jersey. Glenn smiled. "The world isn't made up of atoms," he said, "it's made of stories." And with that, he proceeded to tell me some, starting with his childhood.

I remembered, when I was a kid growing up in Scotland, seeing pictures in magazines of American families on fishing trips. They seemed magical to me, impossibly exotic. Junior, with freckles, would be holding up a trout he'd just caught; Dad would be smiling benignly at his son and puffing away on a pipe; Mom, with a tight head of curls and wearing those 1950s blue jeans that were always rolled up halfway to the knees, would be crouched over a skillet frying up dinner. Craggy mountains rose up in the background. Sometimes there were horses tethered to a tree.

It sounded as if Glenn Brackett, growing up in the San Francisco Bay Area, had had that kind of idealized upbringing. "Water was always in my front yard or my backyard, at my feet, always in my imagination," he said. "I was always out on the dock with a line and a pin. I remember going up into the Sierra foothills with my grandfather, or rowing out on some little farm pond in a leaky boat. Those were great times, great memories."

Glenn's grandfather had known some people who owned a bamboo rod shop off Market Street in San Francisco, and he took the boy to visit one day when he was ten or eleven years old. The small enterprise had been founded in 1929; originally it had been the Winther-Stoner Manufacturing Company, but later that was contracted to R. L. Winston—an amalgam of the initials and first syllables of the names of its two founders, Robert Winther and Lew Stoner. Glenn was mesmerized by the Winston shop. "It got into my blood," he said, "the smells, the sense of things." Listening to him reminisce, I found myself thinking of what Sam Carlson had told me of his own memories, at a similar age, of smelling the pungent odor of varnish as he swept the floors of Eustis Edwards's shop in Mount Carmel, Connecticut.

Lew Stoner's fluted hollow-built rods had captured every record at the Golden Gate Casting Club—the same place where

Per Brandin would later perfect his Zen of fly-casting. But Stoner was getting on in years by the time of Glenn's first visit. He was cranky and hard of hearing, and to a boy of ten or eleven he was a little intimidating. But Stoner's protégé and partner, Doug Merrick, was a different matter.

While Stoner dressed in bib overalls and suspenders and looked like a dairy farmer, Merrick was a suave-looking man with a pencil mustache on his upper lip that made him look a little like Errol Flynn. Glenn fell under his spell. As he grew older and went to college, studying fisheries biology at Humboldt, he took to hanging around the Winston shop, picking up tips from the master, scrounging castoffs to experiment with rods of his own.

He agreed with what Per Brandin had told me: these West Coast craftsmen—Lew Stoner, Doug Merrick, E. C. Powell—were mavericks, indifferent to the traditions of the East and, in Merrick's case, openly disdainful of them. "Doug would get a Leonard or a Payne," Glenn said, "and he'd shake it around and say, 'Jesus Christ, that's terrible. You'd never want to fish with this—it's a club!' And I had no reference point, so I was going, 'Hmmm, what makes it a club? Feels all right to me.' "

Merrick had an uncanny sense of the innate qualities of the raw material. It started in his fingers, Glenn said. "He would pick up a rod, even before it had a handle on it, and swish it in the air. Then he'd put it down on the bench and hit it with the sandpaper—*here...there.* He knew *exactly* what he was looking for. He even backed up to the point where he would take the individual strips before they were glued up, and he'd say, 'Look, *there*, right there, see?' *Swish, swish*"—Glenn made a quick sandpapering motion—"and then, '*There!* That's it!' And he'd throw it down on the bench and grab the next one. Jesus, this guy could work so fast!"

Although Merrick was a tournament casting champion, the rods that he made were strictly for fishing. "What he did," Glenn continued, "was pretty much to follow what nature had done in growing the bamboo, the way it flexed in the wind. There was no stress at any point, no shearing. With Doug's rods, you could feel it in the hand, you could really get in touch with the material. He just knew bamboo so well."

Inspired in this way by Doug Merrick, Glenn never abandoned the dream of rod making, though it took the better part of twenty years for the dream to materialize. After college he thought about the Peace Corps, but the draft put an end to that. He worked for fifteen years as a biologist, traveling the world, consulting with governments in Argentina and New Zealand, fighting one losing battle after another against big dams and hydropower developments. "There were unbelievable challenges," he said, "tremendous trade-offs to be made. All these unique resources—salmon, steelhead—just went by the wayside." The work politicized him, turning him into a lifelong environmentalist.

In the early seventies he worked briefly as a fly-fishing guide. He lived out of a 1959 Airstream. On the Henry's Fork of the Snake River in Idaho he met an aspiring young East Coast rod maker named Per Brandin. In 1977, when the opportunity arose to buy a share of R. L. Winston, Glenn jumped at it. His new partner, Tom Morgan, had bought Winston in 1973 and decided to relocate the company to somewhere quieter than San Francisco, somewhere that hadn't changed much in the last thirty years and wouldn't change much in the next thirty, somewhere out of the way where there would be mountains and clean air and great fishing. He looked at northern California, at Oregon, but settled eventually on Twin Bridges.

The move to Montana was really the only break with the past, however. Glenn told me that he'd never felt the need to depart much either from Stoner and Merrick's ideas about rod making or from the ethos that the company had embodied, a certain ideal of integrity and tradition. Winston rods, Glenn once told an interviewer, were not only tools for catching fish, but tools around which a human story was woven. I remembered something else he'd written in a book on rod making, in which he'd quoted another Winston craftsman: "We try to use our hands to bring useful beauty to the world. In that process, at least, there is mercy, love, skill and hope." It reminded me a lot of how Hiram Hawes had described the bamboo fly rod, almost a century earlier: "A useful thing, beautifully made."

While the skills and the ideals remained the same, the business arrangements changed somewhat over the years, bit by bit, notch by notch. First, in 1984, Brackett and Morgan sold off the retail side of the business. Then, in 1991, the company was sold to a California screenwriter and venture capitalist named David Ondaatje; Glenn would be free to concentrate on his first love, bamboo, and Tom Morgan went off to start a rod shop of his own. Four years after that, bamboo and graphite filed for an amicable divorce. Graphite production migrated to a newly built plant on South Main; the "boo boys"—Glenn, Jerry Kustich, Jeff Walker, Wayne Maca—stayed where they were. They made Quadrates and six-sided rods, though always with what Glenn called the "Winston action"; Jerry Kustich had a fondness for making five-sided rods; the "boo boys" even made *eight*-sided ones, something that hadn't been seen or tried in almost a century. Pilgrims came from all over the world to visit them; Glenn told me that he wanted them to experience the same sense of wonder he'd felt as a child walking into the old Winston shop in San Francisco. The number of pilgrims who came to see the green graphite rods being made is not recorded.

The "boo boys" made a hundred rods a year, and their shop seemed to keep an emotional as well as a physical distance from the parent company. The arrangement with Winston's new owner had given Glenn a great deal of independence. "I'm left alone here," he said. "This is where I belong, this is where I grew up. And I hope I die at the bench.

"This is an open shop, and there are no secrets," Glenn continued. "I keep that alive and the owner knows it. And he hates it. He wants to shut the door and pull down the shades and make rods and shove them out through a little hole, never have any kind of contact with the public. Doesn't work for me; my policy is, it's all about the people. That's what keeps the spirit of the craft alive."

Listening to this, I couldn't help wondering if Glenn's independence, and the passion that went with it, might not be a double-edged sword. He would say things in print that must have raised the corporate hackles, even though they were said without malice or hostile intent. They were simply based on his well-grounded convictions about seventy-five years of tradition—his own view, if you like, of what the Winston brand stood for.

The rest of the company's operations appeared not to interest Glenn much. Graphite was a substance that seemed to leave him cold. I'd heard him quote approvingly, for example, from an author named Harry Middleton, who once wrote, "I'm allergic to synthetics of any kind, whether they be blended in my underwear or my fly-rod. Dacron, polyester, nylon—all those things are a danger to my health, happiness and peace of mind." How did this kind of talk sit with Winston's new owners, who were, after all, joined at the hip to synthetics? Glenn made no secret of the fact that his raison d'être, the thing that got him out of bed in the morning, was the pursuit of the perfect bamboo fly rod; but he sometimes wondered—out loud and on the record—whether that spirit was compatible with the pursuit of profit.

"Three thousand dollars is a lot of money for a fishing rod," I said.

He groaned. "Oh, that price is so way off. It attracts all the wrong kind of people. The people who end up buying the rods aren't the ones you want."

"So what determines that it's worth three thousand dollars?" I asked.

"Well, *I* didn't," he replied indignantly. "I would never have done that, but somehow it was jammed down my throat and I didn't put up enough of a fight. I just said, 'Oh shit, this isn't going to go well at all.' And it puts an awful big burden on the maker. Because now you've got to make it *look* like a three-thousand-dollar rod. It has to reach a certain standard that it's almost impossible to reach. I've gone from making fishing rods to making pieces of art, and I don't want to go there."

"But it seems to be what the market wants," I said, "and the market is the voice of God."

Glenn was quiet for a moment, then he said softly, "It's a terrible place to go. I hate what's happening, what's driving the craft. But I suppose it's always been there."

It was obviously time to change the subject, because Glenn looked up, gave me an inscrutable smile, and said, "What are you doing on Thursday? Feel like going fishing?"

As I told one of my kids later, being asked to go fishing with Glenn Brackett felt a little like being invited to play tennis with John McEnroe. But I had a couple of days to quell my nerves, and I spent them in the Bitterroot Valley, which seemed to be home to a lot of what Glenn had called "the wrong kind of people."

Cheapskate as always, I found a motel in the small town of Darby that didn't seem to have changed much since the 1950s. Darby is a cluster of motels, gas stations, trailer homes, and souvenir stores that specialize in elk antlers and huckleberry preserves. Darby is not, you might say, the fashionable end of the Bitterroot Valley. But things change as you drive north toward Missoula on Route 93, and fly shops, upscale real estate agents, and espresso bars begin to rub shoulders with the billboards, minimalls, and fast-food logos—the ugly street furniture of any American landscape.

The Bitterroot is—or was, depending on how you look at it—

as gorgeous a valley as you could contrive, the broad river winding its way northward between the sheer granite peaks of the Bitterroot Range to the west and the gentler Sapphire Mountains to the east. The Bitterroot and the Big Blackfoot enter the Clark Fork of the Columbia River only two or three miles apart, but the valleys could not be more different, each reflecting its own distinctive pattern of settlement. The Blackfoot is a patchwork of vast ranches, public lands, and timber company concessions; in sharp contrast, much of the flatland of the Bitterroot Valley was subdivided a hundred years ago into apple orchards, a reflection of the Bitterroot's more benign climate. Twenty-acre lots became the norm, and that encouraged denser development.

The architect of this transformation was the Butte-Anaconda copper baron Marcus Daly, and the centerpiece of his empire in the valley was a twenty-six-hundred-acre spread called the Bitterroot Stock Farm. In 1996 the Stock Farm was bought by Charles Schwab, owner of the famous brokerage house. It was a year of significant acquisitions by Schwab, since he also bought the famous California rod shop that was owned by E. C. Powell's son Walton. That deal degenerated into an ugly lawsuit, in the course of which all the surviving family members were ousted from the Powell company. For Schwab, however, the acquisition of the Powell brand was an added touch of class for someone who already had all the money that money could buy.

In the wake of his purchase of the Stock Farm, Schwab divided up the property into 125 house lots—arranged in a hierarchy of "mountain homes," "ranch houses," and "cabins"—with an eighteen-hole Tom Fazio–designed championship golf course. The handy airstrip at the small town of Hamilton quickly began to fill up with Learjets and Citations. The valley's new "residents" might visit the Stock Farm only a couple of times a year, but no matter: it was only a couple of hours from the West Coast and the fly-fishing was first-class. The Stock Farm was the latest iteration of the old theme of Fly Rod Crosby's "wilderness with all the comforts." From your cabin or mountain home, there were great views of snow peaks and grazing elk herds, even if they were views across the golf links.

To critics of the Californication of the Bitterroot Valley, the Stock Farm was the paradigm for all that had gone wrong; to those who flooded in to take advantage of the valley's beauty, it was the consummate expression of wealth and prestige. It was also a perfect symbol of the pressures that were bearing down on Glenn Brackett's bamboo shop and its three-thousand-dollar rods.

These thoughts were in my head as I turned off Route 93 and left the Bitterroot Valley behind, climbing to the east to cross the Skalkaho Pass, 7,260 feet up in the Sapphire Mountains. Glenn had suggested we meet at noon at the confluence of the East and West Forks of Rock Creek, one of the most celebrated trout streams in Montana, and I had plenty of time on my hands. The air was clear and pure and hung with pollen, and if there was a more beautiful road in the United States, I hadn't driven it. At the Skalkaho Falls, I stopped to stare over the precipice. On the far side of the narrow defile the ponderosa pines seemed to have been painted onto the sheer rock face in defiance of the laws of gravity and perspective.

As the dirt road descended from the pass, I could see the sparkle of the West Fork through the trees to my right, beginning as a rill and then gathering volume to become a swift-flowing stream twenty feet wide. In the distance I could hear a sound of mooing and bellowing, and then around a bend came four real cowboys with real hats on real horses with real rawhide whips, driving the herd before them. The cattle blocked the road in an impenetrable traffic jam, taking turns to poke around between the streamside rocks for patches of grass to nibble on. I was stuck there, but I didn't mind. Through the trees I could see a long amber pool strewn with large boulders. Time was on my side, so I strung up one of my Eustis Edwards rods and whiled away a half hour catching small cutthroat trout and rainbows as wild as the mountains.

The West Fork of Rock Creek had been steep and rugged, so I was surprised when the East Fork revealed itself as a tranquil, spring-fed meadow stream. I followed Glenn's battered camper for two or three miles until he pulled over and stopped at the edge of a field. Under the big sky, the little river snaked its way across a vast carpet of yellow and blue wildflowers, rimmed by the distant snow peaks of the Anaconda-Pintler Wilderness. I began to walk upstream and Glenn headed the other way until he was only a speck in the meadow. As the writer David James Duncan once said, "Disappearing in the opposite direction is the greatest gift a fly-fisher can offer his partner," and Glenn Brackett seemed to me someone who was full of gifts.

When each of us had caught enough trout to fill a kid's dreams, we went back to the camper. Glenn had fixed sandwiches for lunch, and lettuce soup, and there was cold beer, and as we ate I asked him about the photograph of the Dalai Lama I'd seen over his workbench in Twin Bridges. It had just been a simple photograph up there—no shrines or bells, no lotus flowers or dharma wheels.

"Oh, he's definitely one of my heroes," Glenn said. "I've gone to his teachings, been in his presence. You like to fashion your life on that kind of model."

"Is Buddhism something you practice actively?" I asked.

"In kind of loose terms, yeah. I certainly meditate and read his teachings and try to apply them to everyday life. I mean, this is one of the great individuals of our time."

It didn't altogether surprise me when he went on, "Plus it was the outgrowth of working with bamboo, reading some Zen stuff, reading about how bamboo was so influential in certain Asian cultures."

He told me about his first-ever trip to China three or four years earlier, when he'd visited the bamboo-growing areas in Guangdong Province. Bamboo was everything there, he said; when you were born, they cut your umbilical cord with a bamboo knife; when you died, they made your funeral pyre of bamboo. The trip had brought things full circle for him. The cane that he'd seen growing on the hillsides along the Sui River had been bent and shaped and strengthened by Chinese winds, cut and worked by Chinese hands, and now he was assuming his place in the cycle, honoring that spirit as he turned it into something else, a tool for catching fish.

He showed me a book he'd been reading, about a Colombian architect named Simón Vélez whose buildings were made exclusively of bamboo. We looked at some of the photographs together. There were seventeenth-century bamboo fences around the imperial palace in Tokyo, a bamboo-paneled yurt in Turkmenistan, a rural clinic of woven bamboo in Vietnam. Market traders in Hong Kong carried a batch of piglets in a woven bamboo sling. Children in a field near Kathmandu swung ecstatically from ropes strung from a bamboo frame twenty feet high.

"I was walking through the San Francisco airport recently," Glenn said, "going from my gate to the BART station, and suddenly there's a wall of bamboo in front of me, forty, sixty feet tall. It's absolutely remarkable, I feel right at home. So I go through there, I say my little piece, I rub the culm, and here's the living plant! These things really add up."

We agreed that things like that had a way of happening in San Francisco.

"Oh yeah," he laughed, "you can't help but be influenced by any number of things living there. You know, driving down to the Golden Gate Casting Club and seeing everyone there doing their tai chi. And then stepping off the airplane, first time in China, and right there next to the runway, exactly the same thing I'd been seeing at the Golden Gate. It's an awareness thing, constantly building awareness, staying sharp, always staying alert to what is there in front of you and what you're meant to learn from it."

But our talk of China took a darker turn, and it brought us back to what Glenn had said two days earlier about the price of maintaining his uneasy independence from Winston's corporate owners. A Winston bamboo rod cost $3,000, which he'd said attracted "all the wrong kind of people." But even Winston's green graphite rods were priced in the high hundreds, and that put them out of reach of the entry-level fly fisher. With tens of thousands of neophytes flooding into the sport every year, the company had decided to enter the brutally competitive lower end of the market, and like so many other American corporations, it had decided to outsource the work to China. The tentacles of globalization had reached Twin Bridges.

Winston's employees had taken the move as a betrayal of that seventy-fifth-anniversary slogan—"uncompromising." They had written an open letter that said:

> *This outsourcing goes against everything that R. L. Winston stands for. We have been building rods in the United States for 75 years, and we plan to keep building them for the life of the company in the United States... to send them to a country that has such human rights violations is inconceivable.... This outsourcing of America must stop. Large corporations and small companies all over the United States have been bleeding our country dry with this practice.*

Glenn had echoed these feelings in a series of interviews with the local papers. He told them that "the moral integrity of the company is very much in question now." He said he regretted selling Winston to an absentee owner living in Malibu. "If I had to resell the business again, I would not have sold it to a person who wouldn't live here with the business. That was my biggest mistake." These were tough, perhaps irrevocable things to say.

"I'd have had a hard time dealing with the kind of anger you must have felt," I said.

He thought about this, then said, "The Dalai Lama was asked once if he ever got angry. And he said, *'Every day.'* And that says it all. I get angry with bad work sometimes, with the kids, the influence of management and ownership, but you always come back to some kind of a base—this is what you're here for. There are constant challenges; you can't minimize them. You've got to deal with them, get things straightened out so you can say, this makes sense. And Per shares a lot of that, he practices it, and we compare notes."

The remedy, he said, lay in the rituals of the craft, rituals that couldn't easily be explained or intellectualized. There was a circular flow to the process of making a bamboo rod, a kind of feedback loop. You needed intense focus and discipline to perform the task, and performing the task brought you intense focus and discipline.

"It becomes a mantra," Glenn explained. "It clears your senses. There's something about that one-two-three-four-five-six-seven-eight. And I walk away every day saying, yes, today was something different, something learned. Hands, eyes. Hands, eyes. Put out a product. Feel good about what you do. And think, *This too will pass.*"

Later, in the slanting light of the late afternoon, we fished Rock Creek itself. The trout were much bigger than they'd been in the upper forks—easy enough to hook but hard to land in the high, fast water. They'd streak away into the heavy currents downstream and keep running until there was a faint snap and you realized you were holding a line without a fish on it.

Weary from wading, I sat on the bank to wait for Glenn. He came into view at last around a bend, and I realized that he was going to cross the river by way of a deep, shelving run of fast water with a bottom of loose cobble and rocks the size of basketballs. Glenn is a small man, well into his sixties, with an elfin demeanor that makes him appear even smaller, and I grew more and more nervous as I watched him wade deeper and deeper until the powerful current was thrumming against his rib cage. He had no wading staff, only his own sense of balance. He held his bamboo rod high above his head. His face wore an expression of beatific calm.

Without thinking what I was doing, I lay down flat on the riverbank and stretched my fingers out to help him, feeling absurdly like Cary Grant reaching out for Eva Marie Saint on the face of Mount Rushmore in the climactic scene of Hitchcock's *North by Northwest.* I imagined being the one to call 911 and break the news that Master Glenn, the bamboo guru, had been swept away in the currents of Rock Creek. But Glenn just smiled up at me, eyes beaming behind his glasses, and said, "Don't worry. I've done this a million times."

With every rod maker I'd met, I'd asked the same question: how does this man keep body and soul together? With Glenn Brackett, I found myself asking the same question, although in this case it had other layers of meaning.

CHAPTER 13

Back to the Future

A few weeks after I got home from Montana, a letter arrived. At first I didn't recognize the tiny, precise handwriting, but then I saw the Butte return address. Glenn Brackett was writing to say that he was just back from a fishing trip to what he called "the great North fjord lands." But there was a definite melancholy undertow to the message. "I'm having a hard time getting back to the ole rod bench," he said. And he ended, "Well, I must face humility again." I could almost hear the sigh.

Part of me waited for the other shoe to drop, and drop it did—within a month. As with most other news these days, it was preceded by a chatter of static on the Internet. Glenn Brackett had resigned after thirty years; the apostolic succession was broken; the R. L. Winston Company was planning to outsource its entire bamboo rod operation to China. As the smoke of battle cleared, the nub of the problem came into focus: Glenn had been asked to identify a successor, someone he would groom to replace him when the time came eventually to retire. Glenn had found such a person, but Winston had rejected his choice and Glenn had felt this left him with no option but to quit. He'd wanted to turn a hundred at his bench; he'd had every intention of dying at his bench. Now none of that was going to happen.

After a couple of uncomfortable days of rumors and speculation, Winston issued a statement saying that "Glenn Brackett, who manages our bamboo rod building area, [has] notified us that he will be leaving the company." There followed a lot of happy talk about tradition and excellence and commitment, and promises that Winston would be "continuing our goal of building the finest bamboo fly rods in the world." To accomplish this, two guys from the graphite factory would be taking over the bamboo shop. They had ninety days to learn a craft that Glenn Brackett was still learning after more than thirty years.

The Winston press release read as if it had been vetted to within an inch of its life by the company's lawyers and PR advisers. I called Winston to see if I could talk to the company's owner, David Ondaatje, or its CEO, Mike "Woody" Woodard. Some chance. That left me in the familiar reporter's limbo, where all you can really say is "Winston's management declined repeated requests for further comment," and leave your readers, rightly or wrongly, to draw their own conclusions.

A few days later, I ran into Per Brandin in Massachusetts. "It's all so reminiscent of what happened at Leonard," he said.

At first I thought he meant the breakup of Leonard's original supergroup in 1890, when Eustis Edwards, Fred Thomas, and Loman Hawes had left to make the Kosmic rod, no longer able to tolerate the bottom-line pressures of corporate ownership. But Per was talking about the final ignominious decline of the late 1970s and early eighties, the period after Jim Frank had ended his stint in the Leonard shop. It was one thing for Hiram Leonard to have been bought out by the Mills family, who had specialized, after all, in outdoor recreation. But in 1976 Leonard was acquired by S. C. Johnson & Son, maker of Johnson Wax, a corporation whose products were mainly to be found under the kitchen sink. To run the operation, Leonard's new owners installed what the rod dealer Len Codella once described to me as "a bunch of javelin-throwing jackasses with MBAs," people who thought you could make a fly rod the same way you made a furniture polish.

After a few years of hemorrhaging money and several more changes of ownership, Leonard had fallen apart. Seized for nonpayment of taxes, the contents of the celebrated rod shop were auctioned off in the parking lot. Lot 14, which included one of the Leonard bevelers and 750 culms of Tonkin cane, went for $300.

Going back to the events at Winston, Per said, "Bamboo rod

making just isn't conducive to today's world of bean counters and corporate acquisition. It requires a level of personal commitment that comes very naturally to people who have spent a long time conceiving and executing the rods out of their own passion and imagination. But it's simply not a commodity that can be bought."

I nodded, agreeing with every word and thinking, well, I guess that's how my little Montana parable ends. Stamp it, seal it, wrap it up with an angry red bow. But then I stopped and thought about it some more, and, well . . . it would be going too far to say that I had second thoughts, but I had *more* thoughts. It wasn't that I had any doubts about where my core sympathies lay—Glenn Brackett embodied everything that I'd found seductive about the craft. But at the same time I was reluctant to see my Montana parable as a simple morality play, a black-and-white tale of evil triumphing over good.

I was sorry that the Winston execs didn't want to talk, because I'd been genuinely curious to hear what they might have to say about the economics of making bamboo fly rods in the twenty-first-century economy. The bean counters might not be richly endowed with the higher human qualities, yet I couldn't help but feel a certain compassion for them for being trapped, as so many Americans are these days, in the kind of existence where you couldn't even use the English language to express your thoughts without worrying about lawyers and liability and bad publicity. I had no reason to believe that these people beat their wives or kicked their dogs or even voted Republican. There was no evidence to suggest that they were the kind who wanted to clear-cut the ponderosa forests or build a cyanide heap-leach mine on the nearest trout stream. If you wanted to find examples of blind corporate villainy in Montana, a small fly rod factory in Twin Bridges probably wasn't the first place you'd look. The Anaconda smelter stack was right there on your doorstep, telling you everything you needed to know.

Rather, the point was that the imperatives of making a profit and the imperatives of building the perfect bamboo fly rod had never had very much to do with each other. The market is a cold force, value-free; it allows no room for sentiment. Leonard and Mills; Edwards and Winchester; Edwards and Bristol; Leonard and Johnson Wax. It was a story with many reiterations. What was surprising was not that Glenn Brackett and Winston had parted ways, but that the quality of Glenn's craft and the power of his sense of tradition had held things together for so long.

Would the bean counters find another individual with comparable gifts, someone capable of building a three-thousand-dollar fly rod in Twin Bridges, Montana? Perhaps, though I doubted it. And if Winston decided one day to outsource the work to China and make five-hundred-dollar rods? Surely that was heresy, and I rebelled against the idea as viscerally as anyone. The entire mystique of the bamboo fly rod was based on an ideal of perfectionism that was bound up with 150 years of American history. But might the tree of tradition grow a new branch? A hundred years ago, after all, no one would have predicted that the craft would migrate from Maine and the Catskills to the wild frontier of the American West. The purist might say that no Chinese craftsman could ever bring things full circle, because he doesn't have the trout. But then again, we don't have the cane.

I couldn't help thinking back to the encounter I'd had with the Taiwanese travel agent in the backyard of Bill Edwards's old rod shop in Mount Carmel, Connecticut. He'd looked at the Quadrate rod I had in the trunk of my car, learned how much it was worth, discovered that the raw material grew in China, and then let his eyes do the math. *Maybe we could export to United States, make a great business.*

By now I'd heard of one or two people who had begun to import modestly priced fly rods from Chinese workshops. Those who'd tried them out told me that the American craftsman had nothing to worry about; the Chinese-made rods were somewhere between a poor imitation and a bad joke. But I wanted to find out more.

I tracked down one of these importers in Westchester County, New York. His name was Allan Liu, and oddly enough, he had known Per Brandin back in the days when Per was taking his first baby steps into the world of bamboo. I was taken aback by the voice that answered the phone at the Liu residence. Despite the name, and despite the fact that his father had been the chief physician for the Bank of China, Allan Liu sounded more like Tony Soprano. I asked him to tell me more about his rods. There were three tapers so far, he told me, all based on the designs of Jim Payne. "There was no greater rod maker than Jim Payne," he said.

The first model in the new line, as I heard it, was called the See Payne.

"*S-e-e Payne?*" I said, spelling it out.

"Naah," Liu said, "*C.* Pain. Letter *C. P-a-i-n.* The *C* is for my grandson Christopher. The 'Pain' is 'cause he's a major pain." He chortled.

"So where are the rods made?" I asked.

"Fujian Province. A guy called Zhu Youxin makes 'em."

"How often do you go there?"

"*Go there?*" he exclaimed. "I've no intention of going there. Don't like to fly—I've never even spoken to them, in fact. Fujian? Never even bothered to look it up on the map."

I was perplexed. "So how do you do quality control?"

"QuickTime video," he said. "Do the whole thing over the Web."

American craftsmen, it seemed, had little to fear from C. Pain rods.

And yet . . . These days even the most die-hard patriot would have to acknowledge that here and there—in Austria and Argentina, in England and Norway, to name just a few places—there were individual craftsmen turning Tonkin cane into exquisite fly rods. If there, then why not in Asia? The fact that C. Pain rods were not going to turn the bamboo world on its head wasn't necessarily the point; after all, for years people had thought Japanese radios were a joke, too. I'd already seen one or two bamboo rods that Japanese craftsmen were beginning to bring to the American shows. These weren't the postwar clunkers from the Tokyo PX, like the red-lacquered monstrosity with which I'd started my own journey into the world of bamboo, but delicately crafted rods that were made not only from Tonkin cane but from other species of bamboo that were native to Japan. To botanists they were *Sasa borealis v. purpurascens, Pseudosasa japonica, Phyllostachys aurea.* Japanese rod makers called them *koyachiku, yatake, hoteichiku.*

Ironically, Glenn Brackett himself had offered a glimpse of this possible future as we'd sat together in that luminous meadow by the East Fork of Rock Creek. We'd been talking about Winston outsourcing its low-end graphite rods to China and I'd asked Glenn, "Why not bamboo?"

"Yeah," Glenn said, "I've struggled with that"—a comment that was probably more heartfelt than I'd realized at the time. "And they'll do a damn good job, they'll get it down real fast, like the Japanese. Craftsmanship? They've got it; they *know.* And this is home ground for them—they're growing the stuff. When I was in China I lived with a family, and the guy was making bamboo rods, six-strip, and I helped him out a little. He was a grower, but he wanted to take it the other way. Just like I'd like to be a grower! And why not? I mean, the world's turning into that kind of place."

Bamboo fanatics talk about Brackett-era or Merrick-era Winston rods. Was it possible to imagine a time when some comparable Chinese craftsman might emerge? Would the collectors talk one day about Winston rods from the Wang Xiaofeng era or the Li Baoxiang era? Again, I doubted it. But that didn't mean there wouldn't be a market for decently executed work with which no American craftsman could compete economically. From talking to musicians, I knew that this was exactly what had happened in the last decade with Chinese-made violins. There would never be a Chinese Leonard or a Chinese Stradivarius, and the top-of-the-line luthiers might still work out of small artisan shops in Europe or the United States. But if you were a competent high school violinist looking for a serviceable, well-made instrument for five hundred bucks, chances are it was coming out of a Chinese workshop—even if the name on the label was Andrew Schroetter, Alfredo Medici, or Johannes Köhr. As Glenn had said, the world was turning into that kind of place.

After the events at Winston, somebody asked me—someone who knew much more about the history of fly-fishing than I ever would—if I thought this was the beginning of the end of the bamboo rod making craft, or the end of the end. Neither, I said. While the apostolic succession at Winston might have been broken, I had little doubt that Glenn Brackett would go on building wonderful bamboo fly rods for as long as his brain and his hands remained connected. And there would be other apostolic successions for as long as there was the passion to keep the craft alive. Inevitably that made me think again, as I often did, of Sam Carlson.

I'd last seen Sam at one of the Holiday Inn shows in Massachusetts. He was wearing a baseball cap with a Pfizer logo, a Fair Isle cardigan zippered up the front, and a brown-and-yellow plaid shirt that didn't begin to match. At his neck was a Western bolo tie with an incised motif that appeared to be of a llama. Sam's wife, Verna, was standing quietly by his side, not saying anything, and she shook my hand with the same faint, inscrutable smile I remembered from our earlier meeting.

I became aware of a buzz of whispers in the room. One or two of the high rollers were gawking at the old man in the baseball cap, and I heard one of them say, "Is that really Sam Carlson over there? *The* Sam Carlson?" You almost expected them to usher him into the greenroom, like a movie star. The regulars, the fellow rod makers and professional collectors, just glanced up and said, "Hey, look, there's Sam."

We looked at some fly rods together, which for me was like a free history lesson. There were three Winstons, two of them from the San Francisco period and one from Twin Bridges. There were five Paynes, and more than a dozen Leonards from various times in the company's history. There were a couple of handsome rods by Fred Thomas, a rare one by E. C. Powell, and a sweet eight-footer by Gene Edwards. There were also three rods from Sam's own hand. Two of them were Quadrates in short lengths, and I knew they would be fetching big money, as much as $5,000 each, later in the day. Dana Gray had spent years cajoling Sam to raise the prices on his new rods, stressing the fancy amounts collectors were paying for them on the secondary market. In the end Sam had agreed, grudgingly, to break the two-thousand-dollar barrier, though he found it unfathomable that anyone would pay that much for a fishing stick.

Now he picked up the third of his rods that were on display, a six-sided rod signed "Sam Carlson" in white ink, and frowned with displeasure.

"That isn't even one of mine," he growled. "That's from when I was first working with Gene, just after the war. It's made from some old Bristol sticks that were lying around. It's a terrible rod. I didn't even put the wraps on it. All I did was write my name on it in ink, just fooling around, practicing my signature." He shook his head. "These things come back to haunt you, I guess."

"Even so," I said, "I'll bet someone in there is going to shell out a couple of grand for it. All that money for one of your rods, and you'll never see a penny of it."

It was a stupid, tactless remark, and I wanted to bite my tongue. Instead I tried to make up for my blunder with a lame joke. I said, "Maybe you should just sign your name on a piece of paper and sell it for a couple thousand bucks."

Verna cracked a smile.

"You know," I said to Sam, "after the last time we talked, I thought of a million things I still wanted to ask you. Can I come up to the shop again sometime?"

He smiled warmly and said, "Sure, only it would have to be a Monday or a Tuesday. I'm still working three days a week for a company up in Milford."

The man was eighty-seven years old and still working three days a week.

I found a free Monday on my calendar and called Sam again about a week ahead of time to make sure the date still worked for him.

He hesitated. "Why don't you check back with me at the weekend? I've had a couple of doctor's appointments; haven't been feeling too good."

Always vigorous, Sam said he was puzzled by recent bouts of lethargy and exhaustion. The doctors were running tests, giving him shots. Anemia, they thought.

But Sam didn't make it to the weekend. It wasn't anemia, the doctors finally told him, but advanced leukemia. He was dead within days, hanging on just long enough to tell Dana Gray that the time had come for the apostolic succession.

When they buried Sam, the church was filled with Swedish choral singers. After the music was over, the Lutheran pastor asked if anyone would like to say a few words. There were a lot of taciturn Swedes in the pews, so Per Brandin stood up and talked about Sam, about how he'd been one of the truly great bamboo fly rod makers. The minister looked at him and said, "You know, I'd heard that. But to us he was always a singer."

I drove up to New Hampshire later that summer to pay my respects to Verna Carlson. Dana was there, cleaning out Sam's shop.

"I've got to put some mousetraps down in there," Dana said to

Verna. "I had one trap down there that was sprung, but nothing in it."

Verna pursed her lips and said, "These mice are getting real intelligent."

Dana turned to me. "We had a rod, Sam and I were working on it, one of the new eight-footers I think it was, and didn't the mouse take a few bites out of the cork grip?"

Verna said, "They're very intelligent animals."

Later Dana and I crossed the yard to the rod shop. Dana looked around at the disorder and the dust and scratched his head.

After a moment he said, "I fully expected Sam to be working here in the shop until he was well into his nineties. He was just that kind of guy, so sharp, so able physically. His mind, his eyes, he could still pick up the most minute details, things you wouldn't even notice."

He looked around some more and sighed. "There's so much stuff in here that should be tossed out. Sam didn't like to throw anything away. I mean, there's vacuum cleaners and old clothing irons and stuff that he was eventually going to fix one day, which was really not a very good idea, I guess is the best way to say it. Maybe from growing up in the Depression; that probably has a lot to do with it."

"Same thing with my father-in-law," I said. "Can't see a garage sale without buying something. He's got twenty-eight coffeemakers in the garage that don't work."

"Look at all this old machinery," Dana said, waving a hand at Bill Edwards's sixty-year-old beveler. "That Bridgeport over there is probably from the fifties. That Atlas lathe came from Gene Edwards. So did that wood lathe. This one's from Thomas. That milling machine is a dinosaur. I mean, nowadays you could buy a machine like that for fifteen hundred bucks. They're not that expensive. I even saw one in the *PennySaver*, a want ad, free if you could get it out of somebody's basement.

"Well, be that as it may," he went on, "I'm hoping to continue with the Carlson name. Obviously it won't be 'Sam Carlson, Maker,' but I'll try and set up a shop that I can put everything in. It's something that Sam wanted, and if he's looking down from somewhere I think he'd be happy to know that I'll try and carry on in his tradition."

There was one part of Sam's legacy that went elsewhere, however. Back in the late fifties, in misbegotten fashion, Sam had bought the remains of the old F. E. Thomas company, the grand old name that was synonymous with the fly-fishing traditions and the classic sporting camps of the Maine woods. But as the years went on and Sam's independent reputation grew, the Thomas name steadily faded from memory.

It wasn't alone in this regard. Despite the renaissance of the craft since the 1970s, all of the grand old names were defunct. Edwards and Hawes were long gone. Thomas, Payne, and Leonard existed only on paper, in the form of records of trademarks and patents tucked away in forgotten corners of some lawyer's filing cabinet. But in the 1990s, in what I now thought of as the post–Brad Pitt era, there was talk of revival. Part of it was a desire to keep the flame alive; part of it was another chapter in the story of commercial branding. There were even rumors that the current owners of the Leonard name were planning to dust it off and market a new generation of Leonard rods through Kmart.

To head off that kind of affront, a collector in Houston bought what remained of Leonard and contracted with a couple of craftsmen in the Northeast to build a few rods a year. An aspiring rod maker in the fashionable little resort town of Sisters, Oregon, acquired the rights to use the Payne name. A lot of people sniffed and said these weren't real Leonards or Paynes, which of course was true. But at the same time there was a certain grudging respect for anyone who wanted to keep the old names from being forgotten.

At around the same time Sam Carlson found himself fending off people who were interested in acquiring the Thomas name. On one occasion, a group of Japanese investors approached him and offered him a lot of money for a three-year lease. They proposed to make bamboo fly rods in Japan and then affix the name of Thomas to them. Sam just grunted and said the F. E. Thomas Rod Company wasn't supposed to end up in Japan.

But then a nervous young man named Steve Campbell came calling. He asked Sam if he'd had any thoughts of selling. Verna Carlson answered first. She said, "Yeah, take it all, stick it in a U-Haul and get it out of here."

Sam was intrigued, because the young man said that he was from Brewer, Maine, and although he hoped to make a few rods, his main goal was to take Fred Thomas home where he belonged. Sam agreed to the sale, liking the idea of things coming full circle.

I met Steve Campbell a couple of times on my trips to Maine. His bona fides really did seem impeccable. He gave me a tour of the Penobscot Salmon Club, where he was an active member— despite the fact that dams and pollution had all but wiped out the salmon. He told me of his dream of one day opening a museum that would be dedicated to Maine's fly-fishing tradition. He showed me where he wanted to locate it, right in the heart of Bangor, just steps away from where Hiram Leonard had built his first bamboo rods in the 1870s. He said he was turning out a handful of rods in his spare time, no more than a dozen each year. He knew he could be charging a lot more for them, but he was wary of any accusation that he was trying to cash in on a famous name. Look at Indian Motorcycles, he said. The company had been defunct since the fifties, but now someone had bought the rights to the name and was selling the new machines for premium prices, exploiting the cachet of the brand.

Sam had been dead only a few weeks when Steve and I met for the first time. "You know," he said wistfully, "Sam never came to Maine in his life. Not once. Never even came here when he bought the Thomas business in 1958. Ray Gambordella took care of that side of things. Never came here after he moved from Connecticut to New Hampshire, even though it's so close. But we'd finally persuaded him and Verna to visit. He called me up to say they had no intention of imposing on me, even though I wanted them to stay at the house. He said no, they'd just find a motel somewhere. He said the thing he really wanted to do was to eat lobsters. Then he called again one day, out of the blue. All he said was, 'You know, I've been thinking about it, and I think I want to have some clam chowder, too.' "

Other things, too, had come full circle, in the person of Jim Frank. After his four years with Leonard, Jim bailed out as soon as Johnson Wax entered the picture and returned to his peripatetic lifestyle. He moved back to the Pacific Northwest. By a chance deal, through an ad in a magazine, he acquired Eustis Edwards's old beveler, which had been lying unused for many years. The Leonard beveler had done its best to eat Jim's fingers; now the Edwards version, too, threatened to compromise his sanity.

"That machine was a nightmare," he said. "I had all sorts of copper foil and shims and everything else, trying to get it to operate consistently. I had it for almost a year and a half, but most of that time was just trying to get it to run properly."

Whenever a strip came out right, Jim would set it aside for later use, and over the next few years he managed to make about two hundred rods under his own name. Jim Frank rods went to some notable clients: Secretary of State Cyrus Vance bought one; so did William Ruckelshaus, the first administrator of the Environmental Protection Agency. "But most of them," he said, "ended up in the hands of friends of mine, working-class fisher-men who paid me thirty bucks a week until it was paid off."

After a few years of this, Jim's restlessness grew, in inverse pro-portion to the size of his bank account. The Edwards beveler found its way to a new home with a rod maker in Pennsylvania, from whence it disappeared into the mists of history, and Jim took to the road. Missoula, Montana; Telluride, Colorado; Colorado Springs. He was as much the stormy petrel as Eustis Edwards had ever been. His marriage fell apart.

"I was never home hardly," he said. "Lived in a trailer, all over Kansas, eastern Colorado, Idaho, working on big commercial building projects. Lived in Dodge City. I forget all the school dis-tricts. I mean, there was about as much craft in what I was doing as a sledgehammer and a cold chisel. Welding, shuffling paper."

But once Jim had put his son through architecture school at the University of Oregon, he wended his way back to the East Coast, back to the craft that had always been lurking at the edges of his life.

He went on, "I always wanted to get back to it. But I had some criteria. Like I was not going to put myself in a Mills situation. I wasn't going to do this for Johnson Wax. I wasn't going to have somebody be my patron. Investors? Yeah, I'm real interested in in-vestors. *Control* for investors? No. You either have faith in what we do, or . . . *next case!*"

The "we" in this case was a group of three men who had been around the block more times than any of them cared to remember. Jim brought his Leonard background; his friend Dave Decker had worked at different times with Leonard and Payne; the third part-ner, Hal Bacon, had owned what was left of the Payne company for a few years in the late seventies and early eighties. For a while he even owned the original beveling machine that Loman Hawes had designed for Leonard in 1878. After that he acquired another beveler that had been made by George Halstead, a metalworker of genius who had made parts for Payne and a small number of well-regarded rods of his own. Hal Bacon was still making Payne clones as well as a few rods on contract for the new Leonard company in Texas. The lineage got very complicated, in other words, but the important thing was that it was still there.

It was like tracing the line of Adam in the book of Genesis. Hiram Leonard, the patriarch, had begotten Edwards and Thomas and Hawes and Payne. All four had passed the torch to their sons. Gene and Bill Edwards, and then Leon Thomas, had in turn passed their legacy to Sam Carlson, and Sam had passed it on to Dana Gray. Steve Campbell had taken F. E. Thomas back home to Maine. Now Jim Frank and his partners were gathering together the dispersed threads that ran through Leonard and Edwards and Hawes and Payne.

Keeping the lineage intact had become an obsession with Jim Frank. And by staying faithful to the old Maine-Catskills masters he meant fidelity not just to the *spirit* of their work, but to every last perfectionist detail of its execution—something that Jim was singularly equipped to do.

He reached for some papers on a shelf and selected a sheet to show me. "These are E.W.'s patterns," he said—meaning Eustis William Edwards, the man who had inspired my own personal journey into this arcane and beautiful subculture. There were penciled lines, plotted in graph fashion, with tiny numbers expressed in thousandths of an inch, and the taper of the rod stipulated in one-inch increments. Jim said, "When I worked at the repair bench, I had any number of Paynes and Thomases and Edwardses, took them all apart to strips of triangle. You look on the Internet and everybody's got this bloody taper and that taper, but they're all measured at five-inch intervals. The complexity is lost in the translation."

"Now, look at this." He fetched an exquisite Eustis Edwards rod, a Deluxe model from the Mount Carmel period. "How old's

BACK TO THE FUTURE | 221

this one? Seventy-six years. Hide glue. All in one piece. See, they last! They're not fragile. That's total mythos. People keep trying to tell you how rarified this thing is. They push their rods up on a pedestal." He parodied a grave expression and his voice dripped with sarcasm. " '*I'm the great rod maker and these are my fabulous rods.*' It's basically about ego. And to me it all gets a little fey. Pretty soon, everybody's scared to pick 'em up! You know, they're not made of blown glass!"

Now he took another rod from the bench. "Here, let's go outside."

It was a rod he'd made precisely to Eustis Edwards's pattern. I studied the three sections admiringly, and now he transferred some of his scorn to me.

"Oh, come on, for Christ's sake," he said impatiently, as if I were handling the crown jewels. "Remember what I just said about blown glass? Put it together! People do this to me all the time. Why wasn't that the first thing you did, put it together?"

"A little nervous, I guess . . ."

"OK, OK, I understand. But here's the deal. Why did I make it? What's the point of having a rod in your hand if you don't bend it, feel it, learn from it? Here's my thing about fly rods. They're built to be bent. Fished, not fondled."

So I put it together, attached the reel, strung the fly line through the guides, made a few tentative casts. Incredible.

But Jim, amused now, said, "No, no. Stop working so hard. Let the rod do it for you!"

I relaxed. Forty, fifty feet of line streaked out, arrow-straight, effortless, utterly forgiving of my mediocre skills. It was close to an out-of-body experience.

I said, "Wow!" and Jim Frank grinned. Now he was happy.

Back inside, he said, "Fourteen ninety-five. I won't charge two thousand dollars for a fly rod. It's nuts. There's a limit. You price yourself out of the marketplace, because who's going to buy it? A collector. And where does it go? In the closet. On his wall, like antlers. *But it's got a job!* What it is is a very sophisticated crowbar. So start using it, put it to work."

He went on, "I want us to be selling these things like you sell cars. Why? Because I want the money to come in so we can hire kids and teach 'em. The mission of this company is to teach the Catskill style of making fly rods."

The craft was now well into its fifth generation, and Jim was already looking to recruit the sixth.

"But where are you going to find your apprentices?" I asked. "In this day and age, in this economy?"

He gave another of his wolfish grins, looking more than ever like the actor Woody Harrelson. "Damn, have *you* got any ideas? Sure, it's always the biggest question. But I showed up at Leonard. Did Leonard come looking for me? See, I think it's like that. People come, a certain number of them are good, and they stay, and you fish through the pile until you find a group of people who really fall in love with it. Once the word gets out, someone's going to come along and say, 'Hey, man, I really want to know how you do this stuff.' Because they're out there. And I hope some of them will be higher-minded people who'll see it for what it is. The chain. The chain of knowledge."

Jim was spinning elaborate dreams now. There would be half a dozen people in the rod shop. It would make three hundred rods a year. It would be an old-style production company like Leonard, like Thomas, like the team Eustis Edwards had finally put together in the last years of his life. I couldn't begin to fathom how the economics of this would work, whether a market of that size existed, where the higher-minded apprentices would come from. But as Jim spun out his visions to me that afternoon, those questions seemed earthbound and mean-spirited. What counted was his capacity to dream. What counted was the chain.

And what would the company be called?

"Well, it was just an idea that popped into my head one day when Dave Decker and I were talking on the phone. Hal went out and found this thing and saved it. Here, I'll show you."

He reached into a drawer and placed a small, hard object in my hand. It was an old metal rolling die stamp from the 1890s, and it said, "The Kosmic Rod."

"All the people came from Leonard," Jim said. "And that's what Dave and I come from: Leonard. We cooked this thing up because we're the same as them, we're from the same root. We're new, it's a different century, folks, but our core is that. Thomas, Edwards, and Payne. Those were *astounding* fly rods."

Thomas, Edwards, and Payne. And now Bacon, Decker, and Frank. They'd just completed the first prototype, and Jim showed it to me. On the butt cap, the roll stamp had incised those three words, "The Kosmic Rod." And the serial number: *001*. This time I put the sections together without being asked.

CHAPTER 14

Making Nine Mistakes

Fall. Foliage and catalogs. Half the forests in the United States were turning shades of orange and cranberry and gold, and the other half, it seemed, had been chopped down, pulped, and turned into the junk that was jammed into my mailbox every day. Fall and winter offerings from fly shops, craft suppliers, and rod dealers, from L. L. Bean and Orvis and Abercrombie & Fitch.

In the L. L. Bean catalog, men who looked like Richard Gere were going skiing with women who looked like Michelle Pfeiffer, while Denzel Washington look-alikes were joining them for *après-ski*.

A&F's days as a stuffy gentlemen's outfitter next door to Grand Central Station were long gone. Since its rebirth from bankruptcy in the late eighties, the company had concentrated on upscale teen apparel, with less and less emphasis on how much clothing the teens were actually wearing—just as long as they carried the A&F logo. After howls of protest from religious conservatives, the Abercrombie catalog had curbed some of its earlier excesses; there might not be any bamboo fly rods in there these days, but at least they'd put some clothes on their teenage models and dropped the articles about whether it was a good idea to have oral sex in movie theaters.

Orvis at least still offered a page or two of bamboo: "We built our first rod when Lincoln was just a Whig," the catalog boasted. "In the overwhelming techno-wilderness of the early twenty-first century, the Orvis bamboo rod represents a lasting bastion of workbench craftsmanship." True enough, perhaps, but you had to struggle a bit to find the fly rods among the other lifestyle signifiers—the snowshoe sconces, the three-hundred-dollar dog beds, and the twenty-three-hundred-dollar St. James tufted leather chairs. ("Just like those found in London's private clubs, this tufted leather chair is oversized with a specially designed seat cushion for ultimate comfort, covered in distressed leather for an already broken-in look and feel. . . . The only thing missing is the single malt and cigars.")

The fly-fishing catalogs weren't much of an improvement. They tended to confirm the worst fear that the conservationist Aldo Leopold had expressed in the 1940s, that our love of the outdoors was fast being overwhelmed by an addiction to gadgets. Anglers could now clank their way to the river weighted down with a dizzying assortment of guy things: digital thermometers, telescopic wading staffs, streamside entomology kits, head-mounted Ion lights, and a collection of pliers, clamps, clippers, scissors, forceps, and hemostats that made you look like a surgeon heading for the operating theater.

Many of the catalogs also advertised high-priced remedies for the cold-weather blahs. With no apparent irony, they delivered the message that no corner of the "wilderness" was beyond the reach of those with means. For $4,500 (plus airfare), I could enjoy five days in an exclusive architect-designed lodge in deepest Chilean Patagonia, with fine wines and gourmet dining and a side trip to the Torres del Paine. For a little more, a refurbished Soviet military helicopter would whisk me to the wilds of Kamchatka, where I could be one of the first humans to present a fly to gargantuan salmon and sea-run rainbow trout.

I opted instead for Maine.

Like many people who go to the Maine woods in the fall, I was drawn by the prospect of landlocked salmon, which I hoped would be making their fall spawning run up the rivers that ran into, or emerged from, Moosehead Lake. To get there, I took the modern Route 15 from Bangor to Greenville, following the old stagecoach road on which Thoreau had encountered Hiram Leonard in 1857.

Moosehead Lake is still a place of singular beauty. From the crest of Indian Hill, on a clear fall day, you can cup your hands around your eyes to screen out the motel and the gas station and the general store and see the lake much as Thoreau must have, its chain of green, forested islands stretching away across the blue water as far as the horizon. In Greenville itself, you can stock up with supplies at the Blushing Moose, or relax over a drink at the Moose Breath Bar or the Stress-Free Moose Pub. There's a large statue of a moose by the railroad depot. Nearby, a flotilla of sea-planes bobs at anchor on Moosehead Lake, ready to take you on thirty-minute moose-watching flights. Greenville is what you might call a thematic town.

My destination, a camp on First West Branch Pond, was still an hour away. I'd chosen it because it was one of the oldest Maine sporting camps still in existence, its physical structure little changed since it was built in 1889. The road to the camp hugged the east side of Moosehead Lake until a dirt logging road branched off to the right, along the south shore of Roach Pond. A sign at the intersection told me I was entering land owned by the Plum Creek Timber Company. It was the first intimation that this remote and apparently timeless Maine landscape might be on the brink of transformation.

The name rang a bell, and then I placed it. Plum Creek was the Seattle-based corporation that had achieved notoriety for clear-cutting the valley of Norman Maclean's Big Blackfoot in Montana. Notwithstanding the "Timber Company" part of its name, Plum Creek was structured as a real estate investment trust, and its focus was increasingly on the recreational development of the forestlands it owned. Its largest holdings, more than a million acres, were in Montana, and until 1998 hardly anyone in Maine had even heard of Plum Creek. But then it had bought up 905,000 acres of forest—half of them in the vicinity of Moosehead Lake— that had formerly belonged to Sappi, a giant South African paper and pulp company.

Since Thoreau's time, development in Maine's vast unorganized territories had always occured in piecemeal fashion. What that meant was that a particular hillside or lakeshore might look pristine today, but you never quite knew what might happen to it tomorrow. The state's Land Use Regulatory Commission had to examine each application individually. Plum Creek now proposed to change the old paradigm. Late in 2004 the company announced a thirty-year plan for its acreage in the Moosehead Lake region. Most of this land would be set aside for "forest management," which meant that Plum Creek would continue to harvest timber there but guarantee to refrain from further development. But twelve thousand acres would be given over to new housing lots and two "destination resorts." Among its other impacts, Plum Creek's plans would double the population of Greenville.

All this sounded ominously Montana-esque. Here was another impoverished state, its traditional economic activities in decline. Like Montana, what Maine had to sell was its beauty, by which it was both blessed and cursed; and like Montana, its remotest corners lay within a day's travel of major urban centers, places where people had lots of disposable income. As I pulled onto the road for West Branch Pond Camps, I was smack in the middle of one of Plum Creek's planned subdivisions. Today there was only a signboard; soon there would be bulldozers.

It was dusk when I reached the camp, a cluster of peeled log cabins at the water's edge. I was greeted by a young man named Eric, who said he was the fourth generation in his family to own the place, and by Alice, a self-described gypsy from New Zealand who had somehow fetched up here in this remote corner of Maine as camp factotum. Alice showed me the common room. It held an old upright piano, a broken-down harmonium, and a collection of battered armchairs. The floor sloped at odd angles. A variety of stuffed critters lurked in shadowy corners and on the walls there were moose antlers, brook trout mounted on strips of birch bark, black-and-white photographs of mustachioed gentlemen with dead bears hung by the heels.

To describe the accommodations as spartan would have been generous. There was a sharp chill in the air, and I stuffed pine logs into the ancient cast-iron stove until I had a good blaze going. It warmed an area that must have been all of ten feet square. At the stroke of ten, the electrical generator gave one final cough and fell silent and the cabin was plunged into utter darkness. I groped my way across to the sagging bed frame on the other side of the room, collapsed onto the lumpy mattress, and pulled six wool blankets around me. The temperature had dipped into the thirties. Once or twice in the night I heard the faint howl of a coyote.

I dreamed of a French monastery in a deep valley. An ancient bell was tolling. But as I stirred from the dream the sound resolved itself into the clanging of the breakfast bell. I'd slept the sleep of the dead, missed the early morning fishing.

The breakfast crowd was emphatically blue-collar; these were people whose grandfathers had been guides, not sports. As I waited for Alice the gypsy to bring my pancakes and bacon and maple syrup I fell into conversation with a good-natured elderly man named Jerry. In an impenetrable Boston accent he told me he'd been coming to West Branch Pond Camps for close to half a century. I could see why. The place was already beginning to cast its spell on me.

Outside, in the crisp morning air, the lake shimmered under tendrils of mist. Whitecap Mountain rose up on the far shore. On its slopes I could see a replanted clear-cut, a long, razor-edged rectangle of Plum Creek Christmas trees. Out on the water, a fisherman was silhouetted in an Old Town canoe, his fly line describing long, graceful arcs in the air. A pair of loons twittered at each other. I was suddenly aware of a movement in the trees by the water's edge, not fifty yards away, and as I watched, a huge cow moose lumbered into the water to feed, followed by her twins. It was as if someone had assembled the scene from a kit called Timeless Maine.

The fishing was lousy. I'd missed the best part of the day on the lake, and the river where I went in search of salmon was elbow-to-elbow with other anglers, this being a Saturday.

On the second morning, craving solitude, I followed an old logging road that paralleled the river for about six miles. When I came to a rough timber trestle over a swift-flowing brook, I stopped to study the topographic map. It looked as if I was about a mile from the main river. Time, then, for some serious bushwhacking. The only practical dilemma was deciding which rod to take with me. The brook was choked with trees and boulders, which meant I'd need both hands free to negotiate the obstacles. I'd have to strap an aluminum rod tube to my backpack. But which one?

I knew by now that one of the pitfalls of falling in love with old bamboo fly rods was that there was no end to the number you could collect. You could rationalize this in various ways. You could say, for example, that going on a fishing trip with only two fly rods was like playing a round at Saint Andrews with only two golf clubs. Rationalization or not, I had four rods with me to choose from. There was a grand old F. E. Thomas Brownstone Special that was ideal for casting the large streamer flies that anglers favor in Maine. There were a pair of Eustis Edwards rods—an eight-and-a-half-footer with a slow, old-fashioned action, and a quicker-tapered seven-foot rod that was ideal for smaller streams. But in the end I chose the eight-foot Quadrate that Eustis's son Bill had made, the same rod I'd used on the East Fork of Rock Creek in Montana.

The descent to the river took me through what Thoreau would

have called a damp and shaggy forest. I squelched through bogs and forced my way through tangled underbrush, thorns tearing at my face and arms. I clambered up slippery rock faces and teetered on rotting deadfalls. In the swampier sections, I had fantasies of being stomped by enraged fifteen-hundred-pound cow moose protecting their babies. Bears of my imagination lurked behind every tree. Thoreau would have been proud of me. Well, OK, his squeamish traveling companion, Edward Hoar, would have been proud of me.

It took me a full hour to reach the river. The brook joined it in the middle of a shallow, stony flat that stretched for hundreds of yards in each direction. The sun was high in a cloudless sky, and the riffles glittered in the brilliant light. There was pleasure in the solitude and in the rhythms of casting, but that was all. Despite the nighttime chill, the water temperature had risen to sixty degrees—the river was far too warm and far too low to trigger the salmon run. I waded upstream for the better part of an hour in search of the deeper pools and runs that fish use as staging areas during their annual migration. Eventually I caught two salmon and a marvelously colored brook trout, but they were all small fish, yearlings. I turned an ankle painfully on a boulder. I thought gloomily of the hike back to the car—uphill this time, and in the heat of the afternoon. The whole exercise began to feel futile.

I headed back downstream until I glimpsed a cove in the distance, and behind it the expanse of Moosehead Lake. A quarter of a mile or so from the lake, the river at last entered its homestretch, carving out a long, deep run that was more a trench than a true pool. The sun was directly overhead now and the light was harsher than ever. I waded waist-deep, bracing myself against the flow, and cast a nymph into the head of the run. Almost at once the fly line stopped in its drift. There was a pause—three heartbeats— and then something silver erupted from the river in a great vertical leap.

I've never been good at estimating the size of fish, and at the end of the day the inches and pounds don't really matter, but suffice it to say that this salmon was big and heavy. It streaked clear to the other side of the river, pulling the fly line deep to increase the resistance, and then went vertical again, three or four feet in the air this time. Then it tore off straight downstream toward the lake, using the faster current to its advantage, with me stumbling after.

Now I had a problem. The salmon was in deep water thirty or forty feet below me, sulking on the bottom, biding its time, regaining its strength. To wade any deeper, with the force of the river at my back and loose rocks under my feet, would be asking for trouble. The bank was too high, too far away, and if I tried to reach it and race the fish downstream, I risked putting too much slack into the line and losing control of the situation. I dithered; I overcompensated; the line went taut as a guitar string, and my fish was gone.

What had I done wrong? Well, let me count the ways. For a start I should have held off on the trip for at least a week, maybe two; impatience had brought me here too early for the spawning run. To make matters worse, I'd come to the river at the wrong time of day, when the sun was too high and bright for good fishing. Then I'd compounded my frustration by wading for hours in the wrong direction. And when I finally did hook the big salmon, I was hot and tired, and my haste had led to a series of small miscalculations. A run too deep, a line too tight.

Yet back on the riverbank, sitting on a sun-warmed rock and listening to the music of the water as it rushed toward Moosehead Lake, I realized that the moment of anger had passed. And I had to confront the question, what added more to the quality of the day, a fish caught, or a lesson learned? The moment was rich in its own way, if far from perfect.

But of course there was no such thing as perfection, there was only the constant striving for it. "Perfection" was the name that Eustis Edwards had given to his finest fly rod, but he must have known that it was less description than aspiration. Streamer's pursuit of the same ideal had been expressed in those three barely visible turns of purple silk that he'd added when he restored the rod for me. But he'd also acknowledged that no rod is ever perfect; you just get as close as is reasonable—"proper," as Jim Frank would say. Hoagy Carmichael had put it slightly differently, that "a good rod, a really good rod, is one where you make maybe nine mistakes." When I looked at it that way, I felt less bad about losing my salmon.

In the final analysis, my rod was only a tool for catching fish— although that was something you could also say of dynamite. But catching the fish, it seemed to me now, was really the least of it. On a day like this, being on a river with a split bamboo fly rod could approximate a state of grace, and as Norman Maclean had written, "all good things—trout as well as eternal salvation— come by grace and grace comes by art and art does not come easy." Try as they might, not all the glossy tourist brochures in the state of Montana could turn that line into advertising copy.

The Edwards fly rod in my hand connected me to a universe of meanings. It stirred buried instincts from a time when we were hunters and gatherers. It was a magic wand that connected the visible and invisible dimensions of the natural world. Its fibers flexed and dampened with a subtlety, a tensile strength that had been imprinted by the winds and monsoon rains of a Chinese river valley. Skilled hands had taken it from there, cut it and stripped it and scoured it and straightened it and rafted it downstream. Other hands had picked it up in a workshop in a small town in Connecticut, where they had cut it again, tapered it, glued it, wrapped and varnished it, passing the skills from father to son to new apprentice.

This was not necessarily romantic work, since food still needed to be put on the table—and often wasn't. The rod maker was rarely free of the corporate demand for profit, the exigencies of retailers, the whims and vanity of clients. Yet his bench remained part of a world before mass production, the world of *Homo faber,* in which a man's identity was formed by the intertwining of what he thought and what he made. As Lewis Mumford wrote in *Art and Technics* in 1952, the craftsman

> took his own time about his work, he obeyed the rhythms of his own body, resting when he was tired, reflecting and planning as he went along, lingering over the parts that interested him most, so that, though his work proceeded slowly, the time that he spent on it was truly life time.

The rod makers I'd come to know were, in modern terms, irrational people, favoring intelligence over cleverness, useful beauty over the bottom line. They worked in small rooms and lived in small places—Warren, Connecticut; Shelburne Falls, Massachusetts; Twin Bridges, Montana. Yet they weren't the kind of people to indulge themselves with nostalgia; they weren't Luddites in Birkenstocks and homespun. You couldn't meet anyone more wedded to the idea of tradition than Glenn Brackett. But at the same time he'd told me admiringly of another of the Montana "boo boys" named Wayne Maca, who had once made snowboards for Olympic athletes. Wayne Maca had embraced advanced technology—experimenting with new adhesives, using sound waves to create an acoustic profile of the power fibers in each strip of cane—and Glenn was sure he would revolutionize the design of the split bamboo fly rod. "This is still a young craft," Glenn had said. "You're only looking at a hundred and fifty years, and that isn't long for something to develop." At the time that had seemed to me a very un-American thing to say about a quintessentially American activity. But perhaps there was more to this America business than I sometimes chose to see.

Back in Greenville, I stopped for one last look at Moosehead Lake. A sudden stiff breeze, of the sort that tormented Thoreau during his crossing, had whipped the surface of the water into whitecaps. There's a small park by the lakeshore now to commemorate his third journey to Maine. It's a pleasant spot, with manicured lawns and neat rows of flowers in cement planters and a sign prohibiting bicycles, ATVs, skateboards, and Rollerblades. I wondered what the great transcendentalist would have made of it.

Another sign carries a quotation from Thoreau. "A lake is the landscape's most beautiful and expressive feature. It is earth's eye, looking into which the beholder measures the depth of his own nature." The other side of the sign tells the visitor that this is the spot from which Thoreau, Edward Hoar, and their Indian guide, Joe Polis, launched their canoe at 4 A.M. on July 24, 1857.

I dried off my Edwards rod with a clean cloth and put it back in its case for the flight home to New York. A hundred and fifty years, I thought. And counting.

Postscript

It took Dana Gray a full year to clean out Sam's workshop. At his home in Massachusetts, he used his construction skills to build a new two-story shop to house everything, beveler on one floor, lathe on the other. The machinery of the Carlson Rod Company is now humming again; Dana has carried on the tradition, just as Sam wanted.

And even as this book was going to press, Glenn Brackett wrote again from Montana. The "boo boys" from Winston were staying together, he told me. "Have moved our bench across the street and within casting distance of the Beaverhead, under an old golden willow tree. Should be up and running in the next two months if lucky."

Did the new shop have a name yet? I asked. Yes, Glenn wrote back. "We're calling it Sweetgrass Rods."

Sweetgrass is the name of a county in southern Montana; the Yellowstone River runs through it. And "sweetgrass" is a fine translation of *Arundinaria amabilis*—which others call "the lovely reed."

Index

Page numbers in *italics* refer to illustrations.

ABOUT THE AUTHOR

GEORGE BLACK was born in the small Scottish mining town of Cowdenbeath, north of Edinburgh, in 1949. He has a master's degree in modern languages from Oxford University and has worked for twenty-five years as a journalist and magazine editor. He has written for *The New York Times*, the *Los Angeles Times*, *The Nation*, the *New Statesman*, *Mother Jones*, *The National Law Journal*, *Fly Fisherman* magazine, and many other publications. He divides his time equally between *OnEarth* magazine, which is published by the Natural Resources Defense Council (NRDC), and a variety of fiction and nonfiction projects. He lives in New York City with his wife, author and playwright Anne Nelson, and their two children, David and Julia.

ABOUT THE TYPE

This book was set in Walbaum, a typeface designed in 1810 by German punch cutter J. E. Walbaum. Walbaum's type is more French than German in appearance. Like Bodoni, it is a classical typeface, yet its openness and slight irregularities give it a human, romantic quality.